Terminal Velocity

Terminal Velocity

Jim Thurston

This book is published by:
Jim Thurston
Email: terminalvelocitybook@gmail.com

ISBN: 979-8-35092-777-1

First Printing, 2023

TERMINAL VELOCITY

An Autobiographical Journal by James W. Thurston

Just about every senior I know perceives that the passage of time accelerates with age. For my entire life I have been living in the future, excitedly anticipating challenges and experiences yet to be lived. Now, all of a sudden, as I approach an unknown termination date, it has dawned on me that time is short, its velocity is increasing rapidly, and all those dreams that used to be of the future are now the realities of my past. At some unknown point, this increasing velocity of time as I perceive it will terminate, and so will I. I have had a full life and wish to leave a footprint. For the benefit of my family, relatives, and friends, I am writing this journal of the active period of my life with the hopes this may be of some interest.

Jim Thurston
January 2023

Harry Barr was an Iowa farm boy. I grew up in New England. Our paths in life crossed in 1967 on the remote Red Devil airstrip in western Alaska, which was serving as a logistical staging area for fighting multiple wildfires. Harry had a Huey helicopter and I had an Aero Commander. He was transporting firefighters and I was working the air tankers.

During the following years, his skills as an aviator amazed me and we became close friends. Over 55 years later, I have decided to dedicate this book to my special friend, Harry Barr.

Harry's M35 Lear Jet erected in his
memory by the Seward Municipal
Airport at Seward, Nebraska

ACKNOWLEDGEMENTS

Thanks for the "You need to write a book" motivational guidance I received from my wife, Janet Thurston, my son, J.T. Thurston, my daughter, Joy Eto, and neighbor, Diana Tillion of Halibut Cove, Alaska. Also thanks for editing support undertaken by Katie Yee of Blue Jay Editing Services. Book cover photo editing services were provided by Beka Thoning of Stillpoint Lodge, Alaska. Finally, for layout and the task of assembling all the pieces into a coherent package for shipment to the printer, I owe my gratitude to my son-in-law, Youske Eto of Vancouver, Washington.

Preface

Preface

As a youth in New England, I was extensively exposed to outdoor living, camping, and hiking at Lake Winnipesaukee and the White Mountains in New Hampshire. I loved the forest. This infatuation led to the decision to enter the field of forest management, which in turn led to gaining seasonal employment as a U.S. Forest Service smoke-jumper in Idaho. Later, I was hired by the Bureau of Land Management (BLM) as a fire control forester in Fairbanks, Alaska. (BLM is a bureau in the Department of the Interior.) In 1958 I acquired a pilot's license, purchased an airplane on floats, and started accumulating experience flying in remote areas.

Because wildfire management and other BLM programs in Alaska require extensive aircraft support, the BLM had an Aircraft Division, which years later invited me to join their ranks, and I did—in effect starting a new career. Because of my fire control experience, I initially started out by running the air tanker firefighting program. Later, I flew a Learjet on high-altitude thunderstorm patrols to detect storms producing lightning fires. Also, I designed a comprehensive aircraft cost accounting system to guide decisions affecting aircraft acquisition and maintenance.

Eventually, I was chosen to form a task force to evaluate the various aircraft programs throughout the department and recommend changes. In 1973 the decision was made to create a department-level Office of Aircraft Services (OAS) to consolidate the management of Interior's aviation programs under one roof. Its stated management objectives were to raise aviation safety standards, improve department-wide avi-ation efficiency, and achieve economic savings. I was assigned to the position of OAS director.

This book contains a mixture of exciting ground and aerial firefighting narratives, colorful Alaskan aviation anecdotes, and my tumultuous experiences fighting to establish the Department of the Interior's Office of Aircraft Services.

1

1934 - 1952

My Roots

In 1889 my father, William R. Mowrey, was born in Topeka, Kansas, on the family farm. At 16, he changed his last name from Mowrey to Thurston (which was his brother's first name) and ran away to California, where he lied about his age and joined the U.S. Army. He was then shipped to China and the Philippines. Years later, at 27, he had risen to the rank of major and was serving as an artillery officer during World War I in France.

In 1890 my mother, Estelle W. O'Brien, was born in Bridgeport, Connecticut, and with her sister, Hazel, became orphaned at a very young age when their only surviving parent suddenly passed away. In the mid-1890s, social services generally did not exist, and there was no family member or other adult available to help them. Clutching each other's hands and sobbing, they walked to a YWCA and sought refuge. After high school, they split paths, and my mother entered nursing training, eventually becoming a registered nurse in the U.S. Nursing Corps at Base Hospital No. 10 in France during World War I.

My father-to-be (now Major William R. Thurston) and an army captain signed up for a blind date with two nurses. The captain was to pair with my mother-to-be, but when they laid eyes on the nurses, Major Thurston pulled rank on the poor captain and paired up with Estelle himself. Had not this unsavory treatment of a fellow officer occurred, I wouldn't be here.

After the war, William (Bill Sr.) and Estelle were married in New York City at the famous "Little Church Around the Corner" and moved to Brooklyn, where they had their first child, Bill Thurston Jr., in 1921. Due to my father's success in the field of financial advertising, my family later moved into an upscale gated community in Stamford, Connecticut, where in 1934, 13 years after my brother's birth, I was born.

The Beginning

Due to the Great Depression, the Thurston's run of financial independence gradually evaporated, and the family eventually declared bankruptcy. As a result, the family became dysfunctional, and my parents divorced when I was three. My Aunt Hazel had by this time secured enough financial stability as a needlepoint artist with a prestigious New York City firm that she had built a home and moved into an upscale section of Darien, Connecticut. Because we had nowhere else to go, our family of three would have been out on the street had Hazel not taken us in.

Her house was where I experienced the first memory of my childhood when I was about three. A red balloon was being inflated very close to my face. It got larger and larger, closer and closer, and the rubber fabric was stretched so much that I could see individual threads holding it together. I instinctively knew it was going to explode inches in front of my eyes, and it did! I woke up screaming, and my mother rescued me. She held me in her arms in a rocking chair until I went to sleep again. It became a recurring dream.

During this period my father was a shadow figure in my life who occasionally came by to take me with him for walks or visits to a little creek somewhere where I could catch small fish in shallow pools with my hands. He had a stern demeanor, was always formally dressed, and didn't speak much. I cannot remember any conversation I might have had with him of any consequence. One Fourth of July, he took me out to a field to set off fireworks he had purchased. The weather was dreary and rainy, the tall grass was wet, and the mosquitoes were fierce. Most of the fireworks were too damp and fizzled. The visit registered very high on my disappointment index.

I still remember my first exposure to world politics during the late 1930s. Over the dinner table there were frequent arguments between my brother and mother about Russia and communism. Often these would take place while I was crawling around under the table eating fake bones out of our dog's dish. I can't recall who was on Russia's side and also have no memory of any discussions specifically about Adolf Hitler.

At 5:30 p.m. each weekday afternoon I would avidly listen to "Uncle Don," who hosted a very popular kid's radio show for tots like me. One day, just after the show ended, my mother walked by, and I asked her, "Mom, what does bastard mean?" She stopped dead in her tracks, slowly turned around, and asked me where I had heard that word.

I told her that after uncle Don said goodbye, he said, "There. That ought to fix the little bastards." That was the early days of hot microphones.

In 1940, brother Bill had departed our home and entered the Massachusetts Institute of Technology (MIT) to study electrical engineering. Because of his engineering acumen, and as a part of his MIT experience, he was recruited into the General Radio Company, where he worked in their radiation lab which was developing the Airborne Warning and Control System (AWACS). Due to the nature of his work, he was exempted from the draft. At one point the ultrasecret atom bomb project in Los Alamos tried to recruit, him but since he had no idea what they were up to down there, and because he believed AWACS was too important to abandon, he turned them down. Many years later, Bill became the president and chairman of the board for this company, now known as GenRad.

So back around 1939, with brother Bill gone, I was the five-year-old my mother had to unload somewhere so she could find work and get out of Hazel's hair. Somehow, she managed to find Wallace Greene Arnold, a veteran of the WWI trenches, whose summer camp took in some kids without charge and made them more self-sufficient. That took care of the summers. Later she enrolled me in an Episcopal boys' school on 5th Avenue in New York City that was also free because the boys sang for their keep and education in the famous Saint Thomas Church 40-boy choir. I loved the camp and despised the choir and the city life that went with it.

New Hampshire

Hanson Cove is located in the northern portion of Lake Winnipesaukee, the largest lake in New Hampshire. When I first arrived there in 1939, it was very remote. Wallace Greene Arnold, a veteran of World War I, had established a boys' camp at the head of Hanson Cove, and except for his work, the area was pure white pine forest with no other man-made structures for miles around. Mr. Arnold was a charismatic person who inherently projected a presence not only as a person in charge, but also as a person imbued with significant wisdom. He did this naturally, quietly, and with humility. He was referred to and addressed by everyone as "the Boss."

To me this was paradise and the beginning of an intense spiritual connection with the wilderness. The camp discipline, however, would probably be regarded as harsh by today's standards. Minor infractions, such as swearing, usually generated a "red hand," which was a very hard slap on the bare back with an open palm administered by a counselor. When administered upon a back recovering from a recent sunburn, it hurt like hell. The more serious violations resulted in multiple red hands. For an extreme violation, such as stealing, the entire camp would be divided into two columns facing each other, and the violator would have to run the gauntlet while being fiercely pummeled on both sides. I only saw this once, and there was a certain barbaric feeling to it.

Speaking of barbaric, one day the camp cook decided to cook veal, and a calf was selected to be dispatched. I was unaware of this, and while walking along a dirt road I noticed several people clustered around a calf. One person was petting it. I ran forward, wishing to pet it too, when another one of them suddenly slit the calf's throat with a large knife and the blood gushed out in a huge stream onto the ground. I stood paralyzed for a moment and then turned and ran away in a state of horrified shock.

The Boss had a goal of developing youngsters into independent and self-sufficient men. He had spent World War I in the trenches of France and had observed many young soldiers breaking down and unable to cope with the battlefield situation. Without someone else to lead them and prop them up, they were helpless. His belief was that these deficiencies should be addressed at an early age. With that in mind he instituted a camp banner and awards system fueled by earning points for mastering various tests demonstrating self-sufficiency.

One example was "The Mile Away Test" in which the camper was required to wander into the forest at least a mile away from camp and spend the night all alone with virtually no equipment or shelter. For a little boy, this took a lot of nerve. Consequently, I never did it.

Several years later, a favorite pastime for me at Lake Winnipesaukee was fishing for pickerel and bass. Usually, I would get up just before dawn and slide a canoe out into the calm, glassy water amid morning patches of fog, giving the scene a real deep-in-the-wilderness feeling. Because I was barefoot and only wore a pair of shorts, it was a chilly undertaking, but I loved it. I was an avid fisherman. One morning I hooked on to a 14-inch pickerel with my Daredevil spoon and spinning rod. When I hauled it into the canoe, it was thrashing wildly about as I attempted to extract the three-pronged Daredevil hook from its mouth. As bad luck would have it, the pickerel flopped onto my right foot and one of the barbed prongs sank into the meat of my big toe causing me to react so violently I capsized the canoe.

For a moment I treaded water while the fish struggled, still attached to my toe, while the spinning rod plummeted toward the bottom. Almost immediately the hook tore out of my toe, and both the fish with my fishing gear waved goodbye. The camp was almost a mile away around a corner, and since there was nobody around, I had to stop crying and fend for myself. Camp training had been good. I managed to beach the canoe, empty it, and swim out to recover the floating paddle, but the sight of so much blood unnerved me. I made it back to camp, whimpering every foot of the way in a canoe with a bloody bilge. Memories.

The camp also had what were called "Labor Gangs." From 9:00 a.m. to 11:00 a.m. we all worked in small groups, each with one boy in charge. Gang activities included logging, mowing grass, carpentry, painting structures, dock repair, etc. The labor gangs instilled the concept that all work was not bad and provided opportunities for learning some basic skills and leadership. I don't recall these experiences being distasteful.

Five-to-seven-day mountain trips were the highlights of my camp experience. These were again part of the survival training doctrine the Boss espoused; we traveled very light and sometimes had to cope with cold, wet storms above the timberline with no shelter. In New Hampshire, we hiked the Presidential Range, the Franconia Range, and the Green Mountains in Vermont. My worst night was weathering a ferocious storm under a tiny wind-blown juniper bush on the summit of Mount Washington. These experiences set the stage for decisions I would later make regarding the direction of my life.

Caritas Island

My mother's finances apparently became desperate during this period because the two of us had no real home for a while. On many occasions I would arrive on the train from the New York City choir school on a Sunday evening and be taken to a new place to spend the night, which was often a house owned by one of my mother's friends from the good old days. Usually this was a spare bedroom, attic, or basement space. A week later we would be staying at some other place. One winter Sunday I ended up in a nursing home where my mother was working. She had cut some sort of deal with the manager to let me stay there. I wound up sharing a bedroom with half a dozen very old men lying motionless in their hospital beds. The room was dimly lit, and it was dark and snowing outside. They all looked dead, like skeletons in repose. Some had their mouths open. Others were just staring at the ceiling wide-eyed. None of them talked. I slept poorly that night.

Eventually my mother rented a single room in a rooming house on Summer Street in Stamford. The bathroom was down at the end of the hall. Our room had just one single bed, so we slept head-to-toe. Entertainment was the Sunday evening radio programs featuring Jack Benny and Amos 'n' Andy. There was no TV in those days.

Our situation improved dramatically when my mother landed a job as the home nurse for Percy Bartram, who was a multi-millionaire (or perhaps billionaire). Percy and his wife were very old and bedridden in the upstairs bedroom of their mansion on Caritas Island on Long Island Sound. Percy built Caritas Island on what had been a small, offshore rocky reef. In 1908 he constructed a 150-yard steel bridge to these rocks from the mainland. He then had a rock and concrete wall constructed around the perimeter, which enclosed three and a half acres, after which squadrons of dump trucks filled the whole area up to create the island. Once filled and leveled, he built a large English-style mansion and complex that housed his family and servants. I was told he was the "Sugar King" who cultivated, processed, and sold massive quantities of sugar to the U.S. and other countries.

The landscaping was over the top with full-grown oak, hickory, maple, and other trees transplanted from the mainland. Caritas Island was a unique, beautiful, and breathtaking contrast from our days on Summer Street. The cottage was now our new home. I spent many days exploring tide pools and the fascinating sea-life species around the island.

Various incidental events during our time there remain in my mind, like the afternoon I was asleep faceup on the living room sofa and Smokey, our cat, jumped up on to my chest. I didn't wake up and was snoring loudly with my mouth wide open. Smokey was fascinated by the noises coming out of this gaping hole and was peering in very closely when he sneezed. My mother had been feeding Smokey garlic to get rid of the worms, and I've had few wake-up experiences as disgusting as this one. (Years later, I would have a similar experience involving a porcupine in the Idaho wilderness.)

Fred, the butler, had a good-looking daughter who was about a year older than I was. We hung out a lot, and I kind of had the hots for her but never made any advances because I was shy around girls and wouldn't have known what to do with one anyhow. Looking back, that was very fortunate.

Eventually the Bertram's passed on, my mother was out of a job, and the estate put the island up for sale. We were allowed to continue living in the cottage pending future developments. Wealthy prospective purchasers were given island tours, which also included our cottage. One Christmas I received a film developing kit, which I set up in my bedroom to process my box camera pictures. I had taped over all the cracks around the window and door that could let in light. In the middle of my film developing process, there was activity in the hall, and my mother was trying to push the door open against the tape. I was screaming for her to stop while she was demanding I open the door. Eventually the door flew open, and a man walked in who my mother excitedly introduced as Guy Lombardo. I didn't know Guy Lombardo from Ichabod Crane and maintained a highly pissed demeanor during this brief encounter while my negatives became fully exposed to light

A Rockefeller family purchased the island and allowed us to stay for a while. They were newly married, and the rumor was that the wife received one million dollars from the family for each baby she produced, which was real money in those days. At that time, I was just getting into skiing and needed ski money. Mrs. Rockefeller hired me for odd jobs, one of which was to paint the basement of the mansion.

The basement was huge and occupied the same footprint as the entire mansion. Its central hallway was studded on both sides with numerous concrete rooms, two of which were filled with coal, but most were empty. The environment was poorly lit, very dusty, with bad guys lurking in every corner. After sweeping and vacuuming all the floors (which took forever), I started painting. The color was battleship grey, and I used a brush. It quickly became clear that with the brush I would have no knees left and I would not finish the job until after the ski season, so I bought rollers and pans. The roller on a broom handle worked best, but it still seemed slow, and I was bored, so I put on roller skates and experimented with high-speed roller painting. It didn't really work well but was a fun way to amuse myself for a few minutes. Unfortunately, Mrs. Rockefeller walked in at just the wrong moment and caught me in the act. She was not happy. To this day I have scary dreams about that basement.

Still No Real Home

Eventually it became necessary to move out of Caritas Island. I don't know if we were asked to leave or if we were thrown out by the Rockefellers, but we eventually departed and once again began looking for a home. My mother found a place out on Long Ridge Road in a rural area north of Stamford. It was a cabin with one main room for eating and living, a tiny bathroom, plus a small room for my cot and a pot belly coal stove

The cabin was situated on the grounds of a nursing home owned by Dr. Lenz. He had converted an old farm to this use and had built a cheaply constructed facility to house, feed, and care for the elderly during their twilight years. From what I observed, most of these folks had already progressed so far into the twilight that they probably had to turn around in order to see it. My mother was one of the nurses, and when I was home, she often asked me to come over and help out with one problem or another. Sometimes there would be a patient or two out of control, and I would be summoned to quiet them down or break up a fight. I felt like I was an unpaid teenage bouncer.

Around 1951 we transitioned from Dr. Lenz's nursing home to a house on a Catholic convent on Strawberry Hill Road in Stamford. My mother worked in the emergency room of Saint John's Riverside Hospital a short distance away. Often, I would drop in on my mom after school, hoping to scam a couple of bucks from her. The nuns were there, always in full penguin regalia, and even though I was bristling with pimples during my advanced hormonal transition, they seemed to think I was adorable and would follow me around chitchatting about pretty much nothing.

One day I arrived, and after scrounging two dollars from my mom, I stopped by the small cafeteria for an ice cream. A man in a suit and tie sitting near me suddenly collapsed on the floor and started making terrible sounds. A hospital attendant arrived and told me to help him drag the gentlemen out of the tiny cafeteria to a gurney that wouldn't fit through the doorway. I had him under both arms as the sounds quit, and we managed to place him on the gurney. It turned out the gentlemen died from a heart attack, probably while we were moving him.

Late in 1951 I started thinking about my future and what field of interest I should pursue in college. My experiences with the Boss on mountain trips had awakened spiritual feelings in me about the wilderness. About this time, I became aware of the forestry profession and started exploring what that was all about. The New York State College of Forestry in Syracuse published a book of their curricula, which was fairly detailed and included extensive botany, plant physiology, and other similar subjects. I was enthralled by the thought that forestry could be a profession that could accommodate my longing for the wilderness and decided that this should be my future path. The only drawback was that it didn't pay much. The curricula book estimated that foresters could make as much as $5,000 a year (about $57,500 in 2023), but that didn't concern me at the time.

In June 1952, I graduated from high school and found my first real job with the Bartlett Tree Expert Company in Stamford for the summer.

| 13 |

2

1952

The Bartlett Tree Experts Company

At the tender age of barely 18 years old, they teamed me up with Phil Church, a grizzled, mean-looking, battle-hardened World War II veteran of the South Pacific, thus creating the original version of *The Odd Couple*. When I learned he was a WWII ranger veteran who had fought the Japanese in the South Pacific, I instinctively knew not to joke around with this guy unless I harbored an irrational urge to be dismembered piece by piece. My "coefficient of intimidation" with Phil Church was off the chart. He immediately anointed me with the name "Junior," but with the Maine accent, it came out as "Juniah."

For my first week, they sent me to a week-long climbing school. The instructors had more than a hint of marine-drill-sergeant flavor about them, and they sure knew how to climb trees, demonstrating amazing climbing feats that were hard to believe possible. It was even harder to believe that I was expected to do the same feats by the end of the week. At the school, the trees were very large oaks, tulip poplars, and maples. Limbs had been removed (or maybe I should say, amputated) by generations of climbing school students over the years, so there were long distances along the tree trunks between the remaining ones. Standing on a limb 40 feet up and having to get onto the next one 20 feet farther up was a daunting challenge. Climbing spurs that telephone pole climbers use was not permitted since penetration of the bark provides access for insects and fungus. Spurs were reserved for "take downs," which is the systematic disassembly of a tree piece by piece. The training required the use of muscles I didn't know I had. In the mornings they hurt so much I could hardly walk. Also, the almost constant clutching of the climbing lines made me wake up in the morning with fingers so swollen I could hardly make a fist.

My first two weeks of actual work was on a spray truck with Phil and a large black man named Howard who had an easygoing temperament. The truck had a 1,000-gallon tank and 150 feet of 1" hose with a high-pressure spray nozzle. When spraying, Phil would walk along behind the truck operating the sprayer, Howard would drive, and I was responsible for keeping the hose untangled and out from underneath the wheels of the truck.

Often, we sprayed lead arsenate, which was a white, milky fluid that coated leaves and poisoned leaf-eating insects. The spray gun could reach almost 100 feet up, and often, in a light breeze, the spray would drift back over us with the result that when we went home at night, we were a little pasty looking. That first afternoon, I got up the nerve to ask Phil that since arsenic is a deadly poison, shouldn't we be concerned about being drenched in it daily! Phil gave me a one-word answer: "No." I decided not to push it. At the end of our first day out together, we rolled into the company garage, and there stood an absolutely beautiful young woman in shorts and a halter. I indiscreetly volunteered, "Wow, would you get a load of that!!" and Howard started to frantically elbow my ribs, whispering, "It's his wife! It's his wife!" Phil stopped the truck, leaned over glowering, and said to me, "What did you say, Juniah? What did you say? What did you call my wife?" Then he got out of the truck and said to his wife, "Do you know what he just called you?" Then he turned to me and demanded I tell her what I had said. I managed to barely squeak out that I wasn't calling her anything but beautiful, and, please God, forgive me! Meanwhile Howard was trying to crawl under the truck's dashboard. Obviously, this was not the perfect ending to my first day at work, and I departed quickly.

In the morning I returned with considerable trepidation and encountered Phil. He smiled and then started to laugh. Seems he had a lot of fun yanking my chain yesterday and had never really been upset. It was all an act. Howard was as relieved as I was. A week later I had become "truck worthy" and was driving while Phil sprayed an apple orchard. Howard was tending the hose. We came to a hill, and part way up it, the truck spun out. Through the rearview mirror, I saw Phil motioning me to back up and try again with a head start, so I did. I backed up to what I felt was a sufficient distance, put it in gear, and floored the accelerator to get going. The truck took off, and I had no problem summiting the hill, quite rapidly, in fact.

I was feeling very proud of myself until, through the rearview mirror, I saw Phil way down the hill, struggling to get on his feet, and Howard running up the hill obviously distraught about something. The hose was strung out on the ground behind the truck. Phil had not been prepared for me to challenge the hill at that moment and had been walking backward with a loop of hose around his waist. When I lunged forward, he was pulled part way up the hill before he got disentangled. A close call.

Later the same day, we were spraying lead arsenate again, and Phil asked me to hand him the spray gun that was lying on the ground. I picked it up, and while handing it to him, clumsily brushed the trigger, and Phil received a face full of lead arsenate. I still remember him standing there stone-faced with the milky arsenate dripping off the bottom rims of his glasses, his nose, and his chin. I feared my end might be near.

July came, and the spray season was over, so we took to the trees, which is what I had been trained for. Howard went somewhere else, so Phil and I worked together the rest of the season. He had warmed toward me and was kind of becoming a father figure. I think my climbing ability and readiness to perform arduous tasks may have impressed him. Phil did have one quirk, though. He hated pears and told me if I ever brought one in my lunch, he would kill me. It was obvious he was not kidding about the pears, and killing me was probably an overstatement —maybe.

One day that summer I went to a movie at the Plaza Theatre in Stamford titled *Red Skies of Montana* starring Richard Widmark. The movie was a revelation to me since I had never heard of a smokejumper and wondered if smokejumpers really did exist, because if they did, I wanted to be one. Three years later I would actually be a smokejumper. Later, I emerged as the catalyst for starting the Alaska smokejumper program, but if you had told me that then, I wouldn't have believed you. Life can be unexpectedly exciting.

Courtesy of Everett Collection Inc./Alamy Stock Photo.

By summer's end I had managed to get accepted at the New York State College of Forestry (now called State University of New York College of Environmental Science and Forestry) at Syracuse University, New York, and was ready to leave the nest. As a youth, summer excursions in New Hampshire and Vermont mountain wilderness areas lead me to choose a profession in forestry, which, unforeseen at the time, later morphed into an aviation career initially associated with wildland fire control.

3

1952 - 1953

College Freshman

It was during the drive from Connecticut to forestry school with my mother and brother that I announced a name change. For 18 years I had been addressed as Warner Thurston, which to me sounded a little sing-song-like, if not downright nerdy. Since my full name was James Warner Thurston, I switched over to Jim Thurston, which I felt oozed with masculinity, kind of like Jack Armstrong, the all-American boy.

Syracuse University housed its freshmen at Hilltop, which was a conglomeration of army-style barracks on a large, grassy area at the top of a rolling hill. The housing was all men—no women—and we were two to a room. The campus was several miles away and the school provided free bus service back and forth. The first day at forestry school, they gathered us all in the auditorium for orientation where they told us that, four years from then, half of us would be gone. It turned out they were right. It was a 50 percent survival rate. Forestry was a tough curriculum.

The routine involved morning classroom lectures and afternoon lab work or field trips. New York State seemed to have endless experimental forests, and at the rate of two or three afternoon field trips a week, I never visited the same one twice. Amazing. Our freshman forestry class was small (only about 100 of us), and true to the prediction, it gradually dwindled. During the fall weekends, most of my classmates went to the football games. I couldn't afford not to work, so I had outfitted myself with equipment to work on people's trees like I had for the Bartlett Tree Experts Company. I had purchased a 1948 Ford half-ton pickup truck, a Homelite chainsaw, various pruning and cutting tools, climbing spurs, and lots of rope. On weekends while my classmates were at the football game, I would often be working in the top of someone's tree. In those days, I wasn't particularly interested in football.

Dendrology involves the classification and identification of trees, and at forestry school, identification testing was rigorous. They had leaf tests, bark tests, and twig tests. To take a test we would all file into a room filled with the samples requiring identification along with an identifying number. The twig test contained poison ivy and poison oak twigs. Since in many instances twigs may be identified by their taste, chewing on them was an accepted practice. The forestry school negotiated this obvious potential problem by stressing that there may be poisonous twigs included, so chew with care. (I wonder if they still do this, considering the number of attorneys per acre there are in our country these days.)

Forest sewer systems was another required course. The professor was young, and I guessed probably near the bottom of the school's faculty pecking order. He introduced his course by stating that to many people his subject material was just a bunch of crap, but to him it was his bread and butter. Actually, I thought the course *was* a bunch of crap, but I appreciated his sense of humor.

The entomology professor's name was Jack Crawl. Enough said.

Forest Service Lookout/Smokechaser

The forestry school had a program to help students get summer work related to forestry, and I used the opportunity to apply for a smokejumper position. The U.S. Forest Service turned me down due to my lack of fire control experience and instead offered me a job as a lookout/smokechaser in the Nez Perce National Forest in Idaho. I accepted and, with four other students, made plans to somehow make our way out west for our various summer jobs. Walt Sutliff had purchased an old, very high mileage Plymouth sedan, and we agreed to share expenses. We met Sutliff with his bedraggled-looking sedan under the New York City side of the George Washington Bridge. It looked worse than he had earlier described. We had a big poster on the back that said, "Idaho or bust." The trip lasted two days longer than we expected due to numerous breakdowns, and in northern Utah just short of the Idaho border, we busted.

None of us had ever been west of New Jersey before, and despite the condition of the car, we set off with high expectations. The interstate highway system did not yet exist, and most of the journey was on two-lane roads winding (out west) through open range land. Actually, the car held up fairly well until we entered Wyoming three days later, at which point the tires began to fail. It seemed we were stopping at every other service station (they were far apart) to scrounge used tires. At one point in the high desert country, we stuffed sagebrush in the left rear tire to make it to the next station.

Just outside of Cheyenne the car boiled over as we entered the community, and being on a very gentle downhill slope, all of us except Sutliff, who was steering, jumped out and began pushing. When we arrived at a main intersection, we encountered a parade in progress, which we had to enter so as to not lose momentum. The clapping spectators obviously thought the four youngsters pushing an old, dilapidated piece of junk was part of the show until we veered into the first gas station on the roadside.

Eventually, during a very hot afternoon, the car gave up its ghost in the northern Utah desert on a deserted arrow-straight road to nowhere. The five of us stood in despair on the side of the road discussing our chances of another vehicle coming along before we withered away in the heat. After a couple of hours, we spotted movement several miles away. As it drew closer, we could see it was a truck. Closer yet we could see it was a huge truck with all sorts of signs on it. When it pulled up and stopped, we saw that the signs, which were in large letters, said "EXPLOSIVES." The big, burly driver said he was going to Pocatello and we could join him if we didn't, mind sitting on each other's laps with 40,000 pounds of dynamite behind us. So, we climbed aboard! As we pulled away Walt looked at his forlorn, abandoned car getting progressively smaller in the side-view mirror. I felt sorry for him as I noticed his eyes beginning to water.

We all parted company at Pocatello. I took a bus to Boise and then another north to Kooskia, Idaho, where I had been instructed to meet a Forest Service ranger who would take me to my destination. Dan Chapman met me, and we drove the 40 miles or so to the Fenn Ranger Station in his government pickup. Dan was neither warm nor informative and had a Marlboro Man image—complete with the cowboy hat. I sensed that maybe he didn't care for Easterners, especially young ones like me who knew next to nothing.

We arrived at the ranger station, which was near the end of the road and on the Selway River near Selway Falls. Fenn Ranger Station was the gateway to the Selway Wilderness, a wild, remote, mountainous part of Idaho that had been hit hard by the Great Idaho Fire of 1910. Many thousands of acres of ponderosa pine snags still stood as testimony to that fire's intensity. Heavy, thick brush carpeted the ground under the snags, making travel off the trail system difficult.

My ultimate destination was a Forest Service lookout named "Bear Wallow," 25 miles up the trail from Selway Falls on the north side of the river. Chapman pointedly informed me that for some reason there were hardly any rattlesnakes south of the river, but the north side was heavily infested, especially around my lookout. He emphasized that the brush was thick with them. I figured he was just trying to unnerve me, but later found out he was correct—and also probably trying to unnerve me. (There will be numerous references to rattlesnakes in the following paragraphs because of my preoccupation with the thought of getting bit in the middle of nowhere with no help available. I'm still paranoid about them and have occasional snake dreams.)

During a week of fire control training, I watched the film *Forest Smokechaser*, which made a big impression on me since being a smokechaser would be one of my responsibilities. The main character, John, performed superhuman feats, knocking down flames and felling very large trees with an axe for hours on end in 100-degree heat while never breaking a sweat. There was no chainsaw present since in those days they were heavy, and to get to the fire, John had to bushwhack 10 miles cross-country with nothing but a fire pack, Pulaski, shovel, and compass, which he constantly read to navigate his way through the thick, rattlesnake-infested brush. (A Pulaski is a combination axe and grubhoe tool used extensively in wildland firefighting. It was invented by a Forest Service ranger named Ed Pulaski who saved all but five of his 45-man crew in the Great Idaho Fire of 1910.)

For two weeks prior to moving to the lookout, I did phone line repair and maintenance along the trail system. Occasionally I would head out with Chapman, who had a horse. I did not have a horse. Going up steep trails on hot days often had me in front with Chapman on his horse immediately behind. The horse would repeatedly nudge me to go faster, and I thought I could hear Chapman chuckling, but maybe it was just my imagination.

Eventually, the journey to Bear Wallow Lookout commenced at the Fenn Ranger Station corral where I met the packer, Albert Hendron, and his mule team—which was right out of the 20 Mule Team Borax add. Albert was quite old and appeared to have been mule packing for the Forest Service forever. Helicopters had not come into common use yet, and it was folks like Albert who shouldered the logistical supply requirements of a national forest. The mules were loaded with supplies, some of which were for my lookout.

There were also three horses—one for Albert, one for me, and one for Chapman who would be overseeing my lookout duties. Having had almost no exposure to horses, I was uncomfortable on them, but I thought it had to better than walking ahead of Chapman's horse. The trail followed the banks of the Selway River along precipitous cliffs for 20 miles to Three Links Guard Station and then up the mountain five more switchback miles to the lookout. (The guard station was used to stash supplies; nobody was stationed there. It was located at a horse bridge [built by Japanese prisoners of war] that crossed to the Selway River's south side, which apparently was devoid of rattlesnakes, according to Chapman.)

The lookout was not the tower I had expected. It was a two-story log cabin with a tiny room on top that contained the fire-finder device for locating fires. The first level was all for storage of tools and food, and the second floor was a one-room living/cooking/sleeping space. A quarter mile away there was a spring that gave birth to

Bear Wallow Lookout

a circular muddy area called Bear Wallow. I would trek down there every few days for water and sometimes encounter elk and bears. I would discretely let them depart before taking my turn. The plan was for me to lead a solitary existence here for the next 10 weeks. Chapman reviewed a long list of chores I was expected to accomplish that summer, one of which was to brush out the telephone line to the lookout that lay on top of the dense (rattlesnake-infested) 8-foot-high brush for half a mile or so.

As they departed (taking my horse with them), I asked about the frequency of resupply and was told it would be every two weeks, and sure enough, two weeks later Albert and his mule team reappeared. Unfortunately, this was the last time he came to visit me because numerous fires kept him busy packing out smokejumpers, which had far higher priority than me getting eggs or toilet paper. One of the small patrol aircraft (N447W) would occasionally do a drive-by and drop me toilet paper and spam, but never eggs.

My first morning at the lookout, I reviewed Chapman's list over breakfast. One high-priority project was for me to re-erect a flagpole in the dirt yard of the lookout that had rotted at the base and fallen over. It was a 4-inch diameter lodgepole pine about 25 feet long just lying there by a small wood pile. I didn't know why Chapman had given this chore such high priority since, for the next two and a half months, I would be the only person to see it, except occasionally for Albert Hendron who, I was sure, couldn't care less. I think the Forest Service manual may have specified that flagpoles should be upright and not lying on the ground, and the Marlboro Man made this my priority.

So I dug a hole about two feet deep and planted the base of the pole in it, but the pole still wanted to tip over. While holding the pole with my left hand and looking up at it, I reached out for a stick of firewood on the woodpile right next to me to prop the pole up. Not making any contact, I glanced at my right hand and saw it was only two inches from the head of a huge rattlesnake. Apparently, it had slithered up there to catch some sun while I was digging my hole and loved my company. I abhorred his company and shot him with the 8x57mm Mauser I had purchased to kill the grizzly bears I knew would be constantly attacking me out west.

One night I woke up to scratching sounds directly above me, so I turned on a flashlight. An 8-inch pine crossbeam that held the cabin walls together was above my midsection as I lay in bed. Peering down at me from on top of the beam about six feet above were the beady eyes of a large pack rat. The Mauser was within reach and had rounds in the clip. I jacked one into the chamber, pointed the rifle at the beam under the rat and pulled the trigger.

In retrospect this reflects the thinking of a typical 19-year-old: insufficient consideration of possible adverse consequences. As the bullet passed through the log, it must have expanded enormously with the result that the pack rat disappeared in a cloud of rat blood, hair, and biological mush—much of which coated my face and exposed upper body as it drifted down to my bed. A residual odor from the incident was still noticeable two weeks later.

This was the 1953 fire season, and lightning fires were popping up all over. The weather was hot and very dry, even though most afternoons there were thunderstorms. I'd watch them forming many miles west of me over the Selway River drainage and then observe their relentless march up the river toward me. Since their precipitation was not reaching the ground, I imagined them to be walking on white stilts of lightning. Eventually they would collide with Bear Wallow, and frightening displays of Saint Elmo's fire would envelop the numerous lightning rods and cables on the lookout. Just inches in front of my belly, the Saint Elmo's fire would circumnavigate my circular metal firefinder, which I pushed around with a small stick because I was afraid to touch it. On occasion the lookout would get a direct hit, which was jarring. The Saint Elmo's displays made me think of Joe's Bar and Grill all lit up with neon.

Usually, the early evening after the storms passed was a productive time to locate smokes from lightning strikes, and I would phone in or radio the information to the fire dispatcher at the Fenn Ranger Station. Later, I would observe smokejumpers wafting down to the various smokes and long for the opportunity to be one of them. In the meantime, I hoped for a chance to demonstrate my smokechaser talents, and that opportunity shortly occurred. Lightning hit a large ponderosa pine snag down the mountain about half a mile from Bear Wallow, and it was smoldering. The dispatcher said they were short of smokejumpers and assigned the fire to me. I gathered up my fire pack, Pulaski, shovel, and compass and, just like Forest Service John, I roared out of the lookout into the dense brush, so juiced up I was not worried about rattlesnakes.

I arrived at the snag as dusk was settling in and observed the smoldering area was just a few feet off the ground in a cavity. By the time darkness fell I had the fire completely out, however, Forest Service policy proclaimed one never abandons a fire until 24 hours have passed since being extinguished. The dispatcher had waived part of that requirement and, assuming I would put out the fire, wanted me back at the lookout the next morning in time to enjoy my ritualistic afternoon pounding by the thunderstorms. But that still meant I had to spend the night with that snag in heavy brush.

I thought about stories I had heard about snakes wanting to find warm spots in which to pass the chilly evening hours, and it occurred to me that I fit that requirement. Contemplating a cuddly rattlesnake slithering into my sleeping bag to enjoy the evening with me robbed me of most of the night's sleep. I think I turned on my helmet lamp and searched the brush around me at least fifty times before dawn. The next day there was no smoke, and I headed back to Bear Wallow for the afternoon's fireworks display.

Just to keep me on my toes, Chapman would occasionally call on the phone and ask me test questions out of the Forest Service manual, such as, "What is the maximum sag permitted on a number 9 phone line per 100-foot of run?" These little interludes gave me flashbacks to his goddamned horse pushing me up the mountain.

At 5:00 a.m. one morning I stepped outside to pee and was looking south over the Selway River. Part way up the mountainside near Martin Creek on a hogback ridge festered with multiple snags was one snag that was smoking. It had been another wild afternoon yesterday, and I had reported several new smokes last evening. So, I rang up the dispatcher on the crank phone and apparently woke him up. He was very impressed that I was on the job at that early hour and told me so. I didn't tell him it was because I had to pee. Because they were short on smokejumpers, he told me to keep an eye on it and advise him if it did anything more than smolder. Two days later it toppled over and was still smoldering, so I called the dispatcher who said I better go deal with it since they were still out of smokejumpers.

The route to the fire was via the five-mile steep switchback trail down to the river from the lookout, over the river on the Three Links bridge, and then up the other mountain by following elk trails to the hogback ridge. When I arrived at Three Links, I encountered Albert Hendron and his pack string enroute to somewhere else. It was about 100 degrees in the valley bottom, and Albert knew I would have a tough time getting to that fire. He cut a mule from his pack string that was carrying water and handed me the animal's rope with instructions to turn it loose when I reached the fire; it would automatically return to the corral at Fenn Ranger Station. I tied my fire pack onto the mule and, with a very grateful wave to Albert, started up the mountain. I never saw him again.

By late afternoon I was clawing my way up a steep slope in 100-degree heat on elk trails that kept disappearing. The mule always wanted to go faster and had his nose up my butt constantly pushing me forward and upward. Late afternoon, upon arriving at the smoldering snag, I tethered the mule's rope around a bush and collapsed in a pool of perspiration for a few minutes to recover. I remember thinking that there was no way John, the Forest Service smokechaser, ever had it this tough.

After unpacking the mule, I slapped it on the butt and down the mountain it went, leaving me a little lonely because threatening clouds were approaching from the west. The snag wasn't doing anything spectacular—just three or four little flames flickering here and there along its 80-foot length. It lay straight up and down the slope. The ground was very steep and rocky, making it difficult to travel up and down the slope attending to the flames as well as lacking dirt to mix and extinguish them. At early evening I heard thunder in the distance, so I climbed up to the spine of the hogback ridge for a look. I didn't like what I saw: a dry thunderstorm marching toward me on its spindly lightning legs.

I went back to the snag with renewed vigor to suppress the tiny fires before any wind arrived. It was now overcast, dead calm, and quiet except for the distant rumbling. Things were spooky. Intuitively I knew bad stuff was about to happen. Eventually a breeze came up, and the tiny fires gradually became larger, and I exhausted myself frantically racing up and down that snag making futile efforts to hold the fires down. A lightning strike with a huge clap of thunder 300 yards away on an adjoining ridge accompanied by gusting winds told me it was time to bug out, and I resorted to the only real option I had left: panic!

I saw myself completely immersed in a forest of lightning rods, each of which was pleading to be hit by lightning. I didn't want to be near anything metallic, so I sprinted 100 feet up the spine of the hogback ridge and threw away my Pulaski and walkie-talkie, which was useless since I couldn't talk to anyone anyhow. Then I ran the opposite direction 100 feet and tossed away the shovel, frying pan, and the rest of my fire pack, which contained food and necessities (such as toilet paper). Halfway in between and as far away as I could get from a lightning rod, I crawled under a clump of very dense brush where I could calmly consider the rationality of my actions. There wasn't any.

My little hogback ridge was mercilessly pounded by lightning and horrendous claps of thunder. The huge snags were so plentiful that I could get only 20 feet away from any of them, and I quivered at the thought of a nearby strike ruining my day. A howling gale only added to the drama. Eventually, as the wind backed off a little and the lightning moved on, I stuck my head out of the brush and was awed at the sight of hundreds of ponderosa pine snags on fire from the bottom to the top against the darkening sky with the wind creating a scene like tattered flags flapping in a hurricane. As it turned out, I was on the extreme upwind perimeter of a fire that was roaring out of control and headed away from me.

So now it was time to take stock of my situation:

1. Throwing my stuff away resulted in the destruction of govern-ment property by fire. I possibly could be in trouble. (This was not to be the only incident of its kind in my life.)
2. The Forest Service will not be happy. This fire sat there for two days doing nothing, and they will probably think I came along and pissed it off.
3. I have nothing to fight the fire with. Everything except my helmet and lamp burned up. I don't even have anything with which to wipe my ass.
4. Nobody knows about this problem except me. I'm in the only lookout that can see into this part of the country, and I'm not there—I'm here.
5. This fire is running wild. One man can't stop it—even with unburned equipment.
6. It's dark, and I don't want to sleep with rattlesnakes again, even though Chapman says they're not on this side of the river. I don't trust Chapman.
7. If my helmet lamp battery holds out, I can make it down through the heavy brush to Three Links by midnight. If it doesn't, I'll be sitting in thick brush until first light with nothing except my snake-infested imagination for company.

I decided to abandon the fire! Around midnight I stumbled into the Three Links Guard Station and furiously cranked on the antique wall phone handle. The groggy dispatcher answered and immediately asked how I had put the fire out so fast. I said no, it's not out—it's probably 300 acres and going like hell! (Actually, it was probably only 30 acres, but I tend to exaggerate when overly excited.) The dispatcher exploded with anger and said I never should have abandoned the fire. I told him he wouldn't even be aware of the problem had I not, and furthermore all my equipment burned up so the only thing I could have done up there was watch it burn and keep myself warm. At that point he cooled down a little and told me to check out another fire pack from Three Links and return to my lookout.

Dawn finally came, and infused with a sense of failure, I shouldered the fire pack and started the laborious trek up the mountain to Bear Wallow. I was concerned about how this would look on my record when reviewed by whoever hired smokejumpers. An hour later I paused to rest while standing on the dusty trail. After a moment I happened to look down at my feet next to which was a rattlesnake all curled up six inches from my right boot. He was covered in trail dust and almost invisible. After recovering from my shock, I dispatched him with my Pulaski. Later I learned that rattlesnakes like to sleep on dusty trails because trails retain the daytime heat at night better than underbrush.

An hour later, I was plodding along a trail that was cut into a side slope upon which the brush was only a foot high. A rattlesnake suddenly darted from the uphill to the downhill side immediately in front of me, so close I almost tripped over him. Emotionally speaking, I was now at war with rattlesnakes and determined to kill them at any opportunity. I reached back and pulled my fire shovel out of the backpack, turned downslope, and started beating the low brush with the shovel. The snake was rattling loudly, but I couldn't see him. Suddenly, because I was bent over so far, the backpack slipped up to my head, and I lost my balance, toppling head first on top of him. Instantly I was back on my feet doing an Irish jig on top of the rattler. Because the soil was loose and sandy, I had trouble gaining uphill traction, and it seemed like it took forever to regain the trail. When I did, the rattling stopped, and I still couldn't see him, so I gave up and continued my trek to the lookout. The snake's rattling may have stopped, but the rattling of my nerves took a while to subside. Chapman was right. I must be on the north side of the river.

As I continued, I heard the sound of airplane engines and turned to look back over the river at the Martin Creek Fire. Multiple parachutes were drifting down from a DC-3 transport, and this only reinforced my self-perception of failure.

Back at Bear Wallow, and without much to do but watch the depressingly large smoke column emanating from the Martin Creek Fire, I decided to review Chapman's to-do list to take my mind off the Fire. Still on it was brushing out the phone line to the lookout, which I had been procrastinating all summer due to my snake phobia. I knew Chapman would eventually jump on me about it, so I bit the bullet and bravely started cutting with my brush hook. About an hour into the project, I felt something squirm under the arch of my right boot, and I reacted violently, severing the snake in half with one swing of the brush hook.

At the end of my tour, Chapman called to inform me that the packer would not be available to pack me out. I could visualize him grinning at the other end of the line as he delivered this news. The weather was still hot, my pack—which I weighed later—was 109 pounds, and it was a 25-mile hike. Halfway back I encountered six overwrought people on five horses coming up the trail. They were three off-duty air tanker pilots and their wives who had just had the misfortune of losing a horse. The animal had misstepped and plummeted to its death into the Selway River off a 120-foot cliff near the trail's edge. Somehow the rider had jumped free at the outset and survived uninjured. She was extremely lucky.

At Fenn Ranger Station there was no sign of Chapman, so I took over a small cabin, un- loaded my pack, weighed it, and collapsed on a sofa facing the open door to cool off. Suddenly, four large, bushy pack rats came through the doorway like a welcoming committee. They were looking for a handout, and I scared them off. As things turned out, this would be my only welcoming committee because the next morning a driver showed up to unceremoniously deposit me at the bus stop in Kooskia. During my return to Syracuse, the phrase "Roast in hell, Chapman" kept churning in my mind and continued during the four-day bus ride back east.

4

1953 - 1955

Forestry School

When I returned to Syracuse from Idaho, my financial status could best be described as "dubious," so I resumed working on people's trees through the winter with vigor. I needed to be a tree expert salesman. Selling something to others has always been difficult for me due to my introverted personality—it was uncomfortable, especially since this required that I go from door to door making "cold calls" with a very high risk of rejection. I hate rejection. Also, I sensed my sales effort was difficult due to my age since I probably looked too young to be responsible enough to guarantee I wouldn't drop a log through the roof of their home.

Later that winter, my old foreman, Phil Church, contacted me. The Bartlett Tree Company had moved him to Syracuse to be a tree expert salesman, and I hardly recognized him in a suit. The two of us teamed up on the weekends and worked the tougher jobs that required two men. This often involved dismembering mammoth elm, cottonwood, and oak trees that hovered over improvements and had phone or electric lines in proximity. I continued to sell my projects that did not compete with Bartlett business. Phil became a close friend and mentor.

I spent the summer of 1954 at the required sophomore forestry summer camp at Cranberry Lake in the Adirondacks. Inconveniently, the camp was several miles over water from the nearest road and required private boats (skiffs) to access civilization. Only a handful of us had these, and those who did were very popular. The camp director was an older gentleman named C. C. Delevan, whom everyone referred to as C-Square. I never saw him crack a smile, but looking back at what he had to contend with (us), I can't blame him. The course activities were timber cruising and appraisal, engineer surveying and leveling, and other outdoor forest management activities. I had brought my home-made diving rig with me that summer, and for recreation, I searched the bottom of the lake for outboard motors or anything else of interest. I found absolutely nothing. All in all, the Cranberry Lake experience was slightly boring for me, and I was happy when it ended.

I was fortunate, however, to survive that summer due to a freak occurrence. One day I stopped at a service station to fill the Ford gas tank. The filler cap was just behind the driver's door, and the gas tank was immediately behind the backrest of the driver's seat. I started pumping and the process seemed to take forever. Eventually I quit filling, replaced the cap, and went into the office to pay the bill. While walking back to the truck, I lit a cigarette and was casually puffing on it while entering the cab. As I reached for the ignition, I noticed that my feet were in water on the floor. A nanosecond later I had the horrific realization that my shoes were in fact enjoying a good gasoline soak, and I bailed out, rolling on the ground. The truck did not blow up. Later, I found that the filler line to the tank had a flexible hose section which had come loose and was allowing gas to overflow into the cab compartment. I believe this was probably my closest encounter with death in my life experience to date.

At the end of the season, I was driving back to Syracuse in the Ford with my diving rig in the back. While going through a small town, the local policeman pulled me over. He was both suspicious and humorless as he cross-examined me about the nature of the contraption in the bed of the truck. When I realized he thought it was a still, I started laughing. At this point he started threatening me, so I stopped laughing and started patiently explaining the components of the rig. It took an amazing amount of time to convince him it wasn't a still, but even then, he seemed disappointed it was not.

My junior year was a continuation of forest management courses which involved numerous afternoon visits to experimental forests, which I found very interesting. Most often the subject was silviculture, or the growing of timber for harvest. The practice of silviculture requires an understanding of multitudes of ecological realities associated with tree cultivation. Routinely, the silviculture professor, after his onsite lecture, would throw out the question, "So what would you recommend to be an appropriate management plan for this forest?" Routinely our immature group response was a chorus of, "Clearcut, burn, hardtop, and set up a hotdog stand." Usually, the professor smiled tightly and probably contemplated how underpaid he was.

That winter I again applied to be a smokejumper with the hope that my Bear Wallow experience would only be superficially reviewed, and the Martin Creek fiasco would somehow go unnoticed. The winter tree work continued with Phil Church, and I managed to meet basic living expenses. When spring arrived, I received notice of my acceptance for a smokejumper position in region 4 of the U.S. Forest Service in McCall, Idaho. I had difficulty believing I had actually been accepted.

5

1955

Smokejumper—Year 1

For my second venture out west, I decided to go it alone in my trusty Ford truck, and the trip must have gone well because I don't remember it except for dodging cattle at night on the open range in Wyoming. Also, I remember arriving in Boise broke with no money for gas; I found the U.S. Forest Service office downtown, walked in, and hit up an employee for a cash loan by waving the letter of my smokejumper appointment under his nose. (I paid him back with my first paycheck.) McCall, Idaho, is a beautiful small community on the southern shore of Payette Lake surrounded by mountains and pine forests. The smokejumper base was close to town and contained many of the smokejumper training fixtures I had seen in *Red Skies of Montana*. Unfortunately, Richard Widmark was not there to welcome me, but "Paperlegs Peterson" was.

Paperlegs was a tall, blond, Norwegian smokejumper with a Harley-Davidson motorcycle and a penchant for gambling. During training days and at lunch break after eating, we would relax on our bunks and either snooze, read, or tell each other exaggerated stories. Paperlegs, reclining on his bed, would spy a fly on the wall and immediately solicit bets about what the fly would do next: move in a certain direction, fly away, etc. Bets were about $2, which was big money to me then.

Paperlegs had no real expectation of what the fly would do. He simply would take any position opposite yours, and you were expected to take the lead. Inexplicably he appeared to win significantly more than he lost. I don't recall hearing how Paperlegs got his nickname and assumed it had to do with a successful recovery from an especially hard parachute landing.

One day Paperlegs talked me into taking his Harley for a ride. After some initial resistance (due to fear of crashing), I took it out and crashed. I was on a dirt road that ran next to a pasture and barbed wire fence. When the front wheel hit a rock, I lost control, powered through the fence, and tangled with the barbed wire. Paperlegs was upset that his beloved Harley got scratched and seemed unconcerned about my sudden need for an entire box of Band-Aids.

The initial training consisted of firefighting techniques, calisthenics, running the obstacle course, and most of the usual body-conditioning exercises. Since I had been actively scrounging a living in other people's trees until recently, I was in reasonably good shape compared to many of the others. An unusual conditioning device was the torture rack, which consisted of a 10-inch horizontal log supported 14 inches above ground upon which were pairs of straps. Below the log was a 2x8 board on its edge, against which you were supposed to butt your toes. After fastening the straps around the back of each leg just below the knee, your feet could not move forward and lower legs could not move backward, thus allowing you to lean backward until the back of your head touched the ground. That was easy. Returning to the vertical position, however, was cruel to the abdominal muscles, and the resultant muscle pains lasted many days.

As we advanced through training, we encountered the shock tower, which was designed to simulate the opening shock of a parachute. That parachutes had a significant opening shock was a brutal revelation to me upon my first experience on the tower—it really hurt! The exercise involved suiting up in the padded smokejumper suit, helmet, and harness. Instead of a parachute being attached to the harness, they attached a 1-inch manilla rope which had slack in it. After jumping off the elevated plank at the top the tower, and after having obtained suitable downward velocity, the rope would run out of slack and snap you to an abrupt stop. About half a dozen shock tower jumps were required and they served the purpose of teaching the correct position to assume when exiting the aircraft. The shock tower was my least favorite exercise.

Next was the letdown and riser training. Risers were the two main shoulder straps that connected the jumper to the shroud lines of the parachute canopy. In addition, there were two guide lines leading to slots in the canopy which enabled maneuvering. The riser training device simulated these situations by suspending the trainee above the ground in full smokejumper regalia so he could manipulate these lines. Letdown training was with the same device and simulated what you do if your chute hangs you up in a tree. Occasionally there are ground conditions for which it is advisable for the jumper to purposely attempt to have his canopy drape over the top of a tree. Such conditions include rocks, cliffs, and jack-strawed blown-down timber which would make ground impact risky. Other times, jumpers wind up suspended in trees unintentionally, but for either case, a way to get down is required. This was accomplished with an 80-foot nylon letdown line carried in a large pocket on a lower leg of the jump suit. The training objective was how to disconnect yourself from the parachute and secure the letdown line without accidentally free-falling out of the tree.

Eventually it came time to learn the beloved Allen-roll, which was the method by which a jumper absorbed the shock of ground impact. In recent years, I've observed that smoke- jumpers have far better equipment that provides for improved maneuverability and softer landings. In many instances I have observed landings in which the jumper performs kind of a landing curtsy and casually strolls off. By comparison, we were told that under normal (high-terrain) altitudes, we would be experiencing ground impacts similar to jumping out of a second story window with no parachute at all. The Allen-roll attempted to distribute landing shock across four points of the body: feet, butt-cheek, diagonally opposite shoulder, and toes, and it had to be accomplished in a nanosecond. The Allen-roll was a challenging maneuver that gave us great problems and frustrated the instructors.

Finally, the morning for our first parachute jump arrived, and we assembled at the McCall airport. The aircraft was a vintage 1929 Travel Air that held four jumpers and the spotter. Spotters were senior jumpers who guided the pilot to the jump spot using hand, light, or intercom instructions. The jump area was a vacant

Posing for the first jump at McCall in June, 1955. Aircraft is a 1929 Travel Air.

sagebrush-sprinkled field close to the training area, and our landings were our first real Allen-roll attempts, which by and large were so awful we spent the entire rest of the day doing Allen-roll practice.

The next morning, we jumped again, and the landings were even worse! After lunch we observed two 3/4-ton pickup trucks that had been modified to provide pipe hand rails on both sides of their beds. Suited up in jump gear with helmets, we stood in two rows facing forward clutching the rails with the tailgate down while the driver took off through the sagebrush field. He accelerated to 20 mph, at which point he blew the horn, which was the signal to jump off the back, which we did. After a series of jarring impacts, we had to do the same thing again only facing rearward. I remember the backward landings not being four-point Allen-rolls. Instead, they were two-point landings: heels and back of the head. After an hour of this, they stopped the torture so we could receive half an hour of creative tongue-lashing and take a piss break. The exercise then resumed, except the drivers upped the speed to

25 mph and the hard knocks continued. The next morning the landings improved slightly, and the pickup truck torture was discontinued.

When the training ended, I learned I was being assigned to the 20-man smokejumper base in Idaho City, about 40 miles northeast of Boise. It was here I became acquainted with several people I would know for decades. I enjoyed being in a small contingent that was full of colorful personalities.

At Idaho City, a pickup truck was the mode of transportation from the fire base to the airstrip for a fire call.

The overall smokejumper supervisor was Smoky Stover (Jim Stover), who had five daughters and apparently had given up on a boy. The dispatcher was a thin, old chain-smoker named Slim. The parachute loft supervisor was Dave Caldwell—a huge, quiet, intellectual muscle man who rarely smiled and intimidated the hell out of me. Larry Looney was a second-year jumper who befriended me (actually, he befriended everyone) and with whom I shared some unusual jump experiences. In later years he became the Idaho State Tax Commissioner. Dick Hensel (nicknamed "The Tea Pot Kid") was also a large person who would cuddle up next to me at the bar, put his arm around my shoulder, and with a broad smile on his face say, "Wanna fight?"—and he meant it. Later, he became the Kodiak National Wildlife Refuge manager for the U.S. Fish and Wildlife Service in Alaska. And then there was Crukshank, who one morning strolled naked down the isle of our barracks on the way to the showers, proudly suspending his bath towel in front of him with no hands. He received applause, even though the bath towel wasn't wet.

As luck would have it, my first fire-jump partner was the intimidating Dave Caldwell. It was a tiny lightning fire smoldering in heavy timber, and nearby was a small opening that looked OK from the air. Actually, it wasn't that great because the spot was all loose granite shale rock on a very steep slope out of which projected a small invisible rock outcropping upon which I planted both feet on impact. An acute pain in my ankle radiated up to my temple as I cartwheeled down the slope, rolling myself up in the parachute as I went. There was no resemblance to an Allen-roll. It was essentially an arrival. Since we had jumped separately and Dave had gone first, he had a ringside seat to my embarrassing display of awkward gymnastics, but I was determined not to let on that I had in any way compromised my firefighting capability. We put the fire out, and Dave spent the evening reading something intellectual with his headlamp while I silently endured my throbbing ankle.

The airplane that dropped us was a rare Cunningham-Hall fabric biplane owned by Jim Larkin. Only six or seven were ever made. Jim was a contract pilot for the Forest Service and had purchased the airplane in Fairbanks, Alaska, that winter with the thought it would be a good jumper plane, and it was. While enroute to Idaho

Thurston, Smokey Stover, and Caldwell prepare to board the Cunningham-Hall.

in the spring, he encountered clear weather and took the opportunity to cut across the Canadian Rockies on a more direct route. At one point the gas tank in use was almost empty, and it was time to switch to the other tank. The fuel selector valve was recessed behind and under the edge of a hole in the plywood floor near the pilot seat, and Jim reached down to turn it. The valve was frozen, could not be turned, and if he forced it, it could shear off, thereby assuring fuel starvation to the engine and his almost certain death. First, he attempted to pour hot coffee from his thermos on it but couldn't since the floor edge covered it. After a moment of near heart-stopping contemplation, he grabbed his pack and pulled out a machete. Placing the tip of the machete on top of the valve under the floor lip, he poured the coffee onto it so it would run down the blade onto the selector. It worked, and with just moments to spare, he switched tanks thereby demonstrating a unique feat of ingenuity.

After depositing Caldwell and myself on the fire during the early evening, it was too dark to return to the Idaho City Airstrip, which had no lights, so Jim diverted to Boise for the night. The next morning, having an extra 5-gallon can of gas on board, he decided to pour it into the wing fuel tank, which he did while standing on a ladder. The gas suddenly ignited due to static electricity, Jim fell off the ladder with his clothes on fire, and the starboard half of the airplane's fabric burned off. Jim had only minor burns, but the Cunningham-Hall was a major problem. To meet his Forest Service contract obligations, he had to come up with a replacement airplane quickly, and somehow, he managed to do that by acquiring the use of a Fairchild 71. This was another vintage airplane that had a large high wing, was designed for doing aerial photography at high altitudes, and was so slow it had difficulty getting out of its own way. Meanwhile, he had the Cunningham-Hall recovered with fabric in Boise, and it returned to service later that summer.

The 1929 Fairchild 71 - a golden oldie.

The summer of 1955 was hot and dry to the very end. On September 5, some berry pickers ignited a fire at the summit of a road between two ridges in the Robie Creek drainage in the Boise National Forest. The temperature was somewhere near 100 degrees. Thirteen of us arrived to find a 30-acre fire burning aggressively on the uphill side of the road; our plan was to keep it from crossing to the downhill side. After only a few minutes, the fire did a massive flare-up that caught a breeze that carried embers back over our heads into a heavily forested valley behind us on the downhill side. At this point, we fell back and redeployed to a ridge top above the valley to construct a hand line which could be burned out to stop the fire's spread when it moved up out of the lower terrain.

Meanwhile, ground crews arrived, and many vehicles congregated in a wide area of the road's saddle far below us. After about 30 minutes, the valley fire suddenly blew up and started quickly advancing toward us with a solid wall of flame at least 100-feet high above the trees. The fuel was a dense stand of mature ponderosa pine, and from our vantage point above, we could see a small army of people in the saddle scrambling into the vehicles and racing back down the road to escape the fire. Since we were between the fire and the road's saddle, it didn't take a genius to realize we'd better get the hell out of there, and discarding our tools, we broke into a gallop down the steep slope toward the saddle. Looney was in front of me when some brush caught the wire on his portable radio and literally ripped its guts out. Fueled by panic, we never slowed down and could see that the arrival at the saddle would be a margin call between us and the fire.

Fortunately, the departing fire crews had abandoned a 3/4-ton Forest Service pickup at the saddle with the keys in it, which we frantically appropriated. As we roared down the road, I could see spot fires starting on both sides over a quarter mile ahead of us. This was the first and only time I saw game running from a fire. There were deer on both sides of us running almost in formation and lots of rabbits. Eventually, we outpaced the fire, and many miles later arrived at a farmer's field upon which the Forest Service was setting up a major fire headquarters.

By the time dusk arrived, the farmer's field was overflowing with trucks, bulldozers, tankers, tents, field kitchens, and lots of firefighters milling about. Miles away, the glow of the fire on the horizon gave the place a surreal feeling. One of the people in charge designated a small section of the field as smokejumper territory where we were to bed down for the night. It was here that Looney did something that Saint Peter must have questioned him about just before letting him pass through the pearly gates. A little earlier a rattlesnake had been decapitated on the road and somehow wound up in our possession. John Payne was terrified of snakes and would recoil in terror if you even threw a shoelace at him while yelling "snake." When Payne wasn't around, Looney stuffed the snake into the foot of his sleeping bag. (It wasn't like Looney was the only culprit—all the rest of us gave him encouragement.)

Upon his return, Payne peeled off his clothes and slid his naked legs and feet into the bag. The rest of us were pretending to read interesting stuff with our headlamps but were, in fact, breathlessly waiting for some sort of reaction from Payne. Nothing happened. Payne started reading something too and time seemed to drag on forever. Somewhere in the bottom of that bag, his warm footsies were destined to contact cold, reptilian skin, and who knew what was going to happen. The minutes slowly ticked by, and suddenly, like a volcanic eruption, Payne ejected out of his sleeping bag screaming, "Looney, you f**ker! I'm gonna kill you!" and he was really pissed. I feared he might react violently, but he didn't, and eventually everyone mellowed out, although I still feel some guilt for being a party to that incident. I never figured out how he knew Looney was the primary culprit.

On larger fires, smokejumpers were often utilized as fire overhead such as crew bosses, sector or division bosses, etc. The next morning after a field kitchen breakfast, we were each given a crew to supervise and then told where to use them on the fire. My crew was approximately a dozen Mexicans, none of whom would admit to speaking English. Packing lunches, tools, and water, we hiked to our assigned area which was on another saddle in heavy timber. During the night, a low-intensity ground fire had chewed its way to this spot, and our job was to secure it with a line dug with Pulaskis and shovels. Since the fire had not gone through the area in the crowns of the trees, the forest was intact except for the burned ground cover. As the day progressively warmed up, we constructed a fire line with me communicating orders via amateur sign language even though I was pretty sure they probably understood some English.

Around 3:00 p.m., I noticed a strange sound downhill from us and stopped to peer in that direction. The sound was kind of like white noise—a continuous surf or static sound—and after a few minutes I sensed its volume may be gradually increasing. Meanwhile the Mexicans were hacking away on the fire line and appeared oblivious to what I was sensing. Aware that we were entering into the peak time of the burning period (highest temperature, lowest relative humidity, afternoon breezes), I was feeling uneasy and continued to stare downhill. Eventually, through the timber stand, I perceived a backdrop that my color-blind eyes concluded was a shimmering reddish yellow. My steel-trap mind realized another major blowup was starting, and it was probably something that we could not outrun.

As a result of yesterday's experience, I had already scouted for and found a nearby thoroughly incinerated area which could serve as a refuge from this kind of event. I pointed downhill and shouted, "Fire!" to my crew to get their attention (bad move), and low and behold, they understood me and started to try and outrun it. This could not be allowed. Since they had thrown away their tools, I was the only one armed with a Pulaski, which I threatened to use as a weapon if they did not go where I told them. They did, and we wound up with a ringside seat as a horrendous crown fire rolled by in front of us. The heat was like a blast furnace, and it still is the most spectacular fire scene I've ever witnessed up close. At times, we stood behind the larger burned tree trunks to shield ourselves from the radiant heat. No longer making a subtle white noise sound, the fire was now a loud roar with a peculiar clacking sound not unlike a railroad train. Eventually, the main fire front moved on, going in the general direction of the Forest Service's fire camp, and we hung out for a few hours to let things cool down before hiking back.

At dusk, we emerged out of the smoldering forest onto the farmer's field which was littered with the remains of what had been the fire headquarters. It was completely deserted. Debris littered the area, and it was evident they had been suddenly overrun, triggering what possibly had been a chaotic evacuation. Standing there in the smokey silence I wondered where everyone had gone, what they expected us to do, and whether they were even aware of our existence. So I gathered up my little troop of Mexicans, and we hit the road, headed for who knows where. Sometime later, we met up with other crews and eventually were assimilated into the fire control effort. This fire has been studied extensively over the years because of its extreme fire behavior and the relationship to weather. The Robie Creek Fire was the grand finale of my first smokejumper season.

6

1955 - 1956

Return to Syracuse

I departed Idaho City and headed back to Syracuse in my truck, which now had a canvas back with a cot for sleeping. Near Challis, Idaho, I had a transmission failure and parts had to be ordered from Salt Lake City. I sat in total boredom for four days before the parts arrived and I was finally able to hit the road again.

One night in the high Wyoming desert country, I was fighting drowsiness driving on the arrow-straight two-lane highway through cattle country. It was overcast, and there was no moon. Miles ahead, I spotted a single light of some sort. When I arrived, it was a post light and a tiny, darkened gas station in the middle of nowhere. A guy in a cowboy hat was standing under the light with his thumb out, so I picked him up to help keep me awake. After impressing upon him how important this was, we headed down the highway, and shortly thereafter, we were both asleep.

I woke up to the truck viciously bouncing through the rocky sagebrush flatlands and came to a stop. When asked why he let me doze off, he admitted he had fallen asleep too. I asked if he had any idea which side of the road we went off, and he was clueless, so I decided to drive in ever-widening circles until we came upon the highway. After bouncing our way around in circles a few minutes, we encountered the road, at which point there was a dilemma: since we didn't know which side of the road we were on, we didn't know which way to turn to resume our trip in the intended direction. At this point, my hitchhiker decided he would prefer to take his chances in the middle of the high Wyoming desert at night and alone rather than ride with me, and he abandoned the truck without even saying goodbye. I took a 50–50 chance, turned left, and luckily chose the right direction.

Back at Syracuse, I started my senior year in forest management and continued working on people's trees. Since I had an interest in aerial photogrammetry, I took a course titled "Photogrammetric Engineering," which went into eye-glazing detail about lenses and focal lengths —of which there were many, such as front and rear focal lengths, equivalent focal length, calibrated focal length, etc. Since we were told that calibrated focal length would be a definite test question, I memorized it:

"Calibrated focal length is the mathematically adjusted value of the equivalent focal length, so computed as to cancel out maximum plus and maximum minus distortions at a selected annular zone in the field."

I have waited decades for someone at a cocktail party to come up and ask me what calibrated focal length was so I could impress them with my awesome knowledge, but it never happened, so I've included it here because it probably will never come up otherwise.

One gorgeous Saturday spring morning, I unloaded my tools at a wealthy client's home to prepare for pruning a shagbark hickory on their beautifully manicured lawn. As the name suggests, this species of tree has exceptionally shaggy bark. My clients were sipping coffee while sitting on their elaborate deck which gave them a front row seat for my forthcoming antics. As I prepared to start climbing this 70-foot tree, they called me over and expressed concerns for my safety, which I diplomatically dismissed, assuring them I'd been doing this forever and not to worry. I then climbed to the top of the tree and promptly fell out of it.

Some explanation is required. When pruning a tree, you always work from the top down, thereby utilizing gravity to assist your moves from one level to another. Reaching near the top, the climber "crotches" his climbing rope over the highest crotch which can support his weight. One end of the rope attaches to his climbing saddle and the other goes over the crotch and hangs down to the ground. By tying a slipknot from his saddle to and around the descending rope, he can swing out into space and the slipknot will support him. Pulling down on the slipknot allows the climber to descend to lower levels. On new ropes, slipknots tend to loosen up quickly and need to be checked frequently. My rope was fairly new.

Shortly after starting work, I stepped off into space and reached for the slipknot. There was none. It had completely unraveled, and I commenced a rapid descent earthward with only the friction of the climbing rope running through the shaggy crotch above reducing my terminal velocity. At ground impact, I luckily performed a flawless Allen-roll, stood up, brushed off my pants, and casually announced to my awestruck clients that I had forgotten a tool and needed to get it out of my truck. I was amazed they actually believed me! When I finished working on their tree, they wouldn't let me leave because they thought I was the greatest thing since sliced bread and wanted to know my life's history. Had the tree been anything other than a shagbark hickory, I would have been dead or severely injured.

The time had arrived for me to make plans for my future, notwithstanding possible intervention by the U.S. Draft Board. (I had been deferred due to my college attendance.) I decided I could not resist a second season of smokejumping and was becoming interested in Alaska as the result of a 35mm slide presentation by a student who had traveled up there. The scenery was spectacular, and my interest in the wilderness was given a boost. In the spring, the recruiters from government and industry visited the campus, and I was interviewed by Homelite (a tool company, the CIA, and the Bureau of Land Management (BLM).

The Homelite people were interested because I was working my way through college with their chainsaw product. I had no interest in working for them.

The CIA mystified me because I had never heard of them, and the interviewer wouldn't tell me anything about the work except the salary and that I would be stationed in Washington, D.C. It seemed their interest was in my photogrammetry knowledge (which really was not all that impressive).

The BLM representative was Harvey Grimm from their Washington personnel office, and when I expressed interest in Alaska and aerial photogrammetry, he informed me that the BLM administered the bulk of Alaska and was engaged in a mammoth photogrammetry program to inventory Alaska's assets. He indicated I would be a natural choice for a position up there. So, I threw my hat in the ring with the BLM and assumed they would be ready to hire me in Alaska by the time the smokejumper season ended in the fall. (This turned out to be a naive assumption because the BLM had absolutely no photogrammetry program in Alaska, and during the course of the summer, they apparently misplaced my application and forgot about me.) This was my first lesson about government personnel offices: often they are incompetent, know little about their agency's programs, and tend to focus their interests on the rights of employees rather than getting the job done.

7

1956 - Part 1

Smokejumper—Year 2

Within hours of the graduation ceremony and having sold my truck, I was on my very first airline flight from Syracuse to New York City in a twin-engine Convair CV-240, which for the young airline industry was a successor to the Douglas DC-3. The flight from New York to Denver to Boise was in a DC-4, and at Boise I chartered a single-engine Beechcraft Bonanza to fly me to McCall. (This was really flying high compared to the cross-country endurance saga three years prior in Walt Sutliff's dilapidated Plymouth.)

After refresher training in McCall, the Idaho City contingent re-assembled with most of the same folks as the previous year. Instead of Jim Larkin's vintage aircraft, the Forest Service had purchased a shiny new twin-engine Beechcraft D18 and had modified it for smokejumping. An innovative addition was a three-position toggle switch back at the spotter's position so he could guide the pilot left and right via two lights on the instrument panel. The center position of the switch was neutral or no light at all. Just before jumpers pushed off out of the aircraft, the pilot would pull back the engine power to reduce propeller wash that could disrupt the exit. The spotter would signal for this engine "cut" by flipping the toggle switch back and forth so the two panel lights alternately flashed rapidly.

Four of us went out on the first, or one of the first, sorties in the Beech to jump a fire. We were jumping one jumper per pass because it was a tight spot that required great precision. I was the first to jump and was in the door poised to shove off. When time came to jump, the spotter toggled the switch left-right-left-right rapidly to signal an engine "cut."

There was one minor problem: because the switch was new and sticky, he was actually toggling left-neutral-left-neutral. With only the left light flashing, the pilot assumed a drastic correction to the left was required and so responded. With the tail down in slow flight and with the wing in a steep left bank, the vertical tail stabilizer presented an obstacle to the jumper (me) just at the moment the spotter gave the signal to shove off. As the chute started to deploy, I bounced off the bottom of the stabilizer and started spinning. When it finally deployed, and because the lines were all wrapped up, my head was locked with my chin on my chest, and I was unable to look up to see if I had a fully opened canopy.

When the lines unspun me, I was able to grab a look up and verify I now had a full canopy but the spinning momentum continued and locked my head back so I could not look down at my landing spot. When I unwound again, I was able to break free and look down just at the instant I crashed into the top of a large ponderosa pine, becoming hopelessly entangled about 60 feet off the ground. By the time I untangled everything and reached the ground via my letdown line, the other three jumpers had contained the fire. The next afternoon back at Idaho City, the spotter and I had "words."

Eventually, I became aware that my most fearful moments occurred when I took my first look at a hairy landing spot. Such a moment occurred one hot, windy afternoon when I saw the targeted landing spot on the spine of a 9,000-foot-high ridge. The ridge was steep and forested on one side and a steep cliff-like bolder slope with 80-foot ponderosa pine snags sticking out of it on the other. A brisk west wind was blowing perpendicular to it, and the spotter decided to let us out a considerable distance upwind on the forested side so we would drift over the forest toward the spot. Since the spot was located on the crest of the cliff, the spotter stressed the importance of not overshooting it unless we had a subconscious desire to come home in a meat wagon. It was a small, smoldering lightning fire requiring only two jumpers—Larry Looney and me.

Since Larry was now a third-year jumper, he went out first, and we observed him as he descended toward the spot, then over the spot, and then over the cliff and into the steep, rock-strewn snag farm. He smashed into the top of a large snag and there was no immediate movement. The spotter grabbed my shoulder, spun me around to face him, and through gritted teeth told me to get my ass down there and see how badly he was injured—and by the way, don't overshoot that goddamned cliff!

The smokejumper head protection was a football helmet modified with a mesh screen to protect the eyes and face. Barfing through it was not an option if you wanted to see anything on the way down, and I was perilously close to doing just that. At the signal, and with my heart in my mouth, I exited the airplane and a very strange thing happened—the opening shock of the parachute knocked me unconscious for a moment. Waking up was weird. I opened my eyes and saw a rugged range of mountains in the far distance and everything was peaceful and serene and I was suspended in the air. It was not until I looked down and saw the ground 2,000 feet below me that I realized I was in a parachute and my feet were traveling over the terrain at a high rate of speed backward.

The realization of where I was and what I was doing hit me and the thought of joining Looney in the snag farm galvanized me into action. I turned the chute around with a guide line to check out the situation and saw I was going to go over the cliff barring any desperate measures. Unfortunately, the penalty for turning the chute to grab a look at the spot added another 14 mph to my already awesome ground speed, and I immediately turned it back 180 degrees. Knowing this would not be enough to keep me from blowing over the cliff, I accelerated my descent by climbing the shroud lines like a monkey to dump out as much air out as possible. This increased rate of descent would, of course, also make my forthcoming impact with the ground even more memorable.

Coming in backward on what was essentially a blind approach, I had no idea where I was going to land, what I was going to hit, or when I might hit it, and because I was coming in so hot, I knew I was going to hit hard. Suddenly there was the prerequisite heels-followed-by-head impact I experienced so often in training. A large snag had fallen over

In the mid-1950s, horses and mules were the most common means for transporting smoke-jumpers off fires.

and was lodged in another tree. I had slipped under it with my head barely clearing while my chute and shroud lines went over the top. If I had hit it in the middle of my back, I think it would have broken me in half like a tongue depressor. After clawing myself out of all my equipment, I raced to the ridge top to help Looney, who unexpectedly appeared swearing vigorously with a trickle of blood running down his right cheek. He told me the impact with the snag had ripped the helmet off his head and gashed his right ear in the process, but the injury was not serious. An hour later a packer and mule string appeared—along with a ground crew to put out the smoldering fire, thereby relegating our whole traumatic adventure to a meaningless exercise.

By midseason I had heard nothing from the Bureau of Land Management, so I wrote them a letter. Providing a vivid demonstration of how tangled up in their drawers their personnel office was, they responded by offering me a job in Coos Bay, Oregon, doing timber sales administration. I answered, citing Harvey Grimm's assurances that the Alaska photogrammetry program really needed me. They came back with the information that there was no such program in Alaska and would I accept a position in Fairbanks as a fire control forester? That Alaska even had a fire control problem surprised me since it conflicted with my uninformed vision of igloos, glaciers, and snowfields, but I accepted with the thought that, after all, Alaska is Alaska and getting a job there is half the battle.

Back in the Idaho City operations, another hairy jump spot materialized with the advent of the Lost Packer Fire up in the rugged Middle Fork of the Salmon River country. The evening before, a carload of us had gone to Boise upon which we had inflicted some of our wild and crazy behavior. We drove back to Idaho City at 2:00 a.m. thoroughly hammered and fell into our bunk beds. At 5:00 a.m., a squad leader came in and rousted 10 of us awake to go on a fire. We suited up and were loaded into a 1929 Ford Tri-motor airplane brought down from Missoula, Montana.

The Lost Packer Fire was in an area of wind-thrown lodgepole pine, most of which was criss-crossed on the ground with few standing trees remaining. Since there was no suitable jump spot, a timber jump was required to avoid serious landing injury. This required jumpers to deploy their canopies over the tops of the stand-

1929 Ford Trimotor coming in to take us to the Lost Packer fire.

ing trees so their descent would stop before impacting obstacles on the ground. When suspended above the logs they would be able to reach the ground with a letdown line. Aiming to place your canopy over a specific tree was tricky at best, and often the target was missed.

Our lumbering Ford Tri-motor arrived over the fire around 7:30 a.m., and we took our first look at the jump area. This could have produced nausea on its own, but coupled with lack of sleep and a horrendous hangover, I felt like I had to get better to die. A total of 104 smoke-jumpers jumped this fire, which was a record at that time. Of the ten on board, I was the last one out, which made me the 104th. As I recall, 60 were from Missoula, 24 from McCall, 10 from Grangeville, Idaho, and 10 from Idaho City. I missed the top of the tree I had selected, and according to a smokejumper witness, the edge of my canopy caught a lateral branch that stopped my descent abruptly, bouncing me up into a horizontal position on my back. At this point the canopy broke loose and my free-fall descent continued toward my destiny with the log pile. The canopy then caught another lateral branch, and when I stopped, my toes were tickling the highest log in the pile. It was a close call. These days, I wonder what OSHA would have thought.

The Lost Packer Fire was at high elevation and evenings were quite cool. Two Forest Service regions were represented on the fire: Region 1 and our Region 4. Sixty jumpers were from Region 1, which that season was conducting a feasibility evaluation of paper sleeping bags vs. the good old down-filled type. Sixty of the 104 testosterone-infused smoke-jumpers on this fire were not keeping warm enough, which resulted in some interregional thievery and fisticuffs after the first night.

Hard feelings intensified into the next day when ground troops arrived to relieve the jumpers. Upon their release from the fire, a twenty-one-mile race amongst the quarreling contingents over rough terrain to the nearest road immediately ensued with our 10-man Idaho City crew in the lead. We won the race, breaking out of the forest to see only one 3/4-ton pickup truck waiting there to meet us. With a mob of angry competitors on our heels, we piled into it and admonished the driver to haul ass. We left two clouds behind us: dust and mob profanity. The road ran along the Middle Fork of the Salmon River; the temperature was very hot in the valley bottom, and many miles later we came upon a tiny store where we hoped to find some liquid refreshment. We cleaned all the beer out of their small refrigerator and continued trucking, glowing with the satisfaction of winning both the race and the liquid prize. Shortly after, we passed several buses on their way to pick up the other jumpers and contemplated their reaction when they discovered the great beer heist.

Late that season, Lamont "Chris" Christensen and I were dropped onto another lightning-struck smoldering snag fire next to a high, grassy, alpine valley. A tiny creek ran through it, and after suppressing the fire, we camped for the night next to a small stream. I've always had a significant snoring problem, and that night was no exception. Later, I awoke to the light of a full moon that was vertically divided into thirds. My groggy mind had problems processing this, and then the realization hit me that the two front legs of a mule deer were the cause since I was looking through them. When I stirred, the deer wandered off.

Later, Chris woke up to my snoring. I was flat on my back and my mouth was wide open. A large porcupine was sitting on my chest peering into my mouth with great curiosity, apparently attracted by strange noises foreign to his wilderness. Chris was uncertain how to react, since the wrong decision could result in a face full of quills for me. Suddenly (according to Chris), with a loud snort I sat bolt upright, and the porcupine tumbled off me and wandered off. I immediately flopped back again and resumed my snoring. When dawn arrived, we both woke up literally imbedded in a herd of sheep. Later we learned the valley was under Forest Service permit for sheep grazing during the summer, and we had camped on the shepherd's salt lick. When we returned to the base, Chris liberally spread my snoring-porcupine story throughout the smokejumper corps.

After completing my second smokejumper season, our little Idaho City band of smoke- jumpers said goodbye to each other, and on September 22, 1956, I flew on the airlines to Seattle to connect with a 7-hour flight to Fairbanks on a Pan Am Boeing Stratocruiser.

8

1956 - Part 2

Alaska

The Seattle-Tacoma airport in 1956 looked nothing like it is today. The terminal was quiet, and there were few people milling around. After checking my luggage, I strolled up to an open-air observation deck on the roof of the terminal and was the only person there. I gazed across the runways to the west in weather that was overcast with drizzle and no wind. Being mindful that I was embarking upon a completely new chapter in my life, I remember contemplating what I might be doing in several years and wondering if someday a wife might be in the offing. If so, I wondered where that person might be at that very moment: Alaska? Somewhere out west? New England? Overseas? Eight years later I would learn the answer: 16 miles north of me in Seattle.

The seven-and-a-half-hour flight in the double-decker Stratocruiser was exciting—for the first hour—and then began to drag, so I killed some time in the lower level, which was a bar. Although I would be flying the whole day, our arrival time in Fairbanks would only be 4:00 p.m. (Alaska in those days had five time zones.)

After landing, I was greeted by an affable gentlemen named Fred Varney who was the BLM fire control officer. This was a great contrast to my Dan Chapman introduction three years ago in Idaho, and I warmed up to Fred immediately. While we talked, a Pan Am official came up to us and asked if, by chance, I had packed ammunition aboard, which

I had. He then politely asked me to follow him back to the aircraft, handed me a broom, and told me to start sweeping up ammunition, hundreds of .357 magnum rounds that were scattered throughout the belly of the cargo hold. Apparently, several of the cardboard boxes I had packed them in had burst. Nobody seemed particularly upset about it —they just seemed to think it would be nice for me to pitch in and help. I couldn't help wondering what kind of first impression I was making on Varney.

The ranger station was near the airport on Airport Road, which had a sign saying, "Welcome to Fairbanks, population 5,002." My new home was next to the Chena River in a barracks building which had about eight or ten bunk rooms, a bathroom, and a kitchen. At the Chena River end, one room served as the fire dispatch office and another as the fire control officer's office. When I entered the barracks, I met Don Burns and Joe Morrison, the second and third persons I would meet in Alaska. Burns was sitting in a chair, and Joe was giving him a haircut. They both would be friends of mine for 20 years. Later, Varney used a large map in the dispatch office to acquaint me in general with Alaska, and I was struck by the number of villages with names that were difficult to pronounce.

Except for Burns and Morrison, the summer seasonal staff had departed, and the permanent employees were few. The next day Varney and I flew in a Cessna 180 to a BLM station in Central, which is about 110 miles northeast of Fairbanks, to secure it for the winter. This was my introduction to Bob Johnson, the BLM pilot in Fairbanks. I was at an impressionable age, and Johnson really impressed me. He spoke few words, had a Lincolnesque stature, radiated supreme confidence, and appeared to really know how to handle an airplane (as if I had any qualifications to make such a judgement). I had always wanted to fly someday and decided right there if I did, I wanted to be like Bob Johnson. During the next few days, we visited several other stations, and I began to get a feel for the nature of the Interior Alaskan landscape, a lot of which was mossy, tundra, and not very high above sea level.

One of my teenage fantasies was to be a big game hunter. In Connecticut I had spent hours leafing through the pages of Stoeger's catalog, which was a virtual encyclopedia of firearms. About four days after my Alaska arrival, I was told to accompany Bob Smith (a BLM forester) on a drive 80 miles northwest to Livengood to survey a campsite. We loaded up a pickup, and when Bob tossed a rifle in back, I asked why, and he said it was moose season and he wanted to get a moose. I thought to myself, "Sure—you just drive out to get one, shoot it, and bring it home for supper! Fat chance." (My Connecticut mind pictured arduous hiking for days in rugged country and all kinds of weather to track down big game.)

Late afternoon after completing the survey, we drove down a long, gentle stretch and observed a huge bull moose in a swamp about 150 yards out from the road. I couldn't believe it—the thing was a monster, and Bob shot it right out in the middle that swamp! What followed was one of the most unpleasant experiences of my young life. Standing, and sometimes kneeling in a foot of swamp water, covered with blood, gutting and dressing out a huge carcass while wallowing in a pile of internal organs, all this in swarms of biting gnats—what a wonderful memory!

Worse yet was dragging the meat to the road through the swamp in the dark because we were still at it at midnight. Even though I was in good physical condition from recent smokejumper work, the hours of moose-dragging thoroughly exhausted me. Bob awarded my effort with half of a quarter of moose (one-eighth moose), but the experience extinguished any desire to ever be involved in big game hunting again.

The refrigerator at the ranger station was not large enough to accommodate even a one-eighth moose, but my cold storage dilemma was solved that night when the temperature dropped below freezing and stayed there for the rest of the fall and winter. I needed to store my one-eighth moose where dogs or other varmints couldn't reach it, so I selected the top of the garbage storage bin next to the barracks. Everyone else had gone, so now I was the night caretaker of the ranger station. Since my hourly wage was $1.67/hour, running to a store and buying steak was out of the question, and therefore, that moose was very dear to me. I would spend much time perched on top of the garbage bin trying to saw off steaks but later, when the temperature was 50 below, cutting that meat was almost impossible, even with a hacksaw.

I am, by nature, somewhat of a loner, but that fall loneliness and boredom nevertheless became a problem. During the workdays, there were a few people around like the maintenance man, the auto mechanic, and occasionally Bob Johnson. During nights and weekends, I became the Lone Ranger of the ranger station and time dragged on with nothing to do. I had no friends, no TV, no car, and little money. As fall progressed, daylight dwindled to almost nothing, the ice fog moved in, and the temperatures sank, however, I was never depressed— only bored and lonely. When the boredom peaked, I'd get the stepladder out, climb onto the top of the garbage bin, and saw away on my one-eighth moose.

My primary task during the fall was the gathering and organizing of fire data from the just concluded fire season. From this, I compiled various fire statistics which I was to present at the annual fall fire conference in Anchorage.

Another of my station caretaker responsibilities included management of the boiler plant which was in a separate building adjacent to the barracks. Years later, Bob Robinson, who was the founder of the Alaska Fire Control Service, told me the story behind that boiler. It was literally a moonlight acquisition from Ladd Air Force Base (currently Fort Wainwright) not long after WWII. The BLM, having withdrawn a tract of land on the corner of University Avenue and Airport Road for a ranger station, needed to somehow provide a power plant with no funds. Robinson and his small band of conspirators, having dug a hole at the station ahead of time, snuck out to Ladd Air Force Base in the dead of night and somehow managed to filch the boiler and get it onto a truck tractor and lowboy that had been borrowed from the air force without their knowledge. They transported it off base without getting caught, promptly plopped it in the hole at the station, and rapidly framed in a building around it. If approached by the air force, they would simply say, "Boiler? What boiler?"

The hours I spent tending to the boiler were unnerving because it was constantly acting up and making threatening sounds. More often than not, it seemed to call me out around midnight or later on dark, frigid (and lonely) nights with ominous rumblings that at times shook the whole building. Fred Varney had informed me that, a few years before, it had exploded and been rebuilt, but the building had largely survived with the exception of the door blowing off and the loss of some windows (in the adjacent barracks building as well). At times I would pester the maintenance man about the problem, but for some reason he seemed to take a general disinterest in my concerns, inferring that I was probably overreacting—which I probably was because I was genuinely frightened of the belching monster.

9

1957 - 1958

U.S. Army

One day I received greetings from the draft board. I had been deferred during my four years of college, and now my military obligation had come home to roost, so my career as a fire control forester would be put on hold for a few years while I fulfilled my duty. I wanted to be a pilot in the military but did not qualify due to red-green color blindness." I learned from discussions with the army that in Alaska, draftees were automatically assigned to the Alaska Infantry after basic training. Since the army had a program whereby one could sign up for training in selected specialties, and due to my aviation interests, I enlisted for aircraft maintenance training and was inducted January 2, 1957 at Fort Richardson in Anchorage. A stern army captain swore me in just outside the door to the barracks latrine, which is where he tracked me down, apparently on his way to other, more important business. He admonished me that, while I was in the army, I had better damn well keep my member in my pants and my fly zipped up and stomped off down the hall to parts unknown.

Basic training formation.

The army had, what must have been, the smallest basic training company anywhere. There were less than 60 trainees ensconced in Quonset huts near the foot of the Chugach Mountains overlooking Fort Richardson and Anchorage. The place had the feeling of a prisoner of war camp, such as in *Stalag 17*. I was the late arrival. All the others had arrived two weeks earlier, and so I took up the "new boy" role, which meant I provided amusement for the two-week veterans as they watched me absorb the shock of being pounded into submission by the half-crazed, neurotic drill sergeants. Little things got to me, such as their preoccupation with belt buckles. Yes, everyone knows they are supposed to be shiny, but I was "gigged" because I had threaded my belt clockwise instead of counterclockwise, which is something barely noticeable and certainly not a threat to national security, much less to keeping my trousers up. My thought was that if this type of concern is what really preoccupies you, you probably should consider getting another life because you are surely pissing this one away.

There were other acts of harassment that, while more significant, were more traditional in my mind, such as the call to formation and inspection outside at night during a snowstorm. We were sleeping peacefully after a good, solid day of healthy harassment when, at 2:00 a.m., the door burst open and a cadre of screaming sergeants flooded the Quonset hut, ripping off our covers, overturning our foot lockers, and generally messing up the place up. At this point, we were ordered to fall into formation outside in seven minutes, fully dressed with our foot lockers and rifles ready for inspection. What followed was army-choreographed panic, with sleep-dazed recruits falling all over each other dragging foot lockers, etc. out the door into the snow. There, in semi-darkness, we attempted to present some sort of passable formation for inspection to sergeants who were figuratively foaming at the mouth.

The Fire Guard Debacle

Being the dead of winter, we wore white camouflage covers over our fatigues when out on field maneuvers, which involved running around in the spruce forest firing blanks at each other with our M1 rifles. Late afternoon they would assemble us in formation and march us to the mess hall for supper, following which we would straggle back and prepare for night maneuvers. We spent the nights out there in 5-man squad tents, and this required the posting of a fire guard to protect government property while everyone else was gone gorging themselves.

One night I was designated the fire guard, and the rest of the troops marched off into the sunset in the general direction of food while I retired to my squad tent to cook a C-ration supper on a wood-fired Yukon stove. I had just ignited the fire and was opening a can of C-ration baked beans when I heard the sergeant calling me to come out to the road. I answered that I had just started my supper fire and quickly found out this was an unacceptable response, so I promptly moved my ass (as ordered) out to meet him. Upon arrival he snarled at me to load 30-cal blank ammunition into clips for the night activities and marched off to supper, grumbling under his breath something about dumb-ass recruits.

Sitting on the roadside snow berm, I loaded ammunition while taking in a glorious view of a winter's after-sunset glow in the clear blue sky with snow-capped spruce in the foreground and the majestic golden Chugach Mountains in the background. This was the type of scene that drew me to the wilderness in the first place, and I was experiencing an almost overwhelming sense of profound spiritual peace and well-being when I noticed a peculiar sound behind me. I turned and observed in horror a large column of dense, black smoke above a 30-foot-high column of bright red flames emanating out of the forest in the general direction of our tent colony.

Dropping the ammunition, I ran through the woods toward the smoke and arrived to that find a tent—my tent, *the fire guard's tent*—had burned down! What remained was a flaming circle on the snow from what was left of the circular structure. In the middle were five glowing mummies that had been our arctic sleeping bags, and next to the tent perimeter there were five M1 rifles with smoldering stocks hanging on the rifle rack. For some reason, this triggered a dramatic mood change in me. Clomping my way through the snow back to the road, I contemplated the probable reaction of my snarling sergeant and decided it was too much to imagine. I was stunned because this was Martin Creek, 2.0. I resumed loading ammunition as both the darkness and my depressed mood gradually enveloped me. It was now dark. Eventually, the troops started appearing on the road from the mess hall. One of them, Ernie Hall—a tent mate, greeted me with, "Hey Jim, how'd it go?"

It's rare in life that a question tees up a chance for such a memorable answer as well as this one, but I probably fumbled it with, "Well, so-so. Where ya headed?"

Ernie responded, "Our tent."

Now was my chance. I recovered with, "Don't bother—it's burned down." Ernie replied, "Yeah, sure. That would make you one hell of a fire guard!" and marched off toward our tent in the darkness.

Then the sergeant materialized out of nowhere, demanding to know how much ammunition I had loaded. I answered, "Sir," (sergeants were addressed as "Sir" in basic training) "we have more important things to talk about," at which point he started erupting.

Ernie suddenly popped up again out of the darkness shouting, "The f**ker's burned to the ground—you weren't kidding!" The sergeant demanded to know what the hell he was talking about. In a quavering voice I tried to explain what had happened, and he just stood there, dumbfounded, wondering how a fire guard's own tent could burn down and probably believing he was conversing with the dumbest idiot on the planet. He was stuck for words. I was hoping he would never find out I was a fire control forester in civilian life.

The next day I accompanied the Fort Richardson fire marshal to the scene of my debacle, and he examined what little was left, which included the Yukon stove and its pipe hardware. Almost immediately he proclaimed the cause: liquid-fuel spark arresters had been issued to us to use with wood fuel. They were incapable of keeping wood sparks from igniting the tent. Case closed. I was greatly relieved that I would not be blamed for the incident. Shortly thereafter I transferred to the Army Transportation Headquarters at Fort Eustis, Virginia, as a student in aircraft maintenance, leaving an indelible memory behind with the Fort Richardson basic training cadre.

Fort Eustis

Spring weather at Fort Eustis was warmer than I was used to, and the classrooms were not air-conditioned. John Stamper was a civilian instructor in all phases of aircraft maintenance, and he always wore a suit, tie, and vest. I was in a pool of sweat almost constantly. The course was general maintenance, which presented an overview after which the student could apply for a specialty. I chose the aircraft engine overhaul specialty, and after completion, the Aircraft Engine and Powertrain section of the training department solicited me to become an instructor. I had some reservations because public speaking terrified me, but after my acceptance, they sent me to a two- week civilian-taught instructor school known as "charm school." The arrangement suited me fine because I planned to use what few funds I had for flying lessons at Patrick Henry Airport, which was just a short bus ride away, and it was better than being shipped to Korea.

While in school at Fort Eustis (also known as Fort Useless and Fort Uterus), we students lived in two-story barracks buildings, and because so many of us were in transient, we hardly knew each other. Inspections were made each Saturday morning, and a student on each level was designated as being responsible for the overall condition of that floor.

One Saturday I was put in charge of the first floor where I was bunked. Just after getting almost everything in order, a second lieutenant accompanied by a mean-looking staff sergeant entered the room. I called, "Attention!" and we all snapped to attention. One by one they inspected each of us, assigning "gigs" for each indiscretion or shortcoming. When done, they headed upstairs, but the lieutenant stopped, turned, and asked why I was not coming with them. I explained the floor responsibility arrangement as best I could, but he rejected it.

"Bullshit, Thurston. You're responsible for this whole building, so get your ass in gear and come upstairs." I had never been upstairs, and when I arrived, I was surprised to see there were few students there. The floor was a mess. There was no indication that the occupants were expecting an inspection. No one claimed to be in charge. Undeterred, the lieutenant worked his way down the aisle checking foot and wall lockers. To my horror, several wall lockers disgorged beer cans and whiskey bottles (both empty and full) that clattered loudly as they rolled out onto the floor. The staff sergeant fastened a wicked gaze on me, and I knew bad news was coming. For the next several days, I became a familiar face in the back room of the mess hall where all the pots and pans were scrubbed.

My Aviation Career Begins

It turned out that there was not much to be had in the way of flight instruction at Patrick Henry Airport near Fort Eustis. I found a dark-complected gentlemen named Hamid in a tiny out-of-the-way office (which was more like a shed) near the main airport building. He wore a suit, had a beard and dark bushy eyebrows, and spoke with a deep, heavy accent. At first, he seemed wary of helping me, but this quickly changed when I pulled some cash out of my pocket. A moment later, a tall, thin, 50-year-old blond guy emerged from the back room, and

Hamid introduced him as Handy, my flight instructor. He only had one working eye and wore a patch over the other. During our walk out to the airplane, I queried him about his flying activity, and it turned out he regularly flew a Piper Super Cruiser to locate fish for commercial fishermen offshore. He pointed out the airplane to me. It had a large loudspeaker imbedded in the right side of the fuselage that he used to communicate with the fishing boats below.

Hamid only had one airplane—an Aeronca Champ, which is a small, tandem two-seat, high-wing, fabric-covered aircraft. I was placed in the front seat with Handy in the rear. When we had climbed to 2,000 feet and leveled off, he turned the control stick over to me, and I struggled to keep the aircraft straight and level. The air was a little choppy with the daytime fair-weather turbulence, and I started to feel slightly nauseous and was perspiring with the effort. Moments later the engine started to sputter, and my first thought was that Handy was testing me to see how well I handled an emergency, which I thought was pretty tough training since my total piloting time was only about eight minutes.

Then the engine quit altogether, and I realized Handy had the controls. We glided down, and he performed a "dead-stick" landing in someone's beet field. The problem was carburetor ice, which restricts airflow to the carburetor and can be dealt with by applying carburetor heat—which we had not done. After the ice melted, we took off again and my lesson continued, this time with the carburetor heat knob pulled slightly out.

Back at the Engine and Power-train section, I found that several coworkers were certified flight in-structors, so I continued my train-ing with them. Handy could go chase fish. After soloing and ac-quiring a student pilot license, I joined a local flying club that had

a J-3 Cub. The airplane had no radio transmitter and only a receiver. In the air, when the control tower gave you directions, you acknowledged receipt by rocking your wings. It was common to hear, "If you read the tower, rock your wings." I always wanted to reply by saying, "If you read my wings, rock your tower," but of course, while that would have been cute, it never happened.

My radio was a Mitchell Airboy Junior. It was only a receiver and was recessed in the wing route wall just above and to the right of my head. On hot summer days, I flew with the door of the airplane open, which opened up a large space on my right. One day, while practicing air maneuvers over the James River, I apparently executed a sloppy, uncoordinated steep turn with the result that I lost my radio. It slid out of its perch, bounced off my right shoulder, and plummeted into the James River below. The Patrick Henry Airport Control Tower was not pleased with my arrival, which was characterized by confusion and uncoordinated light signals.

I had to log 40 hours of flying time to get my private license, some of which had to be cross-country. One afternoon I departed Patrick Henry, bound for some destination I don't remember, and got lost. The summer afternoon haze made it difficult to see very far, the land was flat with no special features apparent, and my ability to hold a consistent compass heading for more than two minutes was questionable. After an hour of galloping uncertainty, I flew lower to more readily spot ground features and concentrated on looking for the name of a town on a roof or, better yet, an airstrip.

Eventually I stumbled upon a small grass airstrip with half a dozen airplanes parked on it next to a cabin. After landing, I nonchalantly wandered over to the cabin, next to which three people sat in lawn chairs looking over the runway. After greeting them, I hurriedly went inside before they could ask me any questions that might reveal I was lost and found just what I was looking for: an aeronautical chart wall map, with a tack, compass rose, and measuring string dead in the center, marking my location. I had blundered into North Carolina (and don't now remember the name of the town). Using the chart, I calculated the magnetic course and distance to Patrick Henry Airport, chatted it up confidently with the folks outside, climbed in the airplane, and took off, arriving home slightly wiser than when I left. Eventually I acquired my private pilot's licence.

One day I was summoned to the commanding officer's office. He handed me a letter from U.S. Army Alaska that said I had been found guilty of negligence for the five-man squad tent fire and I was to reimburse the army the assessed damage of $2,800 (worth $28,300 in 2023). Since my pay as a private was $67/month, I figured that to extract that from me would indeed be quite a feat. It wasn't. Like the IRS, they attacked my paycheck for $60/month leaving me $7/month for my extravagant lifestyle. I slunk out of his office thinking I should probably be thankful they didn't give me 50 lashes.

My snoring became a problem in the instructor barracks, which was now a five-story concrete building. Our floor was open with partitions, and noise was free to echo throughout the entire level, which contained over 100 instructors. We bunked two cots to an enclosure, and Ron Sutherland was my bunkmate. As a civilian, Ron was an astronomer at the Phila-

I am teaching a class how to remove a helicopter engine — known as an engine-ectomy.

delphia Planetarium and came off as highly intellectual. During my first Saturday inspection, the inspecting lieutenant, wearing white gloves, ran his index finger along the upper inside lip of my wall-locker door and presented the results directly in in front of my face: dust! Since any gig in an enclosure was a gig for both occupants, Sutherland's disdain for his new bunkmate was palpable, and it took a while for him to get over it, although we finally became good friends.

But my snoring didn't just bother Sutherland—it bothered the whole third floor of the barracks, and complaints started to fester. I knew of no solution short of sleeping outside or on the roof, which could have worked were it not winter. One night Sutherland acquired a tape recorder and recorded the racket. Then, while a small group happily looked on, he played it back at high volume and woke me up with my own snoring. I responded with feigned good nature, but in fact I was embarrassed and frustrated by a problem I couldn't solve.

I made another friend named Jack Stewart, who was an instructor in the Airframe and Rotor Section. Jack had been an airline pilot with United Airlines. He had been drafted and easily could have flown for the military but hated the peacetime military "with all their bullshit" so much that he just wanted to get through it ASAP. The two of us would escape weekends to fly at the airport and follow up with beer drinking and shuffleboard tournaments at the local taverns. One day we both drew kitchen police (KP) duty. At breakfast I was in back washing pots and pans and Jack was on the serving line. Staff Sergeant Jacobs, who was our cantankerous barracks sergeant, came through the line in his Class A uniform and held out his tray to Jack, who was serving bacon. Jack dropped two strips on his plate and sarcastically Jacobs said, "Aw, come on, Stewart. Are you so cheap that two lousy strips is the best you can do?" According to witnesses, Jack picked up the entire 10-inch-deep pan of bacon that had two inches of grease-soaked bread underneath and upended it on Jacob's tray. The grease overflowed and ran down the front of Jacob's uniform. Working on my pots and pans in back, I heard a combination of swearing, shouting, and laughter but had no clue what was happening. Later, out of the window over my work sink, I saw MP's escorting Jack in handcuffs to a police car and drive off. I never saw him again. Missed that guy.

Up in Alaska, the 1957 fire season was unlike anything anybody had ever seen before; 5.25 million acres burned! Apparently, my brief tenure with that organization had left a good impression because the BLM Alaska State director petitioned the army to release me early under peacetime regulations that provided for such an action in the event one's civilian occupation was more in the public interest than his military one. Predictably, the army rejected the request. After a hassle, the army relented, and I was released. In the spring of 1958 I returned to Fairbanks, primed for a new life.

10

1958

Back to Alaska

I arrived in Fairbanks soon after the 1958 season became active. To my surprise I found that a smokejumper loft building and a new dispatch/office were under construction. The plan was to implement the Alaska smokejumper program in the spring of 1959, and I was informed that my discussions about smokejumpers in 1956 had triggered them to start a smokejumper program in Alaska.

Two days after I arrived, I was in a small, two-seat helicopter, the type used later in the TV series *Mash*, approaching a large fire 50 miles east of Fairbanks named the Chena Dome Fire. This was the first actual fire that I had seen in Alaska, and I was amazed at its size. Upon intercepting the fire, the pilot skirted its perimeter so I could observe the terrain, fuel types, and personnel deployed on the ground. Just skirting the perimeter took 40 minutes. We landed at the fire headquarters, and I met the fire boss, Wayne Fellers. Due to the size of the fire, I assumed he was VIP fire official, possibly even from Washington, D.C., but he was an emergency firefighter (EFF) who had been hired "off the street," and had years of experience. That the BLM was so understaffed that they couldn't even spare a seasonal employee, much less a permanent employee, to run a 60,000-acre fire stunned me, and at that point I began to realize how pitifully small our resources were for handling a fire challenge the size of Alaska's.

At that time, the Fairbanks Bureau of Land Management employed about a dozen permanent people which included the forestry, fire control, and general land office functions. A few more were in field stations in Big Delta, Tanacross, and McGrath. During the fire season, about 10 seasonal fire control aids arrived to round out the Fairbanks staff. Other seasonal fire control aids were stationed at Eagle, Central, Fort Yukon, and later, Galena. This was the nucleus fire control force for all of Alaska north and west of the Alaska Range, including the Yukon-Kuskokwim Delta. Almost all the actual firefighting, however, was done by EFFs who were essentially pickup firefighters like Wayne Fellers. Many returned year after year and were very experienced.

After my "drive-by" orientation with an Alaskan fire, I was assigned as a dispatcher in the back office where Russ Hanson, an experienced seasonal dispatcher, showed me the ropes. The fire season was rapidly becoming active, and I became glued to the dispatch desk and a microphone from about 7:00 a.m. to 9:00 p.m., learning by doing. Before long I came to realize that we had a significant local man-caused fire problem in Fairbanks.

The town was surrounded by homesteads, many of which were still being cleared and developed. Homesteaders had bulldozers that they used to clear land. This involved scraping off the trees and surface vegetation and pushing them into berm piles which they would attempt to burn. Because the berms were a mixture of wood, other vegetation, and peat, they never burned thoroughly once ignited, and smoldered indefinitely into the winter and sometimes the following spring. Fairbanks had no ordinances governing this activity, and much of it was outside the city limits. The state of Alaska did not yet exist; we were still a territory.

During hot weather, many of these dormant fires would wake up almost all at once and take off as crown fires through the adjoining spruce forests. We responded as best we could since often no other organization was equipped or willing to pitch in, but we had little to offer other than hiring bulldozers, which the government paid for. Once that summer,

I stood in the yard of the ranger station and counted 13 large smoke convection columns surrounding town. In the office, my single dial telephone was so swamped with people calling for help that I had to fight to get the line open to call up reinforcements such as—you guessed it—more bulldozers. We were up to our ears fighting private-land fires.

My little dispatch office had a king-sized high-frequency (HF) radio which stood over 5-feet high next to the desk. Our fire frequency was 5,287.5 kilocycles. Actually this was our only frequency in Alaska, so fire traffic had to elbow its way through housekeeping and other traffic to be heard. High frequencies are for long distances as well as short. When you pressed the microphone button, you would be heard next door as well as throughout many areas of Alaska hundreds of miles away (unless the Russians were jamming the frequency which was common). In 1958, a married, seasonal couple were separated for the summer to operate the Big Delta and Eagle guard stations. When evening radio traffic was low, they would come on the air (probably after a drinkie-poo or two) and have marriage spats for all of us to enjoy. This was before TV, but just as good.

A Near-Death Experience

Another homesteader fire visible from our fire headquarters.

In 1956, I had joined the Fairbanks Parachute Club, a ragtag organization focused on skydiving, which at that time was a fairly new civilian sport. We scrounged the use of airplanes from friends and packed our parachutes in the dormitory hallways of the University of Alaska. I knew little about my parachute. A fellow I had just met lent it to me already packed, and it looked OK on the outside, so I used it, and it worked.

One day in 1958, our aircraft chief, John McCormick, expressed interest in observing a jump up close, so I volunteered to provide a demonstration. My landing spot would be a small, deserted pasture near Creamer's Dairy which had only one large spruce tree in its center. McCormick drove out to the field and waited. He was unfamiliar with parachute operations. A friend with a small airplane took me up to 6,000 feet, and I jumped out over the landing zone.

Free-falling is an invigorating pastime—kind of like flying, only without an airplane. To a certain extent the skydiver can navigate and aim for a ground target. I loved the feeling so much that I was reluctant to open the parachute any sooner than absolutely necessary, and on this jump, I carried this to a near-fatal extreme. The main parachute had a metal handle called a "D ring" on the harness on the upper left chest area. Pulling this out of its holder deploys the parachute. Suddenly (it seemed), the ground started rushing up at me, and I reached for the D ring and pulled. It didn't come out! This required a split-nanosecond decision: deploy the reserve chute or look down and see what's with the D ring. I chose the D ring and discovered my bare hand, which had become numb during the fall through the cold air, was trying to pull the harness and not the ring. I promptly ripped the D ring out by the roots, and the chute deployed with a resounding crack.

An extreme oscillation put me at the same altitude as the canopy which managed to settle directly onto the lone tree in the pasture, with the result that I swung into it to become one with a large, cobweb-infested spruce. My descent ended with my toes 12 feet above the ground. McCormick, standing nearby, thought the show was spectacular. I thought it was the dumbest thing I had ever done in my life, bordering on criminal stupidity. I made a decision right there to quit jumping. It was obvious I had demonstrated an inability to control my love of flying without an airplane to any reasonably safe standard.

1958 Fire Season

One evening under the midnight sun, Bob Johnson, the BLM pilot in Fairbanks, flew a Grumman Goose N640 into an unfamiliar lake with a crew of firefighters. After touching down, he skimmed across the lake "on the step" toward shore which was a good distance away. Later Bob told me his first hint of trouble was when he spotted a seagull apparently standing on the water directly ahead. It was actually standing on a gravel bar just below the surface, and the Grumman came to a grinding stop on it, high but not quite dry. The firefighters removed their fire shovels from their fire packs, got out, and started shoveling, but to no avail. The situation looked hopeless, so Johnson called for another goose to help pull him off the gravel bar.

Grumman Goose N640.

John "Mac" McCormick showed up in his goose, and a what-the-hell-do-we-do-now? conference ensued. Mac positioned his goose back-to-back to Johnson's and tied the two together with a line so he could pull him off the bar. Since Mac would not be able to gauge the progress (or lack thereof) behind him, they arranged to communicate via the HF radio, which would be heard statewide and probably well into Russia. Mac fired up the engines, and while the firefighters pushed, he applied maximum power to start the pull. All over Alaska, people on that frequency heard, "*GO! GO! GO!*" followed by, "*DON'T STOP—DON'T STOP—DON'T STOP!*" and probably wondered what kind of activity they were listening to. Fortunately, the maneuver succeeded, and Johnson's goose floated free off the gravel bar.

Because of the lightning fire detection challenges for a state the size of Alaska, the BLM leased a WWII P-51 Mustang fighter that could fly 300 mph and stay aloft about three hours. Its registration was N5448V; it was pink and known as the Pink Lady. Its objective was to respond rapidly to fire weather forecasts that predicted lightning in faraway places. My first memory of this airplane was on or about July 4, 1958, when the pilot, Jim Telford, and observer, Joe Kastelic, took off from Fairbanks International on a morning patrol. Telford called in, announcing, "Fairbanks, 48V is off at 07, and we have a fire to report!"

The fire was immediately out of town on the slopes of Murphy Dome, on top of which was an air force radar installation. It was probably caused by lightning. Telford described it as burning hot and spreading fast in solid spruce. In addition to dispatching everyone I could get hold of, I went to work gathering up—you guessed it—more bulldozers. (Often, we would hire them from the same homesteaders who had started their own fires, but at least they had fire experience.) Before long I had acquired four D8 "cats" and arranged for one of our employees, Boyd Matthews, to be the cat boss and march them cross-country up the slopes of Murphy Dome.

The morning dragged on into early afternoon. Meanwhile the fire was moving rapidly, and the air force was on my back about their radar installation. Eventually Boyd called in on the radio. One of the D8s was stuck in a swamp, and he was using another to pull it out. Before long he called again. Both cats were stuck in the swamp, and he was using the third to pull them out. Half an hour later he called to tell me all four cats were stuck, and could I please hurry and send him more cats? I was furious and announced that better than that, I was sending a replacement cat boss. A day later, an experienced fire boss named Bill Adams showed up and took over the situation, which had become chaotic. I still remember him talking about the air force guys posted in the windows of the buildings on the Murphy Dome summit holding fire hoses at the ready, much like machine guns. The fire never reached there but became the major fire for the 1958 season due to its intensity, proximity to Fairbanks, and the paranoia of our air force.

On Airport Road, the Igloo Motel was situated close to the driveway entrance of the ranger station. It was largely inhabited by EFF who had Hallicrafter radios capable of monitoring our radio fire frequency. When a fire report came in to me (usually from an aircraft), they would intercept this information and start streaming down the driveway into the sta-

A typical active crown fire near Rampart on the Yukon River in 1958. This crew was not in danger because they were camped on the edge of a small lake.

tion where they would be rounded up, trucked to the airport, loaded onto airplanes, and flown to the fire. This was the nucleus firefighting force at Fairbanks. Around the Interior and the coast, in the villages, native fire crews were being formed and eventually would become the mainstay forces for firefighting in Alaska.

An example of this was the Nenana W-30 fire which was, as the name implies, 30 miles west of Nenana. It was a large fire, burning mostly in a carpet of spruce, and there were about 100 EFF villagers fighting it. The fire boss was a Japanese EFF named Herbie Yamanaka. Since we had no helicopters to spare, I rented Herbie a Piper Super Cub with pilot, and they operated off a nearby gravel bar on the Nenana River. One day word spread that Herbie had fallen out of the airplane and survived uninjured, which greatly upset me. At the time I didn't know whether to believe this or not, and still don't. (Maybe he fell out while trying to get in or out of it on the ground and exaggerated a lot.)

Flying a P-51 Mustang on Gas Fumes

Late in the afternoon on August 20, I received a telegram from the village of Unalakleet on the west coast. It said, "Fire in the Old Woman River valley. Smoke blanketing Unalakleet." I contacted Bob Johnson to schedule the P-51 for a recon flight early the next morning, and he asked if I'd like to join him, so I did. We took off at dawn with three hours of fuel and headed for the Old Woman River in the mountains between the Yukon River and the coast. The flight plan was roughly one hour out, almost one hour searching, and one hour back. We were not what you would call heavy with fuel reserves.

Today's airlines have nothing on us. My seat was a wood plank, and the back of Johnson's head was only 13 inches in front of my nose. A parachute provided the cushion for my back against the frame, and I was inside a tangle of safety straps, microphone wire, and earphone wires, all crammed in under the plexiglass canopy. The engine noise was so loud, if you screamed you were unable to hear yourself.

The farther west we flew, the lower the ceiling became, and it appeared we were flying into a textbook warm front situation. Just past the Yukon River, southwest of Galena, we encountered rain. In the Old Woman drainage there was no sign of smoke, and we broadened our search area south along both sides of the Yukon. Eventually we discontinued searching and turned for home, at which point I dozed off. The low weather was forcing us to follow the river under a 600-foot indefinite overcast. Then, abruptly, the engine quit! No warning, no sputtering—nothing except the sound of wind friction. And then it suddenly started again. I've never been more awake in my life!

Johnson came on the intercom. "Jim, the fuel tank that just ran dry was the one I thought we had the most fuel in. I switched over to it when I thought the tank [we are on now] was about to run out. I'm going to try to make it to Galena."

I croaked, "Bob, how long have we been airborne?"

"I don't know. I don't have my watch, and the clock in the instrument panel quit, and I didn't realize it." (It was a windup clock.)

I no longer had my watch because several days earlier I had fallen off the wing of a Grumman Goose amphibian into a lake and ruined it. Thus, I was clueless as well.

Servicing our P-51 Mustang lightning storm patrol airplane.

The prospect of ditching a P-51 Mustang fighter successfully into the fast-flowing Yukon River terrified me, so I suggested we instead use whatever fuel we had remaining, go on instruments, climb to altitude, bail out, and hope we miss the Yukon. I'd take my chance in the top of a spruce any day over drowning. Bob didn't go for this because he said our parachutes were way past their maximum repacking date. Also, I later learned his only jump experience was out of a B-24 with three out of four engines and the bomb bay on fire at 18,000 feet over Germany. He had spent one year, one month, and one day in a German POW camp. This had not been kind of unpleasant, and he did not wish to repeat it.

Desperate to get out of the airplane, I became marginally irrational and asked him to invert the airplane and jettison the canopy so I could bail out and take my own chances, even though we only had 600 feet of altitude. Again, he refused, this time because the canopy balance had not been recertified, and if out of balance, he thought it could decapitate both of us. (And so, I thought, *why in the f**k are we wearing parachutes?*)

Completely out of ideas, I shivered in silence and awaited developments. Johnson then repeatedly tried to call Galena FAA radio. They finally answered, and I listened as Bob told them he thought we were somewhere southwest of them, very low on fuel, and the fuel pressure was starting to fluctuate. He said if we didn't show up in a few minutes they should initiate a search for us. My pulse was pounding like a sledgehammer.

For a moment we entered instrument flight conditions (immersed in clouds) and then broke out almost on top of the Galena runway. Fearing engine failure any second, Bob executed the wildest landing approach

I'd ever experienced, and we plunked down on the runway. After refueling, the meter read 184 gallons, which was exactly the capacity of the airplane. The only fuel left had been in the lines.

11

1958 - 1959

The Search for Clarence Rhode

We had an uneventful trip back to Fairbanks. I walked into my office and almost immediately received a call from the U.S. Fish and Wildlife Service (FWS) that they had an aircraft missing. It was a Grumman Goose amphibian flown by Clarence Rhode, who was the head of the FWS in Alaska. The Fairbanks FWS director, Stan Fredrickson, and Rhode's son, Jack, were also on board. 1958 was the International Geophysical Year (IGY) which was a worldwide program of geophysical research conducted during 1957, and 1958. Rhode had planned to visit the IGY party camped on the very remote Lake Peters in the eastern Brooks Range, over 300 miles north of Fairbanks. FWS requested we dispatch an aircraft there and interview the IGY folks to see if Rhode had actually made it to the lake, and if so—where was he headed next?

Not wanting to interrupt the most adventure-packed summer of my young life, Fred Varney, the BLM fire control officer, tasked me with going to Lake Peters in one of our Grumman Gooses with the pilot, Jim Starkey, to track down the IGY group. We departed early the next morning and, due to having to navigate around some weather, landed at Lake Peters four hours later. Tucked into the desolate mountains of the Brooks Range, this was easily the most unfriendly environment I had ever seen. It was dark, very rugged, cold, and isolated. Everything that wasn't lake was rock—cold, grey, hard rock. I wondered how the fishing was.

Yes, Rhode had been there several days before, but the IGY scientists were unable to help us much in the way of defining his intended route. Apparently, Rhode had been vague, telling them he was headed "westward," providing no particular destination and commenting that he had enough fuel and reserve case gas on board to "go 1,000 miles in any direction." This little gem of information had a huge impact on the search effort, which eventually expanded into the largest search since Amelia Earhart disappeared and lasted well into winter.

Our assigned search area included Lake Peters, so we took off and started looking. Starkey commented that he would't feel safe flying in this country in anything less than a four-engine helicopter. My steel-trap mind surmised he probably wasn't feeling very safe since we were flying in a twin-engine WW-II relic. Finding nothing, we returned to Fairbanks and became participants in an endless search that went on for weeks. (Twenty-one years later, when I was the Department of Interior's aviation director, an employee walked into my office with the news that the airplane had been located—burned and splattered on a mountainside north of Arctic Village on the south slope of the Brooks Range.)

Cabin Fever

Back at the ranger station, thirty yards from the smokejumper loft construction site, was a beautiful three-bedroom log home occupied by Fred Varney and his family. Late summer, Varney transferred out of state and was replaced by Jim Scott from Homer, Alaska. Jim located in private housing in Fairbanks, leaving the log home vacant. It was decided that Joe Kastelic and I could share it, and we promptly moved in. There were bedrooms with beds but no living room furniture—just a big room with nothing. There also was a small, round dining table but no chairs, so we sat on empty Blazo boxes, which are wooden crates that each hold two 5-gallon cans of fuel.

The 1958–59 winter was very cold with minus 50-to-60-degree temperatures and thick ice fog for prolonged periods; this made our daylight hours quite short. Cabin fever became a problem, and after a while Joe and I had coexistence problems. Joe was a good guy but very macho and intimidating as hell—kind of a "my way or the highway" personality. Being an introvert, I tended to withdraw from our conversations because they usually ended in arguments and hard feelings. Joe had a car, and some evenings he would visit a tavern down the street. I often remained in the cabin, sitting on a Blazo box in the middle of the empty living room, wiling the hours away by shooting scurrying insects on the wall with a .22 rifle. (Once again, no radio or TV, etc. But the log walls absorbed bullets with hardly any sign, and one seeks entertainment wherever one can find it—don't they?)

Eventually, Jim Scott noticed the tense atmosphere between us and seized command of the situation, forcing us to reluctantly shake hands like two boys in a schoolyard. After that, Joe and I socialized somewhat, although in those days I had difficulty handling the expected beer input rate at the various Fairbanks bars.

1959 Fire Season

My 1959 fire dispatch office.

With the arrival of early spring, the new dispatch/office building was ready to be occupied. I wanted a wall map to end all wall maps, so I constructed one that covered the entire 20-foot width and the 13-foot height of the wall. It embraced everything from the western Alaska coast east to the Yukon border and from Anchorage in the south to the Brooks Range in the north. Grease pencils would be used to annotate fire information and magnetic symbols could also be used. A library-type rolling ladder enabled access to great heights. A mammoth desk with two side-by-side office chairs largely occupied the room. It was kind of like a mini-situation room for two with phones and radios.

Now I needed to recruit an assistant dispatcher. I had met George Kitson, was one of the experienced emergency firefighters, and "liked the cut of his jib," so I hired him. He appeared to be intelligent, well-versed in on-the-ground fire operations, and equipped with good, old-fashioned common sense. We worked well together in spite of having to endure what would be a highly stressful fire season that was even worse than 1958.

When the fire season was underway, and on days the fire weather forecast predicted lightning storms, I would send the P-51 Mustang out to patrol the forecasted thunderstorm areas. The airplane was now fitted with two wing tanks, which would greatly improve its fuel endurance beyond the three hours we had last year. Having returned from the first patrol with these new tanks, Bob Johnson came into the dispatch office and announced, "Thurston, you should have been with me—the engine quit eight times!" It turned out Bob said it was an easily correctable fuel plumbing problem, but Norm Profit, the Fire Control Aid who had flown with him as the observer, was somewhat in shock from the ordeal and wanted nothing further to do with observer patrol duty. This complicated my morning ritual of finding observers to fly the fire detection missions.

Around 10:30 in the morning I would step out onto the front entrance of the dispatch office and survey the scene in the yard. I'd observe FCAs working on assorted projects that served to fill the voids between fire activity. These used to be peaceful, work-in-progress scenes. Not anymore. Now when I appeared on the doorstep, people were diving under hedges, hiding behind trees, and peeking around building corners. One morning I caught my old tutor, Russ Hanson. In spite of his pleading, I sent him out to meet Bob Johnson at the airplane. After being crammed into the back of the airplane, he asked Johnson in a small quavering voice, "Bob, how will I know if there is some sort of problem?"

To which Johnson responded, "Well Russ, if you smell smoke and see me fumbling with my straps, you'd better start making your own arrangements!" Shortly after, Bob gave poor Russ a real safety briefing, but I doubt he ever forgot the mental picture of "smoke and a pilot fumbling with his straps." (We operated the P-51 from 1958 to 1967 with only one minor incident all those years.)

The late '50s were the early days of retardant bombers in Alaska, all of which were WWII surplus military aircraft. For years we hired a small fleet of B-25s that had large numbers on their tails ranging from 1 to 5. Their call signs were Antique 1, Antique 2, etc. Other bombers we used included

B-25 retardant bomber "Antique 4".

Grumman F7F Tigercat's, TBMs, and B-26 Marauders.

Grumman F7F Tigercat bomber.

Eventually the inevitable happened: I had accumulated enough cash to buy an inexpensive airplane and was scouting for prospects. Nearby at Phillips Field I found a Piper J-3 Cub on wheels that had been converted from a 65hp to a 115hp engine. In my mind this was a "bush airplane," and I bought it. With that kind of power-to-weight ratio, I would be able to slip into and out of incredibly short landing areas.

One morning I landed on a very short gravel bar on the Chena River to go fly fishing for grayling. The fishing was good, and at midafternoon I decided to leave. The weather was hot—almost 90 degrees—and I realized I'd need maximum takeoff performance to clear the alder brush in my departure path. I dragged the airplane back as far as possible until the tail wheel was in the water, fired up the engine, applied full power, and bumped on down the gravel bar. Almost immediately I realized I wasn't going to clear the 12-foot-high alder brush at the other end and chopped the engine. The alders gently embraced my airplane as I settled into the comfortable lap of Mother Nature.

So, there were three things I needed to do: cut down a whole bunch of alders with my machete, drag the airplane by its tail all the way back to the initial takeoff point, and wait until late evening for the temperature to cool, which would enhance flight performance due to denser air. While a machete was not the best hand tool for chopping heavy alder, it was the only tool I had, and I went to work, generating blisters and soaking myself in sweat, which I repeatedly alleviated by jumping into the river. As evening approached, so did hordes of mosquitoes, and around 10:00 p.m., I successfully lifted off the gravel bar and returned to Fairbanks, contemplating how neat it would be to be on floats. Two weeks later I found some, made a deal, put them on the airplane, and embarked upon acquiring a seaplane rating.

July developed into a hot, fire-active month around Fairbanks. The usual spate of homesteader fires was augmented by lightning fires and military artillery practice, which torched off their firing range south of town, smoking everything up. One afternoon a Ladd Air Force Base colonel called, pleading for any fire hand tools we could spare, saying they had a 300-acre fire in their bomb dump. I told him we were down to two shovels, a Pulaski, and one backpack water pump. He immediately sent someone to fetch them. An hour later, a highly excited caller told me I needed to send help to fight a hot brush fire that was burning between four GI homes on the Richardson Highway. I told him to calm down and call the Ladd Air Force Base fire dispatcher who would handle his problem. His response: "Hell man, I AM the Ladd fire dispatcher!"

Meanwhile, just outside the window of our dispatch office, FCA Manfred Keiss from New York City was dutifully trying to execute his assignment of chopping down an aspen tree that was too close to Golden Valley Electric's power lines and our phone lines. Being a city boy, he assumed one chops down trees much like a beaver does—chew all around it until it topples. The tree fell on the lines, we lost our power, and our four phone lines went bonkers—they wouldn't stop ringing, couldn't be answered, and couldn't be silenced.

The broken power line started a creeping ground fire only six feet from our open window, so I sent a runner to the garage to get hold of a pumper truck and douse it. Tanker #30 arrived shortly, but the crew could not get the pump started. Meanwhile, smoke filled the dispatch office while our radio blared with aircraft reporting new fires, our four phone lines rang non-stop, and Jim Scott could be heard from his office yelling, "Hello! Hello! Hello!" and slamming down the phone only to repeat the process endlessly. Outside, the pumper crew finally beat the fire down with hand tools, and I stood next to my desk contemplating the chaos. Functionally, my carefully organized fire control nerve center for most of Alaska was in smokey shambles. Kitson had disappeared. He was in the bathroom vomiting with a nervous stomach. I didn't feel too great either since my breakfast had consisted of only a glass of water and a cigar.

Bran Casler was the BLM radio technician, and he lived in Anchorage. Talking him into coming to Fairbanks to work on our antiquated radio was difficult because Bran hated to fly. When he relented and came to Fairbanks, he drove a car, which took almost 10 hours one way. The radio was a frequent problem but very essential to our operation, so I often had to pressure Bran over the phone to come up and fix it. Often, he would just walk up to it, kick it, and the damn thing would come alive again, at which point he would walk out the door, get into his car, and start driving back to Anchorage. (When I kicked it, it never worked.) On one visit, the kicking didn't work so Bran needed to lower the 88-foot antenna to the ground outdoors and work on it. He told me not to transmit on the radio until he was done working outside since the antenna would provide a substantial shock to anyone handling it if the transmitter were activated. Ten minutes later, one of our aircraft called in a fire report, and having spaced out Bran, I answered the call. Instantly there was a loud howl outside because I had energized poor old Bran from head to toe, following which he let me know how unhappy he was. My profuse apologies seemed to have little effect, and I concluded he probably didn't like me anymore (if indeed ever).

12

1959 - 1961

Kicked Out of Alaska

The U.S. Department of the Interior's attorneys for Alaska (called solicitors) had their office in Sacramento, California. In 1959, frustrated with fighting private-land fires while the public domain lands we were paid to protect were left to burn, I wrote a brief letter to them requesting their opinion regarding the legality of our actions. The Solicitor's written response was that what we were doing constituted a misappropriation of federal funds. In an exhibition of stupendous naivety, and thinking I was being helpful, I showed the letter to Dick Quintus, the district forester. Two weeks later he summoned me into his office downtown and informed me I was being transferred to Salem in thirty days. This made no sense to me. I asked, "You mean Salem, where they used to burn witches?" Patiently he explained that, for my information, Oregon actually had a capital named Salem. I walked out of his office embarrassed, dejected, angry, and disillusioned.

It was mid-September. The night air was getting crisp, and geese were flying south. Sadly, it was time for me to join them. In addition to the airplane, everything I owned only half filled my army duffle bag, which I tossed into the J-3 Cub, along with the landing gear, wheels, and new aeronautical charts. I had been mooring the floatplane on the Chena River next to the barracks, and with a heavy heart, I untied it and drifted out in the current. The Cub had no electrical system which meant I had to start it by hand while standing on the float. After warming up the engine, I lifted off the water and turned south wondering whether I would ever return to Alaska again.

My plan was to take the inland route, following the Alaska Highway down to Fort Saint John, B.C., and then fly over the Canadian Rockies to Prince George and south to Washington State. Adding to my glum mood, the weather for my Fairbanks departure was uninspiring with low ceilings and scattered showers. Due to restricted visibility, numerous flocks of geese were flying virtually alongside me until the clouds opened up south of Big Delta and we separated. Floatplane fuel was available at Northway near the Canadian border, and I overnighted there.

My 115hp J-3 Cub at Fort St. John, B.C.

Whitehorse, Yukon Territory, was my next stop and the place where I made a monumental miscalculation by setting my watch the wrong direction for a time zone correction, which resulted in a two-hour error. I took off from the Yukon River for my next stop at Watson Lake thinking it was 2:30 p.m. when it was actually 4:30 p.m. Later, as I wafted over Teslin Lake, the sun surprised me, and as I watched in disbelief, it set. As the residual daylight faded, I contemplated all sorts of conspiracy theories as to how this unbelievable event could have occurred. That I had set my watch wrong seemed highly improbable. About the time there was barely enough daylight left to successfully land on a lake for the night, a full moon came up, and I spotted the airport beacon at Watson Lake across the flatlands about 80 miles to the east, so I kept on trucking.

My little J-3 Cub had the same radio as the Cub I flew in Virginia with the flying club—no transmitter, only a receiver—so I couldn't initiate contact with Watson Lake. When I arrived close enough for radio reception, I tuned in to Watson Lake aeronautical radio and was stunned to hear they had a surface wind gusting to 32 knots out of the west. This had been a tailwind for me and explained why I was arriving much earlier than anticipated. Looking down at the lake in the bright moonlight, I could see whitecaps—lots of angry-looking whitecaps— and concluded that since my fuel situation demanded I land soon, the chances were high that I was at least going to get wet, maybe lose the airplane, and possibly even my life.

Turning west into the wind, I let down as close to the shore as possible (to decrease potential swimming distance) and landed, meeting the waves head-on. After several vicious bounces off the waves, the Cub survived the ordeal, and I commenced "sailing" backward toward shore since there was no way one could turn the airplane around in that wind. (Airplanes are designed to point into the wind and tend to resist otherwise.) I was expecting the airplane would likely impact shore obstructions and take damage, however, out of nowhere, a person on shore caught the rudder and eased me onto the bank. It turned out he was the Watson Lake aeronautical radio operator, who had heard my engine overhead, knew I was in trouble, abandoned his radio, and left to provide hands-on assistance. That I happened to touch down next to where he worked was extraordinarily lucky. That night he let me bunk in a back room of the radio building.

The next day I flew to Fort Nelson, fueled, and continued on to Fort Saint John, B.C. For two days I attempted crossing into the Canadian Rockies en route to Prince George but had to turn back due to mountain thunderstorms. I succeeded on the third day and, after fueling, headed south down the Fraser River canyon in low clouds and heavy rain to Quesnel, where I encountered an impassable cloud-to-ground weather block immediately south of town. I had to land in the Fraser River, but due to heavy rain, it was a roaring torrent of whitecaps with occasional logs poking up: this provided me a dire warning against landing. There was no choice—the weather had dropped in behind me. On the river's edge of town, there was a narrow strip of calmer water, perhaps forty feet wide, with a sandy shore upon which I hoped to beach the Cub. As I made my approach, I could see people gathering on the beach. When I touched down and went aground, they grabbed the airplane, pulled on it, and beached it. About twenty people were assembled there in the heavy rain. They had observed an idiot trying to land in a log-infested, white-water river in unflyable weather and came out to help. I love Canadians. I wondered if they thought I was at all hairbrained.

By comparison, the remainder of the trip was uneventful. An obvious concern was finding where I could land in Salem, Oregon, since the aeronautical chart provided no clue. Since the Willamette River flows right through the center of Salem, I followed it and discovered a boat marina practically in the town center. After circling a couple of times, I plopped down and taxied up to one of the docks where a crowd of people suddenly appeared. Al, the owner of the marina, welcomed me like I was some god descended from on high. It turned out that floatplanes rarely, if ever, landed there, and Al viewed my presence as a favorable curiosity item for his business. To cement this relationship I gave Al rides, and he provided me free moorage. We became friends.

Life in Oregon

My first impression of Salem was that I was in an ultra-clean and very proper city. This was the first time I had ever seen pedestrian signals at traffic lights that showed when you should walk cross an intersection. My previous reference had been 2nd Avenue in Fairbanks, which was dramatically different. But later, when the wind was just right, the stench of a local pulp mill flooded into my nostrils and made me wonder how anybody could live around such a smell.

After finding a temporary efficiency apartment room, I purchased a car. It was a 25hp Fiat that was very tiny and cheap, but at least I had wheels. I then checked into the Bureau of Land Management Salem District office and encountered my new environment. Unlike my Alaska experience, in which I pretty much operated alone and on my own initiative, I found myself in a room with about 20 foresters (it was an office day) working in a regimented environment. There were three of these units in the Salem office.

The basic BLM mission here was timber sales administration for the millions of acres of federal O&C railroad land grants in western Oregon upon which truly great forests grow. The management objective was to maintain sustained yield, or to manage the forest so that harvesting for lumber did not outpace new growth. The area of our responsibility was a chunk of the Coast Range between Salem and the Pacific coast where the primary timber species is Douglas fir. Due to high annual rainfall, these trees grow fast with some having a rotation (harvesting) age of only 80 years. The environment is very wet, steep, and brushy. In most areas, a machete is required to move through the intertwined vine maple, devil's club, and assorted other vegetation that claw at your every effort to move forward. Logger's boots with spikes coming out of the sole (caulk boots) were a necessary part of the daily field uniform since walking on large deadfall trees was a requirement to get around.

During my tenure at Salem, I primarily worked on timber sale layout, timber trespass investigation, and logging contract inspection. The trespass work was the most interesting because it usually involved actual detective work, such as interviewing people to construct a history going back many years, appraising the value of timber illegally harvested, and locating survey bearing trees, the scribed marks of which were long grown over. At times, due to the nature of the people involved, I worked in conjunction with the FBI. The agent I worked with was Hal Brack, who dressed the role of the typical J. Edgar Hoover agent and came off accordingly. He would ring the doorbell of a house (often out in the woods) to interview someone, and when they opened the door, they would be confronted by a man in a suit and fedora hat who brusquely announced, "Good afternoon. My name is Brack. B-R-A-C-K. I'm with the FBI, and I'd like to ask you a few questions." From that point on, there was no question who dominated the discussion.

I had discovered that my freshman year college roommate, John Roberts, was working as a forester for the state of Washington and that he was married and living on a lake southeast of Olympia. In mid-December I decided to fly up, land on his lake, and get reacquainted. John provided directions which later turned out to be unfathomable from an aerial view, and after grinding around for an hour near the Fort Lewis military base, I figured I had to call him again on the phone. Finding a place to land near a telephone in a floatplane was a challenge, but since the state capital, Olympia, was nearby, I figured maybe I could find a pay phone somewhere near water. Sure enough, a small lake downtown next to the old Olympia Brewery came into view, and a street ran directly into it. It was surrounded on three sides by busy highways and was sporting a large array of floating, lighted Christmas displays, in the middle of which I landed. After beaching the Cub at the end of the road I walked in a couple of blocks, found a pay phone, and acquired new directions from John. Returning to the lake I saw that a small crowd had gathered near the airplane and thought, *Uh-oh! Maybe I have a problem.* Several greeted me with "Merry Christmas," and no one voiced a complaint, but I didn't want to wait for trouble, so I pushed off, fired up the engine, and got out of Dodge.

When I arrived at Salem in late September, I had been concerned about possible snow accumulation on my moored airplane. Al told me it rains a lot in Salem, but there is very little snow. The guys at work said the same thing, so I decided not to worry about it. Most of my work was on the coast, so typically I departed Salem early Monday morning and returned late Friday night. (We were expected to travel on our own time.) One Saturday morning after returning from a week on the coast where a storm had produced very heavy rain, I drove over to the marina with the intent of ferrying the Cub to Kenmore Air in Washington State to have the floats removed and wheels put on.

Unknown to me, during my absence Salem had received over two feet of heavy wet snow, all of which had melted away prior to my return. I arrived at the marina and found that my airplane had sunk. The only things above the water surface were the left float and wing, the engine, and the cockpit windscreen. I could see the airplane logbook floating on the water just beneath the now horizontal windscreen. It was painful to look at. The left float had been secured to a floating dock next to a railroad trestle, and the float struts had buckled under the weight. No one had observed this predicament because this was a secluded area devoid of people during the boating off-season. For the next few days, I salvaged the airplane piece by piece, snaking the wings, fuselage, floats, and tail feathers out through the railroad trestle cross-bracing to the road. Eventually I made a deal with an A&E aircraft mechanic to repair and certify the Cub on wheels in return for him taking possession of my floats.

After about six months, it became obvious to me that the primary skill requirement for a forester in Salem was the proficient wielding of a machete, because virtually everything we did in the field involved cutting brush, often in heavy rain. As time passed, I became more and more disillusioned because the work essentially bored me and did not allow for much creative thought or innovation. Also, I was disappointed with my college training as a forester because I realized that instead of teaching machete-hacking 101, they had schooled me in forest management practices that were not yet practiced and at least 50 years in the future. About this time, I ran across a person who was selling a new vacuum cleaner product to families living in remote areas. He wanted to recruit a vacuum cleaner salesman and had his eye on me. By the spring of 1961, I was so despondent I decided to quit my federal job and become backwoods vacuum cleaner salesman, not realizing that this would be a total dead end, especially since I lacked a salesman personality and couldn't sell a chicken to a starving billionaire.

In what some might call divine intervention, about a week before I was going to hand in my resignation, I received a letter from Jim Scott, my boss from Fairbanks, who had been promoted and was now stationed in Anchorage. BLM had established a fire control training officer position for Alaska and he wanted to take advantage of my military instructor experience. Apparently, he didn't share Dick Quintus's views of my undesirability for the organization and wanted me back. I was ecstatic! In retrospect, Scott saved me from committing a monumental career blunder.

Several days later, as I was making plans for traveling back to Alaska, a fellow from Klamath Falls, Oregon, called and expressed interest in my airplane. He had a Globe Swift that he might be willing to swap, and I agreed to fly down to Klamath Falls and meet with him. The Globe Swift is a two-seat, all-metal, low-wing, retractable landing gear airplane with a reputation for vicious ground loops if not handled correctly. Even though I knew the Swift was not well-suited for Alaska, I thought it would be fun to fly it to Anchorage and eventually sell it for something else. Jim Starkey (of Brooks Range, Lake Peters fame) lived in Klamath Falls and agreed to check me out, after which I swapped my airplane for the Globe Swift and continued preparing for the Alaska journey.

13

1961 - 1962

Back Yet Again

The trip back to the northland was uneventful compared to my trip down in the Cub. The weather was perfect, and the airplane ran flawlessly. I never encountered a problem with its ground handling. I landed at Merrill Field in downtown Anchorage, found transit parking, and was unloading my personal effects when a stranger

My Globe Swift at Merrill Field, Anchorage.

came up to me. He was curious about the airplane, and I proudly pointed its various features out to him. His name was Merrill Akers, and 60 years later we are still friends.

In Anchorage, the BLM occupied almost all of the six-story Cordova Building in town, and there I gratefully reconnected with Jim Scott. BLM also had a fire control base at Elmendorf Air Force Base on Oilwell Road. This is where I would work developing a training program. I was now a fire control training officer who had yet to actually fight a fire in Alaska since all my previous experience was fighting for time on the radios and telephones as a fire dispatcher in Fairbanks. While settling in to this new job, I coordinated some of the training, planning, and organizing effort with Bill Adams, who was running the BLM station at Tanacross, 190 miles down the Alaska Highway from Fairbanks. Bill turned out to be a gold mine of information about Alaskan firefighting techniques and was often called upon to be the fire boss for the more challenging fire problems in Alaska. Much of the information I forged into training curriculum originated from Adams, and during that summer, I practiced what Adams preached as a fire boss on several fires around the state.

Bill Smith from Main Street, Pennsylvania

Late summer in 1961, I met Bill Smith, a bachelor like me, who was transferring to Anchorage from Fairbanks. We decided to share an apartment I had found in Spenard (a suburb of Anchorage), and we moved in the day he arrived. We decided to celebrate this event with a party. Bill opened a checking account at the National Bank of Alaska and wrote check #1 for $89 ($883 in 2023 dollars) to the Cut-Rate Kid, a well-known local liquor store. Our apartment had a large living room, and since its layout was well-suited for parties, its initiation was a huge success and became a central gathering place for friends. Bill, however, was not a big drinker.

One evening he attended some sort of highbrow banquet—for which he rented a tuxedo—and was sitting opposite a distinguished gentlemen who ordered a martini. Having never tried one, Bill gave it a shot and enjoyed it so much he ordered another. The gentlemen was engaging him in intellectual conversation in which Bill pretended to be vitally interested while the waiters distributed the main course consisting of roast beef, mashed potatoes, and gravy. While pretending to be ultra-fascinated with the gentlemen's dissertation, which was way over his head, Bill suddenly woke up face down in his mashed potatoes. Undeterred, he pulled out his handkerchief, wiped off his gravy-soaked glasses, and continued intently listening, just like nothing out of the ordinary had happened. Bill was a quiet intellectual with a sense of humor, and this experience was very unlike him. He used to say he was Bill Smith from Main Street, Pennsylvania, and he actually did live on Main Street. He also loved to tell this story on himself.

Globe Swift Close Call

Shortly after placing an ad in the paper to sell the Globe Swift, Larry, an air force F-102 fighter pilot at Elmendorf Air Force Base, responded, and I took him on a demonstration flight. At one point he asked me about the function of the carburetor heat control, which is so basic to airplanes I wouldn't have been more surprised if he had asked the same about the function of wings. Larry explained he had never flown an airplane with a reciprocating engine—only jets, but he liked the airplane, and we made a deal. On a Saturday morning I had him practicing touch-and-go takeoffs and landings at a nearby gravel airstrip in Eagle River with me in the right seat. The Swift brakes were mounted on the left rudder pedals, and there were none on the right side for me. I discussed the airplane's ground handling reputation with Larry and emphasized he and he alone had the brakes if we ever needed them.

After an uneventful series of touch-and-go landings, we returned to Merrill Field, and Larry executed the landing—almost. As we were rolling out, the airplane suddenly spun about 70 degrees to the right, went between two runway lights, and headed into a small plane parking area. Through our spinning propeller I could see the back of a man working on the engine of his parked high-wing Cessna airplane, and without us changing direction, it was obvious we were going to take him out. I started yelling, "Left brake! Left brake! Left brake!" and seeing no response I looked over and observed Larry had frozen on the controls, so I delivered a healthy backhand punch to his shoulder. It worked. He stomped on the left brake, and the Swift abruptly spun to the left, our low right wing going under the higher left wing of the Cessna. Since we had been throttled back to idle through all this, I don't believe the fellow ever heard or noticed us, even though the tip of our wing had passed within ten feet of him. Later, I suggested Larry spend some time with a qualified flight instructor to brush up on these types of aircraft because I obviously hadn't filled that bill for him. After completing the sale, I started contemplating the idea of a replacement airplane.

Mount Alyeska

That fall, I drove down to the recently constructed Alyeska Ski Resort in Girdwood, about 40 miles down the highway from Anchorage on Turnagain Arm. The scenery was spectacular; this was my first visit there. Turnagain Arm is a fjord named by William Bligh of HMS *Bounty* fame, who was Captain Cook's sailing master on his third and final voyage on their search for the Northwest Passage. The name indicates the frustration of encountering endless dead ends during this quest, evidenced by Bligh's entry in the ship's log, that they had to turn again,

At the time, Alyeska had one chairlift going far up the steep mountain and one small T-bar lift on a bunny slope. The only building was a 20x30-foot enclosure about 50 feet from the bottom of the chairlift. It served as the ticket office, bar, tiny restaurant area, and bathroom facility. The Alyeska manager was Jim Branch who was a party animal, and the small group of us that regularly patronized the place experienced some memorable social events. Sixty years later, I still have friends from this small gathering, such as Merle Akers and Carl Lind, who was destined to become my best man three years later. Eating into my airplane money, I invested in an ensemble of ski equipment, clothing, and a season pass.

The excellent powder snow skiing during the 1961–62 winter on the slopes of Mount Alyeska, coupled with warm, congenial social experiences in the ski cabins of my new friends in Girdwood's Glacier Valley triggered the urge to have a ski cabin of my very own. Bob La Follette, an Anchorage judge who was a direct descendant of the Wisconsin "Fighting La Follette's," had occasional poker parties at his cabin, after which some of us would sleep on the floor because (once or twice) we were too hammered to walk. He was a scary-looking person, walleyed, and built like an ox with a crew cut. Not a person you would want to tangle with. I still remember groggily waking up on the floor after a long poker night and observing Bob in his long johns, quietly gathering up the various wineskins laying around and pouring their contents back into a bottle to recycle for the next evening's poker game.

The following spring, Bob subdivided his lot into eight parcels and sold them. I purchased the farthest lot to the rear left, which was the most isolated and had two sides bordered by the Chugach National Forest. The others sold to bachelor skiers who also had cabin-building intentions, and the subdivision became known as "Stud Alley."

Our Party House

Meanwhile, the apartment Bill Smith and I shared was becoming *the* spot for socializing with our Alyeska ski friends and others both from Anchorage and out of town. In the spring of 1962, we had a party with so many people it was hard to move around. A core of folks were trying to dance, at the center of which was Bob La Follette in a tuxedo, performing exotic gyrations learned earlier in Kenya when he lived with a Maasai tribe. The place was really hopping, and suddenly there was a loud knocking on the door. I opened it and was confronted by two Anchorage policemen who were answering complaints. Telling them to hold on for a second, I grabbed the gyrating La Follette off the dance floor and shoved him in front of the cops. Recognizing the judge, they instantly faded away, and the party rolled on.

My bedroom was next to the bathroom, and in the morning, I groggily awoke to the sound of splashing and got up to investigate. La Follette was sitting in a full bathtub still wearing his tuxedo and holding a can of beer. Fixing a walleyed gaze on me, he intoned, "I've never been to a party this great! You'll hear from my attorneys!" and then splashed around some more. An hour later he had shed the tuxedo, was naked, and still holding a beer as he was walked in circles around the living room shaking his fist and shouting, "Ninety days, you son of a bitch!" at no one in particular. At this moment, there was a knock on the door, and two coworkers walked in. It was Dick Thompson and Alex Kennedy, and it appeared they were unprepared for the scene they encountered. There was no way I could explain the circumstances to them rationally. They just stood there transfixed. I had forgotten that I had arranged to float the Matanuska River in a canoe with them that morning and dreaded the thought due to my horrendous hangover. After stumbling through introductions for which the word *awkward* would have been a gross understatement, I asked them to give me an hourandwe'dmeet up to do the floattrip.

Icy Float Trip

In what was to be a stupid undertaking, we had earlier decided it would be fun to float the Matanuska River in a canoe during spring break-up when there would be abundant ice-cold white water. Fred Rungee, the BLM Glennallen station manager, agreed to drive the "chase car" along the road that paralleled the river. Figuratively speaking, after popping a dumb pill each, we launched the canoe with me in the bow, Alex in the middle, and Dick in the stern. There was thick ice on both banks of the river. For several miles, things went well, and we were having lots of fun.

Then we rounded a corner and headed into an isolated canyon where the river started narrowing and the water started to speed up. Before long, as the water squeezed through the restricted width, it was higher in the middle than at the edges and we encountered "horsetail" waves that were increasing in height. The first one came into my lap, and we took on water. The second one was higher, also came into my lap, and we took on a lot more water. The canoe was now very unstable on its roll axis, and we were teetering toward rolling over. The third wave was higher yet, I went under, and over we went. Now we had reversed positions—I was in the stern and Dick was in the bow and Alex was still the middleman, except instead of being in the canoe, it was more like we were carrying it on our shoulders, but our feet were not touching bottom. For a short time, we floated like this wordlessly, and then up on a cliff above us, Fred Rungee heard a voice wafting up out of the canyon shout, "Jesus Christ! Let's get the hell out of here!"

Moments later he saw us beach the canoe. There was no access to the road, but at the river's edge we found remnant splinters of creosoted railroad ties and started a fire. Two hours later our clothes were dry enough so we could continue, which we did while I contemplated that this was a hell of a way to treat a hangover.

14

1962 - 1963

Girdwood Log Cabin

That summer, I purchased 8-inch spruce logs cut on three sides and started construction of a 16x28-foot log cabin that would be embedded in a thick hemlock forest. I had to drag the logs individually by hand to the building site. One Saturday morning I was installing floor joists using metal hangers secured by short nails hammered in tight corners. At one point I missed the nail and hammered my left thumb, which hurt like hell. With greater care, I picked up another nail, hammered again, and smashed the same thumb in the same place. I dropped my hammer and proceeded to dance around in circles uttering unspeakable profanities. After the pain subsided to a barely tolerable level, and while still seething with rage, I picked up the hammer, another nail, and proceeded to smash my thumb a third time, at which point I threw the hammer deep into the dense hemlock forest and embarked upon another dance of screaming profanity. Later, after getting myself under control, I searched for the hammer. It was my only one, and I never found it; so in deep disgust with myself, I spent two hours driving a round trip to Anchorage to buy a new one.

I was one of many young, single males building cabins in Glacier Valley. We visited each other frequently to check out construction progress and socialize with a beer or two. A traditional way of announcing one's presence on the path to a friend's cabin was to cut off a quarter stick of dynamite, fuse it, light the fuse, and toss it into the woods. Dynamite was often used to blast holes for outhouses. One rainy afternoon a dynamite explosion startled me, and George McIntosh appeared. I was in the process of spiking a corner log wall together with a hand sledge and 8″ spikes. George was obviously under the influence, and he sat on a nail keg in the rain with a bottle in his hand to observe my spiking efforts. Before long, with a very authoritative voice, he proclaimed, "Thurston, I can tell by the way you're handling that sledgehammer you're afraid of it. Let me show you how a man does it!"

He then stood up, grabbed a spike, took my sledgehammer, positioned the spike, took a mighty swing, missed the spike, and tried to imbed his left thumb into the spruce log. My thumb-hammering escapade was a springtime walk in a garden compared to what George did to his thumb. He stumbled off down my path to the road uttering profanity interjected with unintelligible animal-like gurgling sounds, but when I saw him the next weekend, he appeared to have recovered and was even congenial toward me. As the summer progressed, I often visited other projects, such as Julian Maule's construction of the Double Musky Inn and helped out with his effort (for a beer or two).

The Ophir Fire

That summer, the management of the McGrath station had recently changed. Wally Fixen, who had run the McGrath station for years, was transferred to Big Delta. In Tanacross, Bill Adams's kids had been playing with matches and burned the station down, so Bill was moved to McGrath, which hadn't burned down yet. When fires became a significant problem out west, overhead personnel from Anchorage, Fairbanks, and from out of state would be called in to help. I was sent to McGrath to fight a fire called the Ophir N-20 north of an old mining town called Ophir. After doing a recon of the fire in a light aircraft, we asked the U.S. Army to help us transfer firefighters from the Ophir Airstrip to the fire, and this was done using their banana-shaped tandem rotor H-21 helicopters. Adams had procured the use of a small Hiller UH-12E helicopter, which he assigned to the fire and which I immediately appropriated to do recon around the fire.

I had over 100 men who I deployed onto high ground surrounding the north flank of the fire. About half were native crews from Holy Cross and other villages with the rest being "pick up off the street" firefighters from Palmer and Wasilla, north of An-

Courtesy of U.S. Army.

chorage. The higher ground offered the advantage of easy fire line construction (no trees to cut down), easy walking, and flammable fuels like caribou moss, making it perfect for burning out as long as the wind was at our back, which it was. (Once a fire line is constructed, burning out the vegetation between the line and the fire significantly increases the width of non-burnable protection should the main fire later make a run.) Once deployed, our fire line construction progressed rapidly, as did the follow-up burnout operations, and before long I could look back and literally see miles of burned out, secured fire line.

Burning out a fire line.

In our fire training classes, we preached that the fire boss is usually the poorest manager of his own time, and on the Ophir Fire I was no exception. The project was going so well, I didn't want to miss anything by sleeping, and after three days without sleep, I was beginning to run down. It was then that the fire really acted up. A weather front was moving in and producing wind. I now had the fire boxed in except for the last segment, which was where the fire line needed to leave the high ground and connect to a creek in the valley bottom. The line had been dug and only needed to be burned out or this very hot fire was going to overrun it. Not wanting to commit troops into an area potentially uphill of an active fire, I took a burnout torch and ran down the line, setting fire behind me as I went. Suddenly, I realized that below me the fire had already jumped the line and was turning uphill in my direction, so I abandoned the effort and started walking back up the mountain. I had lost the battle and knew that I was in jeopardy. I also knew that if I panicked and tried to run uphill, I would probably not make it, so I concentrated on a "one step at a time" mantra while trying to ignore the increasing sound level of the monster on my heels. When I reached safety, I turned the now out-of-control fire over to the assistant fire boss, Fred Rungee, and collapsed into a deep sleep out in the open. The next day, when I woke up, I was soaking wet from the rains that had moved in on us, but at least the fire had stopped.

Now it was time to demobilize the effort. My request to have the troops helicoptered to the Ophir Airstrip was turned down and meant they had to hike cross-country about 21 miles instead. Bill Adams had made arrangements to have them picked up at the airstrip. This bit of news was met with a sea of resentment from the Palmer and Wasilla troops, and for a short time I feared a mutiny. The native crews couldn't care less either way. Handing a topographic map with the route to Ophir sketched onto it to the FCA who would be the lead scout, I explained there was no need to take food because at midday I would find them with the helicopter and deliver food to them. The long line of men gradually faded from my sight as they disappeared into the spruce forest.

At midday the pilot and I took off to search for the men with the side baskets of the helicopter loaded with boxes of C-rations. At the area I expected to find them, there was no sign, so we started searching, covering an imaginary 5x5-mile grid. Forty minutes later there was still no sign of them, and frustrated, I was now questioning how I was able to so easily lose 100 men in the wilderness when I happened to look up. Just outside of the area we searched was a lone, low mountain peak.

It had fuzz on it. We flew up to it and found them! They looked like a bunch of seagulls perched on a piling, and I wondered what the hell they were doing up there. As we landed, I could see an angry crowd shaking fists and giving third-finger gestures, so we aborted the landing. Instead, we hovered nearby kicking the C-rations out of the basket on my side and then unloading the basket on the pilot's side after a brief landing further away so they couldn't catch us. As we departed the area, I waved goodbye. In return I got the finger.

Jim Thurston: Military Cop

When tensions with the USSR started to increase with the Cuban Missile Crisis in the fall of 1962, I received a letter from the U.S. Army telling me to prepare to report to an army aircraft heavy maintenance depot in Sacramento, California. Before I had to leave, the crisis was averted, and my orders changed. Instead, they told me to report to the Military Police detachment at Fort Richardson for duty as an MP and serve two weeks as part of my reserve training. I thought this was curious. My military specialty was aircraft engine overhaul, and Fort Richardson had a significant army aviation component, so how does training to be a cop fit in with that?

When I arrived at the Military Police station, and after they provided me an MP armband but no weapon, I was posted at various entrance booths to control traffic going in and out of the base. When I asked what the criteria was for stopping people passing through, I was told that the post was mine and I could stop anyone I wanted, so I contemplated how much fun it would be to stop a general and chew the fat. I never did, of course, but having topics like that to think about made the hours cooped up in a booth pass faster. I did stop one BLM property management specialist I didn't like and playfully gave him a hard time about his dirty windshield. He didn't appreciate it.

One day I had to report to the stockade for duty. A sergeant asked me if I knew how to frisk prisoners, and I told him that subject hadn't been included in my aircraft engine overhaul courses. His response was to slam me against the wall spread-eagle me, and frisk the dark recesses of my body for a weapon. Since there was none, he spun me around and lectured me about not being a wiseass, after which I concluded the guy probably lacked a sense of humor. About that time, a guard with a prisoner came by, and I was ordered to frisk the prisoner, which I did, utilizing techniques just used on me that were still vivid in my mind. My frisk job apparently passed muster, so they issued me a 30-caliber carbine and escorted me to one of the guard towers. I was informed that if a prisoner escaped on my watch, I would have to serve his time. Later, during the boredom of standing guard, I checked the rifle. The cartridges were blanks. Fortunately, the guard-tower hours passed without any attempted escapes, and when the two weeks were up, I returned to civilian life unscathed by all these new challenging experiences.

Bill Smith Accident

During the winter of 1962–63, my roommate Bill Smith and I skied Alyeska almost every weekend. We loved the deep powder snow of which there was plenty. Very few people skied there that it often took three or four weeks to ski out a heavy powder snow event. I also spent endless hours working on my now enclosed, heated cabin, which I showed off to the occasional girls I harvested off the slopes. It was a wonderful winter.

Bill had purchased a new Volkswagen Bug, and one weekend in February we both rode in it to Alyeska. In the afternoon on the sunny ski slope, Bill skied up to me and suggested it would be fun to go back to Anchorage and ski while being pulled by dogsled teams at the on-going winter carnival. I had visions of skiing through dog crap and told him I was going to stay and ski—that I'd catch a ride home tomorrow with one of my friends. A couple of hours later, as I was changing out of my ski boots in the lodge, Merle Akers came up behind me and announced that Bill had been killed in an auto accident and I should come with him.

During the ride with Merle back to Anchorage, we passed the scene of the wreck, which was on an icy curve with Turnagain Arm on one side and sheer vertical rock cliffs on the other. A large truck tractor and lowboy laden with oil field drilling equipment was up against the cliff. What remained of Bill's Volkswagen was between the heavily loaded lowboy and the cliff. The VW was so demolished it was difficult to discern its color. A distinctive ski cap that Bill had worn had been found on the edge of the road earlier by Carl Lind, who, driving home earlier, had encountered the scene and was the source of communication back to Alyeska. Apparently, Bill had lost control of his car on the icy curve and had drifted into the oncoming lane where the truck had hit him nearly head-on. As Merle and I wordlessly continued the drive home, my eyes started to water up, so he pulled out a handkerchief and handed it to me.

That evening in the Spenard apartment, I debated myself about when to notify Bill's parents on Main Street in Pennsylvania. It was about 2:00 a.m. their time. Should I wake them now with this devastating news or hold off until morning? I decided to call immediately, which I later regretted. Bill's mother answered the phone, and making my second poor decision, I asked to speak with his father, who, unbeknownst to me, had a serious heart problem. When I broke the news to him, he made a strange noise, and Bill's mother came back on the line, screaming, "What did you say to him?" When I told her about Bill, she refused to believe it, said she was going to call Bill's phone number because this had to be a prank call, and abruptly hung up. Moments later, my phone rang, and I engaged myself by clumsily trying to console a brokenhearted mother I had never met on Main Street thousands of miles away.

Around 10:00 a.m. the next morning, there was a knock on my door. I opened it, and there stood Judge La Follette, clutching a bottle of whiskey. Without saying a word, he handed it to me, turned, and disappeared down the stairs. Later that day, Joe Crusey called and invited me to spend the evening at his place so I could get away from the scene of Bill's living environment. Joe was a well-known bachelor in downtown Anchorage—a connoisseur of precious coins and fine art, and a fellow skier. I remember being with him that evening. He was sitting in a vintage rocking chair wearing glasses with a blanket on his lap, reading the *Wall Street Journal* next to his huge safe, which I assumed was full of coins. I may have had some weird friends, but they sure were great friends.

15

1964 - Part 1

The Taylorcraft

After Bill Smith's death, I needed someone to share my apartment expenses, so Carl Lind, one of my Alyeska Ski friends, moved in with me. Carl was very sharp-minded and had a unique sense of humor. At the time, he was a truck driver for Peninsula Fast Freight which at the time ran back and forth from Anchorage and the Kenai Peninsula. We got along well and eventually decided to purchase a small airplane with floats, wheels, and skis. The lucky winner was a used Taylorcraft (T-Craft) BC-12d that was homeless and we adopted it, arranging to split ownership and costs 50/50. We both enjoyed several years flying this airplane on various winter wolf-hunting outings on skis and summer fishing adventures on floats. The front windscreen, where it joined the fuselage, didn't match up perfectly with the result that there was a half-inch gap in places where my wife would stuff baby diapers to minimize the blast of incoming air. Carl referred to our T-Craft as an all-weather airplane (i.e., you got all the weather!). Years later, when I moved out of Alaska again, Carl remained with the airplane and later sold it. My most irresponsible escapade in the T-Craft was a flight to the Barren Islands, which are between the southern tip of the Kenai Peninsula and Kodiak Island. I was hoping to find a spot suitable for a float landing so I could explore a remote beach. The Barren Islands are well named—they are remote, barren, windy, and subject to vicious seas. They are devoid of any settlement or civilization. After reconnoitering several beaches, the best one I could find was horrible, but I stupidly tried a landing anyhow. The waves were three to four feet high, and I was attempting to land cross-wave and downwind toward the beach. The airplane literally bounced off the crest of the first wave, and I aborted the effort instantly, managed a 180-degree turn without impacting the mountain, and got the hell out of there. Later, upon reflection, my split-second decision to abort saved my life. The airplane could not have survived a second bounce, and my chances of being able to swim to shore were zero. I had a lot to learn about saltwater seaplane flying.

My Useless Manual

At work, my involvement with the fire control training project made me realize that our two-week spring training for fire personnel totally relied on their memories to be effective. This included their need to memorize how to correctly fill out government paperwork, how to set up a complicated fire pump layout, how to construct a fire line, how to organize fire crews, etc. I felt the creation of a fire control quick-reference guide that could fit in a shirt pocket might be useful and set about designing one. Once completed, I had a hundred or so printed and distributed them to the organization.

Jim Scott thought it was a great thing and recommended to the Washington, D.C. fire management office that something similar be adopted nationally throughout the BLM. Meanwhile, as BLM fire personnel in other states became aware of this guide, they requested copies, and the printers started commenting about having a bestseller as we distributed them throughout the western states. Eventually the BLM Washington office responded to Jim Scott's suggestion: "While it appears the fire control handbook may have application for Alaska, we believe it probably would not have application in the Lower 48." Their response amazed us because while Washington was unable to grasp this basic concept, their own people throughout the western states were having us print hundreds of copies. Six decades later, a descendant of this manual still exists, no thanks to our illustrious visionaries on the Potomac River with their sub-level IQs.

How to Park a Floatplane

One cold, windy Saturday I undertook a changeover from the T-Craft's wheels to floats on the old Lake Hood landing strip next to the channel separating Lakes Hood and Spenard. After launching it on floats, the plan was for me to taxi it over to our assigned parking spot at the newly excavated "pothole" while a friend, Don Burns, (of my very first day in Alaska at Fairbanks) drove the car over to meet me. The wind was blowing briskly out of the east which meant that after cutting the engine, I'd coast directly into the spot until the nose of the floats contacted shore, at which point I would hop off the float on to land and secure the line tied to the float cleat.

My plan didn't't work. Being the first float operation of the season, I wasn't thinking float docking procedures and hadn't pre-tied a line to the front float cleat ahead of time. This oversight didn't't occur to me until after I had cut the engine and hopped onto the float expecting to grab a line that wasn't there. As the T-Craft was coasting toward shore in the teeth of the wind, I was frantically rummaging in the storage area behind the seat to free up a line that was tangled up in an anchor and some other gear. Meanwhile the floats gently bumped the shore and the airplane started drifting backward toward several other moored aircraft on the shore immediately behind me. By the time I had a line tied to the front float cleat, the nose of my floats were about five feet from shore and the distance was widening, so I took a running jump for it.

There were three problems: (1) I was wearing hip boots, (2) I just barely didn't't make it, and (3) the water was over six feet deep. Suddenly, I was neck deep in water with my left hand on land clutching a clump of dead grass while my right hand was holding the line to the airplane that was now tugging to get away in the wind and collide with the moored aircraft directly behind. Also, my hip boots were full of water.

About 80 feet away I saw Don Burns park the car, get out, and start strolling leisurely toward me while smoking a cigar. He seemed to be in no hurry. With the airplane's line tugging me, the clump of grass I was clutching suddenly pulled out by the roots, and in a nanosecond, I grabbed another, but it was four inches closer to the water's edge, and there was maybe only one more grab left. I was shouting at Burns to hurry, but he showed no reaction and continued his slow, methodical walk, giving no sign he was even aware of my predicament. The second grass clump pulled out, and I latched on to my last-chance clump while screaming at the top of my lungs. Burns finally arrived, took a drag on his cigar, and pulled me out. His only explanation for his tardiness was that he figured he'd arrive on time. After securing the airplane to shore, we rode home with me being cold, wet, and disgusted.

Chelatna Lake Tragedy

A week or two later, Carl and I flew the T-Craft on floats to Chelatna Lake in the Alaska Range foothills near Mount McKinley. Graham Mauer, an acquaintance of ours, owned the lodge on the south end of the lake, and several other friends also had cabins in the vicinity, so we'd fly up there occasionally to socialize. A short gravel airstrip was located close to the lodge, and on this occasion, we noticed a red and white Piper Cherokee wheel aircraft parked nearby. As a result of our careful planning, we had arrived just as lunch was being served, and we sat down with the guests, one of which was the Alaska director of the National Transportation Safety Board (NTSB), which is vested with the responsibility of investigating aviation accidents.

Three men and one woman had arrived on the Cherokee, and I sat opposite the woman, who told me they had flown all the way to Alaska from Texas in their four-place airplane. She told me she had always feared small aircraft, but that after such a long journey, she was gradually becoming less apprehensive. An exception, though, was this short airstrip that terminated over the water in front of the lodge; she was terrified of drowning. I attempted to reassure her, probably ineffectively.

After lunch, the Cherokee people boarded the airplane and taxied out to the far end of the airstrip. I had donned hip waders and was fishing with a spinning rod off the beach in front of the lodge. My location was close to the center line of the airstrip if you extended it past my location, and I had an almost head-on view of the Cherokee as it barreled toward me on its takeoff run. About two-thirds down the runway the aircraft lifted off and immediately settled back again. Fearful it might hit me, I immediately turned and attempted to run to shore in the hip-deep water, an experience that replicated past dreams in which a monster was chasing me and I couldn't get my legs to move beyond a slow walk.

Looking over my shoulder, I saw the Cherokee's wheels go through the low blueberry bushes at the very end of the runway, at which point the aircraft popped off the ground. A hundred feet later the wheels skimmed the water and the Cherokee popped up again, following which the wheels hit the water a second time directly behind me. Then the wheels con-

Piper Cherokee.
Courtesy of Wikipedia Commons.

tacted the water a third time, after which the pilot cut the engine and the aircraft crashed nose-first into the lake. While I was running from the airplane, the fast-thinking Carl Lind was launching a lodge skiff. We jumped in and rushed to the impact site where people were struggling in the water next to the tail of the airplane that was the only part of the aircraft still above water. (Later we learned the crash impact had blown out the front windshield, producing instant flooding of the cabin.) As we approached, one of the swimmers was yelling that his wife was still in a back seat of the airplane.

Carl had indicated his swimming ability was marginal. I am no Michael Phelps, and my swimming ability could best be described as unnoteworthy, but we had to act, so I removed my outer clothes and jumped in. Meanwhile, Carl was busy rescuing the other passengers. (My reason for removing clothes was my fear of getting snagged on something underwater inside the aircraft. Not factored in at the moment was the fact that the ice had gone out of the lake only nine days earlier and the water temperature was near freezing—something of an inhibition to semi-nude swimming.)

The starboard aircraft door was open, and in the darkened interior I groped the for the passenger, contacting what was probably her right arm. There was no response to my touch, and I tried unsuccessfully to yank her out, following which I placed both feet on the cockpit ceiling and, while upside down, pulled with all my might using both hands. She didn't budge, and the realization hit me that her seat belt must still be fastened. While lunging for her buckle my air ran out, and I had to abandon her. The cold water had played havoc with my stamina, and I barely made in back to the surface. Upon breaching, I yelled that her seat belt had to be unfastened. Half a dozen people had arrived in skiffs, including the NTSB director, and I implored someone to go after that buckle. With only one exception, they demurred, saying they didn't't know how to swim. The exception was Carl Lind, who in spite of limited swimming ability, jumped in and gave it a try but couldn't' get past the door. Minutes later, after shivering in the skiff, I gave it another try and barely reached the door. At that point, the rescue effort was terminated, and an empty 5-gallon gas can was tethered to the tail of the Cherokee so divers could later find the aircraft after it totally sank, which it did.

Later, the NTSB director asked me to provide a witness statement, and I questioned him why—since he had witnessed the entire debacle himself. In spite of my then foul mood, I provided one anyway. Our return to Anchorage in the T-Craft was characterized by sparse conversation as the two of us contemplated the concept of human mortality, and I mulled over the failure of my rescue effort.

A Major Life Milestone

For quite a while I had a girlfriend named Annie who was an Alaska Airlines stewardess. Those were wild times. Eventually, I transitioned to Sally (also a stewardess), and we carried on for several months until she dumped me. This was not an abrupt dump—she just gradually stopped returning my phone calls, and I eventually took the hint. Early in March after skiing, I was sitting on a barstool in what was then the new Alyeska day lodge, sipping a drink and feeling sorry for myself. After several drinks during which I gave myself a dressing down for being such an introverted wimp, I stoked up my courage and decided to strike out for new horizons and find another companion.

Turning on my bar stool, I surveyed the people seated at tables around the room and locked onto two cute damsels engaged in conversation with Elmer Feltz, a ski patrolman I knew. Since Elmer was not in the market, so to speak, I figured he could provide a convenient entry point for me to meet these girls, so I descended upon them hastily before my resolve dissipated. I would ask Elmer something about the condition of the slopes, which was asinine given that I had just been on them, but what the hell—the girls probably wouldn't't notice. I arrived at the table and said, "Hi."

Elmer said, "Hi," and unexpectedly departed abruptly, thereby demolishing my small-talk plot, and leaving shy Jimmy with nothing to do except talk directly with these girls.

They came in two sizes: tall and short. Both were good-looking. I was undecided about which one to come on to, so I made no move, showing no preference for one over the other, pending acquisition of further data. While this may sound cool, it turned out to be expensive. I bought them both rounds of drinks, took them both dancing, and bought them both dinners at the Double Musky Inn, following which we adjourned to my cabin for the night. By morning I had made up my mind. Tall girls tended to intimidate me, and the short one was pretty cute and appeared to be intelligent; so based on this sophisticated selection criteria I chose to pursue Jan, the short one.

Much later into our relationship, it was revealed to me that the decision had never really been in my hands. Jan and the other girl, Pat, had a long-standing policy about who-got-what when meeting men of interest. Pat was tall, and by mutual agreement was entitled to sole jurisdiction over men in excess of six feet, while Jan had jurisdiction of those under six feet. At six feet, they'd fight. Since I was only five feet eight inches, my options had been unknowingly limited. Both women were grade school teachers who shared a basement apartment in Anchorage.

16

1964 - Part 2

The Great Alaskan Earthquake

On March 27, 1964, after working in the Cordova Building all day with Bill Adams designing a fire training exercise, I drove home to my apartment planning to drive to Girdwood to work on my cabin during the weekend. I lived in a two-story wood building, and my apartment was on the second floor. At 5:36 p.m., while changing clothes in my tiny bedroom, I heard what sounded like rolling thunder followed by a small earthquake-like jolt. I had unbuckled and my pants were halfway down. I paused, having my typical reaction, which was, *Oh! An earthquake. I wonder how strong this one will be.*

In the next second I found out. A heavy jolt rocked the building, and I lost my balance and fell backward into my closet, pulling the clothes down on top of me. The building was racking furiously with the sounds of things crashing all around me. I clawed my way up to my little awning window, which was open, and peered out at a horrendous scene of the earth rolling in big waves like an ocean. Power poles were gyrating back and forth with intense electrical arcing, and above the racket of the earthquake itself, there were sounds of glass shattering and people screaming. My windowsill was rocking sideways ferociously while I hung on taking this scene in. Looking down, a fellow was outside below me standing with his thumbs hooked over the rim of an empty 55-gallon garbage barrel that was rocking back and forth. He was a Baptist preacher who lived in the apartment below me, and I called down, "How's it going down there?"

He looked up and replied, "OK. How's it going up there?" At that moment we were two people probably sharing the belief that death was imminent, and to combat it, we were both making small talk. The severe jolting lasted nearly five minutes and kept getting stronger, and we ran out of things to talk about. As of 1964, at magnitude 9.2, this was the second-strongest earthquake ever recorded in the world, and I'm happy I was unaware of this at the time.

When it quit, I pulled up my pants and ran out of the building. The preacher had disappeared somewhere, but Don Burns, who lived in the apartment next to the preacher's, showed up, and we discussed concerns about the electrical integrity of the building and the chances it might catch fire if ever the power was turned back on. We found the electrical box on the exterior rear wall, and Don, attempting to open it, managed to impale his left thumb with a safety wire at the joint that stuck out at the tip of his thumb, which was a gruesome sight. Half a block away on Spenard Road was a small medical clinic I had noticed during my frequent visits to the liquor store next door, and I walked Don over there.

The Montgomery Ward department store just across the street with its large glass windows was apparently the source of the glass-shattering noises I had heard. The clinic was filled with cut, bleeding people. There was no electricity, and we found ourselves in the midst of a crowd of anguished folks illuminated only by flash and candle lights with a couple of medical personnel scrambling from patient to patient. It was a weird scene that suddenly became weirder when out of the darkness, someone tapped me on the shoulder and said, "Jim Scott wants you at the Cordova Building—Now!" To this day, I have no idea who that person was or how he found me.

Turnagain by the Sea
Courtesy of NOAA Coast & Geodetic Collection.

After retrieving my car, I headed for the Cordova Building and encountered earthquake damage areas where I had to drive on sidewalks to get through. I arrived at dusk to a dark, gloomy Cordova Building, finding the main entrance doors in a heap of glass and the building open to anyone. With the exception of sirens as background noise, the area seemed devoid of human activity and appeared to be deserted. Where the hell was Scott? I was unsure how to proceed, but wondered if injured people could still be in the six-story building and started a search from the basement up. A flashlight from my car was a godsend. Things were spooky, and I was fearful of an aftershock. The stairwells were piled high with debris and difficult to navigate.

On the fourth floor I encountered a memorable scene of the U.S. General Land Office. The armada of file cabinets that had apparently been anchored in place did not have their file drawers secured enough to withstand the intense shaking, so they did just what you wouldn't't want them to do—they slid out to their stops and the momentum ejected their contents into the aisles, building 3-foot high piles of all the land records showing who owned what in Alaska. On the fifth floor I checked on the office I had vacated a short time before. The wood-framed glass door into it was locked and the training materials I had been developing for weeks were inside, so I found a chair and threw it through the glass, thereby retrieving my project.

Back on ground level, my boss Jim Scott appeared with several others. He had been in his southeast-corner ground-floor office during the quake and rode it out standing in the office doorway. The main exterior corner of the building started to fail, revealing a massive vertical steel beam being bent into a *Z* shape. (The bent section of this beam currently resides in the Anchorage Museum.) When the quake stopped, Scott hurriedly exited the building and collided with a black janitor who had been working downstairs in the photogrammetry offices. Out on the sidewalk, Scott told me the janitor exclaimed, "Man, that quake scared me so much I almost turned white!"

It was decided we should hightail it to our fire control station at Elmendorf Air Force Base, where there was backup electrical power and HF radios, so we could better gather information about the extent of this disaster and hopefully devise some sort of rational plan. Traveling there became a problem because the military was moving in and starting to restrict "unauthorized" travel due to fear of looting, etc. Scott was some sort of high-level civil defense official, but the native militia, some of whom didn't understand English very well, tried to not let us pass. Scott, a large man who didn't't possess a quiet demeanor in the first place, loudly intimidated them into granting our wishes, and we proceeded to the fire station, where we arrived to find there was no power and no radios, except some portable field sets. Essentially, we accomplished nothing.

Later, I threaded my way back to the apartment by circumnavigating roadblocks and arrived to find our place was now serving as a rendezvous center for a variety of acquaintances, some of whom were from out of town. Several Coleman lanterns were fired up. Bill Adams, from McGrath who had been working with me earlier that day, was there and described his experience of hanging on to a parking meter downtown next to the JCPenney building as the facade of one wall cascaded into the street, crushing cars and killing people. Others described unfathomable scenes, especially in the western part of the city, a portion of which had apparently slid into Cook Inlet. Due to a major tsunami fear, many people had evacuated town to the mountains overlooking Anchorage. With no news available, we were unaware that tsunamis had already devastated Seward, Valdez, Kodiak, Chenega, Old Harbor, and other coastal communities.

Courtesy of U.S. Army.

A tsunami did not materialize in Anchorage. I was anxious about our Taylorcraft on Lake Hood at Anchorage International Airport and wanted to use it to fly to Girdwood to check out my cabin, but I needed airplane gas. Since no electricity meant no gas pumping, Carl Lind and I drove to the main Chevron warehouse down near the shipyard, hoping we could get some case gas. At a spot on the road next to the foot of a hill upon which there were several very large fuel storage tanks, we were about to cross a small creek when the traffic stopped. In front of us was a pickup truck, idling and waiting like us. We then realized the stream was not water—it was fuel bleeding from one of the tanks on the hill and the exhaust of the truck ahead was directly over it. The traffic then moved ahead without incident, and we arrived at the Chevron warehouse, inquiring if we could buy some aviation case gas. The attendant said, "Sure, if you can find it," and waved us through a door where we viewed a huge pile of canned and bottled petroleum products which had fallen off shelves and were heaped in the center of the floor. From it we extracted a couple of cases of aviation gas (20 gallons) and headed for the airport.

Lake Hood is a very large seaplane base tucked into the gut of Anchorage International Airport. In the winter it is frozen over and becomes a ski-plane base. Since Carl decided to stay in town, Julian Maule, who owned the Double Musky Inn at Girdwood, wanted to catch a ride with me in our two-place airplane, so we drove out there together and unexpectedly encountered the world of reality: the control tower at Anchorage International had collapsed and killed a controller; all control tower operations were being managed out of the tiny Lake Hood facility, which was a 12x12-foot box that resembled an old-time

Forest Service fire lookout tower; and the ice on the lake had multiple 8-inch high-pressure ridges on it about 150 yards apart.

I figured the Taylorcraft could get off between the ridges, climbed up to the control tower box to ask permission, and rapped on the bottom of the trap door in their floor. It sprung open, there were about eight faces staring down at me. I made my request, and their response was basically, "Yeah, get the hell out of here—we're busy!" They were now responsible for controlling all aircraft at Anchorage International, Lake Hood, and Merrill Field Airport in downtown Anchorage.

Anchorage International Airport Control Tower.
Courtesy of FAA.

Julian and I climbed in the airplane and attempted to taxi to the takeoff point. We could hardly move due to "sticky snow," a condition that sometimes occurs because the snow tends to stick to the bottoms of the skis rather than allowing the skis to slide on it. Because getting airborne with only me on board would be a marginal operation at best, Julian stayed behind, and I attempted to takeoff. When I encountered the first pressure ridge I had just enough speed to hop over it, but not enough to fly. After failing a second pressure-ridge attempt, I successfully staggered off the ground over the third one, turned southeast, and headed for Turnagain Arm. At Potter, the Alaska Railroad tracks made a right turn and disappeared into the waters of the fjord. Along Turnagain Arm, I observed numerous avalanches segregating portions of the Seward Highway, each segment with vehicles trapped on the road with no way out.

My plan was to land on the Girdwood Airstrip which was on the Turnagain Arm side of the Seward Highway next to the waters of the fjord. Upon arrival, I couldn't' find the airstrip, which was perplexing since I had landed there many times and knew the area well. Then, as

I circled, I spotted the airstrip wind sock. The sock itself on its 12-foot pole was barely above the water between several large floating chunks of ice, which meant the airstrip was probably six feet under water, which also meant this entire part of the country had probably subsided about six feet! I decided to head up Glacier Valley toward Alyeska to look for a suitable ski-landing spot, which I shortly found. It was an uphill opening in an area of ski cabins, and I touched down, coming to a stop near one of them. I spent a short time securing the airplane and then the cabin door burst open and, to my surprise, Jim Branch, the Alyeska Resort manager, appeared on the doorstep with a drink in each hand and called out, "Tell me what happened in Anchorage!" After a two-drink briefing during which I told him what I knew, he gave me a ride to my cabin, which I thankfully found slightly racked into a parallelogram —but still standing.

The scene at Alyeska itself was fascinating. The quake had set off two major avalanches. The first was a dry-snow avalanche directly above the lodge on Max's Mountain, which towers over the resort. Dry-snow avalanches travel at very high speeds. My ex-girlfriend Sally, who was there, told me her story. She and a guy had finished skiing and were in the parking lot securing their skies on the car's ski rack when the quake hit. They heard someone at the lodge cry, "Avalanche!" and looking up, they saw an avalanche high on Max's Mountain that put them directly in its path. The doors of the lodge burst open, and a horde of people poured out into the parking lot running for their lives. The person in the lead was a ski patrol skier in a temporary leg cast that had been injured that afternoon. She had thrown away her crutches and was actually in the lead!

Sally and her friend jumped in the car and raced for the parking lot exit to get ahead of the mob. As they entered the exit road, visibility suddenly went to zero in a dense cloud of snow, and they drove the car into a snowbank. Frantically, he jumped out to push the car, and though the open door, a large German Shepherd materialized, jumped into the car, and ran circles around Sally's head, barking furiously. The car remained stuck, but the snow cloud dissipated, and the avalanche stopped, uphill of the lodge. Then, there was a continuous rumbling sound which was gradually increasing.

A second avalanche was grinding its way down a gorge that ran under the chairlift. This was a heavy, slow-moving wet-snow avalanche that contained whole trees and other debris, and it appeared it was going to take out the day lodge but stopped just short of obliterating the chairlift loading station. When I stood where a skier would stand, waiting for a chair to come up behind, my toes were at the bottom of an almost vertical face of the avalanche. If I had stood on the top of the avalanche there, I would have been able to step over the top of the chairlift cables.

I stayed in Girdwood a few days and was so distressed by the destruction I had seen in Anchorage I became despondent, with a don't-give-a-damn-about-anything attitude. It appeared to me the city was finished, that Anchorage could never rebuild, and I didn't't want to return to it. I just wanted to curl up in my little cabin in the forest and let the world go by without me, but the reality was that I was the fire control training officer and the annual spring fire school—which I ran—was to start in several days in Fairbanks. Before long, I got a grip on myself and realized I had been overreacting. Also, it turned out I was unaware that what I had seen amounted to nothing compared to the devastation that had occurred in outlying communities, some of which had been totally destroyed.

Back in Anchorage, I was stunned to see what was going on at the Cordova Building. While I had been absent, the authorities had condemned the building and had given the BLM a several-day deadline to move out, following which they planned to demolish it completely. Consequently, BLM had knocked out 12-foot-wide wall sections on each level, hired a mobile crane, and were transferring the government property floor-by-floor to a fleet of trucks for transport to the Oilwell Road station. The place was in pandemonium.

During the next few days, "earthquake stories" abounded. One of our pilots, Jim Telford, was returning to Anchorage from Kodiak in a Grumman Goose under instrument flight conditions when the quake hit. He had contacted the Anchorage control tower earlier for his approach, and just before breaking out into visual flight conditions, the tower said they were experiencing a violent earthquake. Telford requested a transition from Anchorage International Airport to our base at Merrill Field in downtown Anchorage and received no answer. After breaking out of the clouds he glanced over toward the tower and saw it was gone. Jim was probably the last person those controllers ever talked to. Unaware the quake was still in progress, he transitioned over downtown Anchorage and started an approach to the east for runway six. Coming up to the Alaska Sales and Service automobile dealership, he saw it collapse in a huge cloud of dust as it passed under the nose of his airplane. When he announced this to the Merrill Field control tower, their response was, "Grumman 640, you're cleared to land—we're outta here!" I never understood why Jim landed in spite of an ongoing earthquake and attributed this to a quasi-state of disbelief. Fortunately, the quake had subsided by the time he landed.

For a few weeks after the quake, and before spring breakup really took hold, skiing continued at Alyeska. Since the whole area had sunk six or seven feet, parts of the Seward Highway along Turnagain Arm, including the small communities of Girdwood and Portage, were under water during the higher of the high-tide cycles. Consequently, for skiers it was necessary to consult the tide tables for the drive to and from Anchorage because these very high tides left large blocks of sea ice on the road at the section called Bird Flats. These were removed by the highway department with heavy equipment. The village of Girdwood was later relocated two and a half miles up Glacier Valley, and Portage village was abandoned. During this period, Jan and I spent considerable time together, and our relationship deepened, but when summer arrived, she and Pat embarked upon a two-month tour of Europe.

17

1964 - Part 3

The Summer of 1964

At BLM, I transitioned from fire control training to the supervisory fire control position for Southcentral Alaska. At this time, the Alaska State government had yet to develop a wildlands fire control organization and was contracting with the BLM to provide it. This served to immerse me once again into private-land-fire issues and brought back memories of Fairbanks. Southcentral Alaska, however, usually does not have fire challenges nearly as acute as Fairbanks, and that, coupled with the fact that the early sixties were quiet fire seasons throughout the state, made my job a walk in the park.

A lot of work on the Girdwood cabin was accomplished that summer during which I contemplated my future. My original life plan had been to remain single until age 30, thus providing almost ten years of time for free, unencumbered activities. Now, all of a sudden, I *was* 30 and starting to get a little long in the tooth, so to speak. Time had passed by faster than I had anticipated. I realized that if I was going to settle down and have a family, I probably should act sooner instead of later. To date, Jan had been the only person I had contemplated as a possibility, and I had no idea if she would be receptive. The thought of broaching the subject with her, much less acting upon it, was fraught with indecision and uncertainty.

One day I received a letter from Jan stating she and Pat were due to return from Europe in two weeks. As I was reading it, the phone rang and a female voice asked, "Jim, do you know who this is?"

To which I stupidly replied, "Sally?"

There was silence on the other end for a moment, and then the female voice, dripping with disappointment, said, "This is Jan. I couldn't't wait to see you, and I wanted to let you know we are coming home early." I was flabbergasted. How frigging stupid do you have to be to not say, "No. Who?" I felt terrible for inflicting this on Jan and wouldn't't have blamed her for calling it quits to our relationship. The thought of our next encounter made me cringe, but when we met, the reconnection was surprisingly smooth.

Before long, things began to progress to the semi-serious state. This was evidenced by Jan taking me to meet her father, Chester P. Lampert (Chet), who lived alone in a log cabin on Fireweed Lane. When we entered the cabin, I was confronted by a heavy, older man seated in a large leather-upholstered chair in the center of a dimly lit room. He was holding a cane in his right hand, did not smile, and did not speak. He was, however, looking squarely at me as if (in my mind), there was reason to believe I may have deflowered his only daughter moments before entering. Jan carried the conversation, and eventually Chet responded to me as we labored through a classic superficial conversation (weather, how long in Alaska? wonderful daughter, etc.).

Later, Jan filled me in on Chet's history, which was substantial. He had been raised in Seattle and migrated to Anchorage in the late 1920s. At that time, Anchorage was a small townsite on a bluff next to Cook Inlet overlooking Ship Creek, and much of the forest to the south was undeveloped. Chet staked out 160-acre homestead one and a half miles south of the original townsite and raised blueberries, receiving a patent signed by FDR's secretary in 1934. Thirty years later this would become the hub of midtown Anchorage. Eventually, in Seattle, he married a woman named Edna with two children and talked her into moving up to his Anchorage homestead, which she did. The home was a tent on what is now the corner of Fireweed Lane and the New Seward Highway, and at this point I was thinking Chet probably missed his calling as a used-car salesman. During this period, Jan was born and the tent family of three kids became a handful for Edna. When the Japanese attacked Pearl Harbor and later the Alaskan Aleutian Islands, the family moved to Seattle traveling on an unlit ship. Chet remained in Alaska.

After receiving the homestead patent, Chet became the classic gold prospector, striking out into the deep wilderness alone, digging holes to bedrock, and living a solitary life for weeks on end. He chartered bush planes to drop him off in the Kantishna and Savage River foothills north of Mount McKinley (now Denali). Years later, I asked Chet how he dealt with the ferocious mosquitoes before the days of bug repellant. I couldn't't imagine how one could survive and not go crazy without the protection from today's products. He said he burned the fungus conks from birch and spruce trees in camp, and I wondered what he did when traveling cross-country on foot, or while digging holes to bedrock. I don't think I could have handled it. A poignant aspect of Chet's wilderness prospecting days was later discovered by Jan: Every so often he would hike many miles to the nearest post office on the Alaska Railroad and hope for a letter from Edna. There never was one. Edna had remarried in Seattle.

Not long after meeting Chet, Jan and I were driving back to Anchorage along Turnagain Arm after a skiing weekend when we encountered a spectacular sunset in progress over the water. We pulled into a turnout where we could enjoy the sight, and being in a magnanimous mood with my arm around her shoulder, I said, "You know, if I ever decided to get married, it would be to a girl like you."

And she replied, "OK!"

Being dense, it took a moment for what had just happened to sink in. I mentally tried to reprocess what had transpired, and thought, *Did I actually just propose? If I think so, does she? If I don't think so, does she? What the hell did I really just do?* In any event, the fact that she didn't immediately jump out of the car and run away screaming bolstered my self-confidence. I could feel myself sliding into the mental state of quasi matrimonial acceptance.

The Seldovia Jail

One Friday after work, Carl Lind and I took off for Homer in our Taylorcraft. It was a beautiful, clear summer evening, but when Kachemak Bay and Homer came into sight, we saw that the area was obscured in low sea fog and Homer was not open. On the far side of the bay, however, we observed that Seldovia was in the clear, so we altered our destination accordingly. Seldovia was a small boardwalk fishing community on the bay with a protected harbor and seaplane ramp. After landing, we taxied in to the harbor, tied up on the seaplane ramp, and adjourned to the nearest waterfront bar, where we walked in to find we were the only patrons at the moment. The lone bartender was friendly, and we each ordered up a beer. While taking the first sip, the phone on the wall behind the bar rang and the bartender answered it, then turned to ask, "Are either of you Jim Thurston?" Since we had arrived in Seldovia only minutes ago, and since *even we* didn't know we would be there until now, how in the world could someone else know to call me on the phone in this bar?

Who else indeed, but good old Uncle Sam! It was the BLM fire control office in Anchorage and they wanted me to go on a large fire in northern Interior Alaska and document its history. I was incredulous. How in the hell did they find me? In Homer, the BLM had a station on a high bluff overlooking Cook Inlet and Kachemak Bay. John Merrick, the station manager, was in the yard raking leaves when he looked up and saw our airplane overhead. John recognized the airplane, knew that Homer was fogged in, and saw us change course for Seldovia. Shortly after, the Anchorage fire control office called and asked him to track me down, since the scuttlebutt had been that I was headed to Homer for the weekend.

When John told them I had gone to Seldovia, they decided to contact the Seldovia chief of police who, it turned out, was our bartender. The BLM planned to send an airplane to Homer the next morning to retrieve me, so Carl and I needed a place to sleep. The police chief said there were no rooms available in Seldovia due to a busy fish canning season, but his jail was available, and there were no customers at the time. To this day, when I am in an up mood, I occasionally break out into a rendition of, "Can't get no bail in the Seldovia jail!"

Our Marriage Ceremony

In Anchorage, discussions about marriage inexorably intensified. I loved Jan. My biggest hang-up was the thought of somehow losing her in the distant future due to an accident or illness. My reservation was brought about by the loss of Bill Smith, which had impacted me severely. This inherent fear made it difficult for me to get too close to people. Then, one day, Jan announced she had missed her period, and that cinched it—we were off to the races. But before we could go further, a formal proposal had to be made. This was accomplished at the old, original Peanut Farm in Anchorage, before it became a sports bar and when they still had floors littered with peanut shells. It was quiet and romantic.

The proposal was not unlike putting a machine into gear. Things started to happen. Things foreign to me. One of the first was to inform Chet that we planned to get married. We invited him to come to dinner one evening at Jan's basement apartment where we would inform him of our intended nuptials. When the time came, I think we were squirming a lot, and Chet probably sensed something serious was up. He was sitting across the dinner table from us reading a women's magazine upside down. We broke the news of our impending wedding to him (intentionally slurring the date) and somehow neglected to mention that Jan had a turkey in the oven too early for Thanksgiving. (This would be bombshell no. 2 to be delivered later after his recovery from bombshell no.1.) Chet did seem to like me just a little bit, and the rest of the dinner was uneventful.

Before long we moved onto the pivotal issue of where to have the ceremony. During several temple-throbbing discussions, Jan pitched a full-dress formal wedding at Saint Mary's Episcopal Church, and I pressed for a "Let's not go overboard here" brief ceremony at a justice of the peace. After capitulating to the church option, I dug in my heels about not having to endure a boring, stuffy, tea-and-crumpets reception impregnated with superficial small talk. I wanted a hell-of-a-party and spiked the punch with 95-proof Ever clear grain alcohol to assure that result. Other preparations included me getting a suit. I didn't't own one and was broke, so Jan lent me $65, and I bought one that she picked out. This was mildly humiliating.

On September 26, 1964, I morphed into another phase of life. The church ceremony was distinguished, marginally regal, progressed smoothly, and we had a full congregation of well-wishers. Carl Lind was our best man. The reception will be remembered forever by every-one who was there, and for this I give Everclear the credit. Even today, the reception is occasionally talked about, usually in the shadows with lowered eyelids and hushed voices. This day marked the termination of the first phase of my life and the start of another, hopefully during which I would begin to mutate into a responsible, mature adult.

18

1964 - 1965

The Newlyweds

After the wedding, Carl moved out of the apartment and Jan moved in. She was teaching first grade at Scenic Park Elementary, and for our first married Saturday, she undertook the preparation of a special breakfast to celebrate our embarkation into domesticated bliss. It was at this point the transformation of James W. Thurston commenced. The breakfast was wonderful, and in a state of intense contentment, I pushed my chair back from the table, crossed my feet on the corner of it, pulled out a cigar, and lit it. This was the last time that ever happened, and thus began the long process of my transition into mature adulthood.

Hewitt Lake

During this period, the brand-new state of Alaska was selecting federal lands administered by the BLM for transfer to the state. Since state finances were challenging, priority was given to selections which would provide a fast return on investment, especially those containing oil and other nat-

Hewitt Lake

ural resources. A supplemental approach was to select and sell lands of value directly to the public. One such program was dubbed "Wilderness Estates," in which desirable lake-front properties were surveyed into lots on numerous lakes outside of Anchorage and sold at auction. In the fall of 1964 they held an auction encompassing hundreds of lots on these lakes. To acquire one, it was necessary (after winning the bid) to pay 10 percent down and 10 percent a year at 8 percent interest to gain the title.

Hardly anyone showed up at the auction, so competition only occurred on a handful of lots, leaving most available at established minimum prices. Lot lines were drawn on large-scale aerial photographs, and I relied on these for selecting my lot. I purchased a 40-acre parcel with a small pond and 1,000 feet of frontage on Hewitt Lake about 80 air miles northwest of Anchorage that was accessible only by float or ski-plane, boat, or snow machine. It cost us the hefty sum of $1,500, or $150 down and $150/year for 10 years. It would be 25 years before I undertook construction of a cabin, so the Hewitt Lake project remained dormant, but was always in the back of my mind as a future retirement activity.

Our First House

Several weeks following our wedding, Jan tried to convince me we should buy a house, which I steadfastly resisted because I felt it would be too complicated and we couldn't even afford a down payment. I had no knowledge of such affairs, and it scared me. Paying simple rent had no financial risk and was a no-brainer for me, and we argued about it for several weeks. One night I came home from work, and spread out on the dinner table was the classified section of the *Anchorage Times*. A handful of houses for sale were circled by red marker. I imagined a bull being led into an arena. Highlighted was a $20,000 house for sale with a zero down payment that demolished one of my arguments. I agreed to at least take a look, and off we went into the dark, snowy November evening, bound for the Anchorage hillside.

Its location was part way up the hillside in the Our Road Subdivision about a quarter mile south of O'Malley Road in a spruce forest. Herb Reim and his wife, Sue, welcomed us into their 750-square-foot home that he had built on a half-acre lot. They served us cookies and coffee, and after a while, I came to realize I had been paying more apartment rent per month

Our road house on the Anchorage hillside.

than the bank mortgage would be if we bought their place. The house, though small, was presentable, and since Herb said he was a home builder who had built several other houses, I figured this house must be OK, and besides that, Jan really liked Sue—she was grandmotherly. Having completed our due-diligence research, we bought the place on the spot and trundled back to the apartment glowing with the thought of the great deal we had just made. My conversion from renting to owning had taken only two and a half hours—I was a born-again homeowner!

We moved in during January 1965. Furnishings were bare, and I remember the first thing we bought was a small, round dining table from Sears. Since we were low on funds, we used Blazo boxes for dining chairs. I have no memory of what we did for beds, and I think the living room was almost empty—but it was a start. Once again, Jan wanted to demonstrate her domestic prowess by jumping out of bed and cooking a special breakfast. In a state of apparent semi-sleep, she put two slices of bread in the toaster, set the toaster on the stove electric hotplate, turned the stove on, and marched off to take a shower. In bed, I woke up to the odor of something nasty burning and could see smoke outside the door. When I ran into the kitchen, I discovered the plastic base of the toaster melting through the yellow-hot coils of the stove top. God, I loved that girl!

The Mouse

One evening as we ate supper, a mouse ran by. Jan grabbed a broom to whop it, and I stopped her—there were far more sophisticated ways to deal with this kind of problem. I had a Daisy air rifle that would work perfectly for this situation: clean, high-tech, and male-ego rewarding! After spraying BBs around the house at the constantly scampering mouse, it became apparent that to eliminate hiding spots, an area had to be cordoned off, so we used LP record holders to erect a wall separating the living room from the rest of the house. Then, because we had moved what little furniture we had in the living room into the kitchen, leaving the mouse nowhere to hide, it jumped into the hot-water baseboard heat register.

I took up a prone position on the living room carpet with the air rifle, poised to shoot. The register cover had a series of oval holes running just above the heating fins upon which the mouse ran back and forth, thus presenting a target not unlike that of a shooting gallery. As the mouse ran, I peppered his moving target with BBs, most of which ricocheted off the register and onto the living room carpet and kitchen floor. About a hundred BBs later, the mouse hid behind the corner plate of the register and no longer appeared in any of the oval holes. At this point Jan implored me to discontinue the BB gun thing and allow her to broom-whop the mouse at her next opportunity. By then, I knew there was no way I was going to let that mouse outsmart me by hiding in the corner so I stood up, marched over to the living room thermostat, and turned it up as far as it would go.

For the next twenty minutes Jan and I argued about the rationality of my actions while the room became warmer and warmer. I was prone again on the carpet with the rifle trained on the corner plate, waiting for the damn mouse to appear. As the temperature climbed, our bickering intensified, and I started to perspire. Her ideas like perhaps resorting to a mousetrap were brusquely rejected—*we're into frontal combat here!* The rifle sights were trained on the right edge of the corner plate when suddenly the mouse made his move: he charged me head-on! The rifle was only three inches above the carpet with my eye on the sights, and it appeared he was going to impact my face, so with an outcry I yielded and rolled to the right. This provided my wife an unforgettable demonstration of what true courage was really all about. I had not even gotten off a shot!

The mouse started doing laps around the living room and came too close to Jan, who whopped him with the broom, stunning him. Before she could administer the coup de grace, I jumped up and intervened, stating that death by firing squad would be more appropriate, following which I positioned the rifle barrel vertically against his ear and pulled the trigger. Nothing came out except a strong poof of air which revived the mouse. It jumped up and traveled about three feet before Jan administered a fatal broom-whop. Mortified, I congratulated her with a forced grin. The combat had been intense, and losing to my new wife was tough. Losing to a mouse was even worse.

Home Improvement

After our daughter Joyce Kimberly arrived, we acquired a black lab dog that was slightly past puppyhood and hyperactive. Now only two other things were lacking to complete our venture into domesticity: grass in the yard and a white picket fence. For the fence I rented a heavy-duty gas-powered post hole digger and had George Kitson, a 300-pound coworker, help me one Saturday with the digging. The post hole digger had two sets of handlebars whereby two operators would face off guiding it while the auger bored downward. At one point, the auger hung up on a rock that wouldn't't move. The sudden hang-up threw both of us off the handlebars, at which point the engine was supposed to idle with nobody's thumb on the throttle. It didn't' idle, and the result was the auger stayed fixed while the whole machine spun around fast enough to make the whirling handlebars unapproachable. Since the gas tank was half full, there was nothing we could do until it ran out, so we both sat down and proceeded to make a serious dent in the six-pack of Olympia beer George had brought.

Instead of the picket fence, I stupidly built a cedar post fence with 1x8 horizontal boards that alternated on the sides of the posts. I thought it looked neat. The fence was supposed to keep our dog in the yard, but the animal simply slithered sideways between the two lower boards and ravaged the neighborhood by stealing children's caps, gloves, toys, freshly baked pies, etc. and delivering them to our front door. To correct this problem, I purchased an electric fence and ran the wire horizontally between the two lowest boards, thus terminating the slithering escapes.

The grass I had seeded quickly took hold during our damp spring, so it soon became necessary to start mowing operations. Two problems quickly made themselves known: a careless lawnmower thrust too close to the fence in wet grass produced an electrocution-type shock through the handles of the mower that resulted in a loud string of expletives, and the presence of rather substantial piles of black lab poop in the grass gave special meaning to a well-known phrase involving a fan. Lawn mowing once a week quickly became a chore I dreaded.

19

1965

The Gulkana River Float Saga

The Gulkana River flows out of Paxson Lake, which is two hundred and fifty miles northeast of Anchorage. This river offers a premier rafting opportunity for a 55-mile float trip in the wilderness (correction: grizzly bear-infested wilderness). It is a small clearwater river that may be accessed at its north end from Paxson Lake and to the south at Sourdough Creek Campground on the Richardson Highway. Between these two points, the river meanders many miles to the west, and by the early 1960s was little traveled as evidenced by an almost total lack of human signs (camping sites, etc.). Huge numbers of red salmon spawn here in the fall, and grayling, which are a tasty trout-like freshwater fish, practically jump into the raft. This raft trip usually takes a leisurely three to four days. I floated it with friends in 1961 and 1963.

During 1965 I flew many trips around the Gulkana Valley, some of which flew over the Gulkana River. Eventually I took notice of a tributary, the West Fork of the Gulkana River, that extended many miles northwest and was born out of a small, shallow, swampy pothole lake in the flatlands north of Lake Louise. I figured the pothole lake was just big enough to accommodate our Taylorcraft floatplane and could be used as the launching point for an extended raft trip. Since the trips on the main Gulkana River were three to four days, my pilot's eye assessed the West Fork to be a six-day trip, and with grayling jumping into our raft, we needed to pack only four days of food. (Since then, I have come to realize that pilots are notoriously proficient at underestimating the time required for non- motorized ground travel.)

In mid-September Jan and I embarked upon our adventure with two friends, Jim Evans and Bob Levinson from BLM. At the completion of a complex logistical operation involving vehicles and multiple shuttles with the floatplane, we assembled with all our provisions on the shore of the pothole lake and watched as Carl Lind disappeared over the horizon in the Taylorcraft, headed for Anchorage. No words were immediately spoken as the four of us stood there in silence letting the enormity of our wilderness isolation sink in. Getting to work in a horrendous cloud of mosquitoes, we started pumping up three rafts that were small, medium, and large: large for the four of us plus most of our gear, medium for more gear, and small for emergency use.

Initially, the creek exiting the pothole lake was only about 8-feet wide, very shallow with no current, and remained that way for the next three days. It meandered in endless oxbow loops with the result that, as far as we could tell, a whole day of paddling placed us only a hefty stone's throw from our morning starting point! A day breeze further aggravated the situation because when we turned upwind with no current to help us, we had to get out and pull the rafts while wading. During this period, no fishing was attempted because all effort had to be devoted to actually *getting* somewhere on what could be 100 river miles. After three days, a hint of some current developed, and we could occasionally leisurely float instead of constantly paddling and pulling. Our poor travel performance was now alarming in view of my idiotic decision to pack only four days of food. Three of those days were already gone, and we were hardly underway. Also, our smallest emergency raft quit holding air and had to be discarded by burial.

Fishing started in earnest, and when a full day of it produced zero results, we started rationing. I still remember the bitter arguments erupting over a block of medium-sharp cheddar cheese and the tattered remains of some beef jerky. As the hours drifted by and our concerns heightened, some minor tension arose between Bob Levinson and Jan on the subject of children's coloring books. While Jim Evans and I periodically exchanged eyeball rolls, Bob and Jan endlessly debated the virtues of having lines in coloring books to guide the child vs. not restricting creativity by having no lines. Bob wanted lines. Jan didn't. Due to its extreme boredom, Evans and I wanted a change of subject. This never happened and they were still arguing about it during the return drive to Anchorage a week and a half later. The next day, Bob pulled out his toothbrush and continued the book debate with it sticking out of his mouth all day long. This rankled all three of us for what was really no good reason—it just did. Now we were bored *and* hungry! The damn toothbrush never left the scene either.

By day 5, the creek had become a river, and we began to cover some miles. At midmorning we came around a bend and observed a caribou standing on a gravel bar. Bob unsheathed a 30–06 rifle and efficiently dispatched the animal, which instantly dropped dead on the gravel bar and patiently waited for us to retrieve him. The cleaning, dressing, meat preparation, cooking, and eating dragged on for several hours, and I was concerned about not making any river miles, especially if the meat cutting, cooking, and eating were going to reduce our daily travel time significantly.

Then an idea hit me: build a small raft out of driftwood, place a layer of wet gravel on it, build a fire on the gravel, and cook our food as we floated with the cooking fire following us on the end of a small line. As luck would have it, we also had a wooden raft panel that could substitute as a cutting board, allowing us to cut up caribou meat chunks while underway. We dubbed these meat chunks "carinuts," which we wrapped in aluminum foil for broiling. To start a new batch, we just pulled the fire to us and threw on the meat. We did not even have to stop to gather fuel for the fire. We'd just break off overhanging deadwood from undercut trees as we floated by the cut banks. The whole operation had a symbiotic feeling to it.

During the next three days, our routine became repetitious. Haul the fire in, throw the meat on it, push the fire out, break off some overhead firewood, cut up more meat, haul the fire in again, try to ignore the ongoing debate about coloring books, try not to focus on Levinson's toothbrush, and study the USGS topographic map to figure out where the hell we were. The river continued to have so many oxbows that we never did really pinpoint our location. Because we ran out of salt, the uninterrupted carinut diet was getting old, so the fishing effort resumed—to no avail. (Many years later I talked to a local who told me the West Fork has zero grayling, and nobody seems to know why.) We never caught a single fish on the entire trip. Thus far, during all the days of rafting, the only sign of human presence had been one dilapidated old trapper's cabin. At this point the second (medium) raft was demonstrating an inability to hold air and we had to move its contents onto our only remaining main raft.

"THIS RIVER TRIP IS THE MOST EXCITING THING I'VE EVER DONE!"

WEST FORK OF THE GULKANA RIVER SEPTEMBER 1965

My darling wife, Jan.

By day 9, the river had a healthy flow, and we were knocking down the miles at full throttle when we noticed that up ahead it widened and sped up considerably. It also became very shallow, and we ran aground in only a few inches of water. The four of us jumped out and started dragging the raft along when suddenly Jan screamed, "Look out—here comes the fire!"

The fire raft neatly slid under our main raft, causing three of us to freeze in disbelief. Jan hopped in and tried to snuff the flames by jumping up and down on the rubber bottom. The rest of us stood there screaming conflicting orders at each other until we noticed that

Jan had dispersed the fire. Some of its logs were floating away with their upper halves still in flames. Downstream we beached on a gravel bar and tried to assess any damage. There appeared to be a leak somewhere since water covered the inside bottom, but we figured that since the inflatable donut was holding firm, the craft was probably river worthy, so we shoved off with fingers crossed and continued downstream.

Day 10 was uneventful, but we continued to make good progress in the increasingly swift current. The weather had turned severe clear, and since we were in mid-to-late-September, the temperature dropped to below freezing by late afternoon and would probably be in the low twenties that night. We also encountered the junction where the West Fork now joined the main Gulkana River, and for the first time since embarking, we actually knew where we were. On a gravel bar during sunset, while munching the last of the carinuts, a council of war was held, and the decision was made to make a desperate run for Sourdough that night. We had gone through two out of three rafts; our rafts's donut could spring an air leak at any time; our boots were ankle-deep in water; we were cold; we were out of food; and a full moon was making its debut for the evening. Not discussed was my fantasy that if I heard another mention of coloring books, the insertion of the toothbrush into an orifice for which it was never intended was a real possibility. This journey had to be ended, and just before dark we shoved off.

Around 2:00 a.m. we were cruising at good speed down the main river when suddenly we entered a fog bank so dense, visibility went to zero in spite of the light from the overhead full moon. The fog seemed to attach itself to everything as frost enveloped our eyebrows, clothing, and even our nostril hairs. Like the others, I was sitting on the donut with my back to the water. Apparently, we came alongside and surprised a beaver which slapped his tail almost next to me, causing spray to hit the back of my neck. I damn near fell out of the raft in a state of shock. Later, in pre-dawn light, we pulled the raft ashore at Sourdough Creek Campground and hurried to the SUV that we had prepositioned eleven days earlier. We were cold, wet, exhausted, and in dire need of some heat. After climbing into the vehicle, I turned the key and there was no response. The battery was dead, creating a fitting end to our wonderful journey.

Thanksgiving in a Cabin

Just before Thanksgiving the snow arrived and a winter wonderland scene materialized immediately outside the large windows of our cabin in Girdwood. We were immersed in a thick hemlock forest, the limbs of which were draped with snow, and after dark the flood lights I had installed under the eaves practically brought the outdoors inside. I could feel Christmas in the air, but first Jan invited her dad, Chet, and his new wife, Helen, to spend Thanksgiving dinner with us at the cabin. She looked forward to impressing them with her log cabin domestic expertise. We also wanted to get on Helen's favorable side because we had been sensing negative vibes out of her.

The day before, the temperature suddenly nose-dived to zero, and it became apparent the electric baseboard heat I had installed was inadequate. Not only was there not enough electric heat, my chic-looking, inverted-funnel wood fireplace was sucking heat out of the cabin faster than it could replace it. When time came to cook the turkey, Jan couldn't find it and realized to her horror she had left it in Anchorage at the store on a counter. The dinner scene still sticks with me as I remember us hunched around the table, shivering under blankets. Dinner was comprised of all the Thanksgiving trimmings without the turkey. Jan was sobbing, and while I was making tortuous small talk with Chet, who was saying very little, Helen was glowering at us for our unforgivable ineptitude. It was a Thanksgiving to remember.

Overcoming Color Blindness

The BLM's land management activities along with several other programs required the use of small aircraft. The BLM's aircraft division grew tired of me constantly bugging them for a pilot to fly me, so the chief, John McCormick, one day said, "Thurston, you've got as much or more experience as some of our Cessna pilots. Why don't you go get commercial and instrument tickets and fly yourself?" So, I did.

But first, I had to jump a huge hurdle: red-green color blindness. Thus far I had been able to fly as a private pilot with an FAA colorblind restriction: no flight at night or by color signal control. In 1956 during an effort to enlist as a fighter pilot, I flunked the aviation color tests for both the navy and air force. In 1965 I learned that the FAA could waive my limitations if I passed a color test administered by an FAA control tower in which they shot actual color signals at me with a light gun. The test was only given once and the results were good for life, which also meant if you failed, it was a life sentence. The aviation colors are red, green, and white. While I could discern the red, I had difficulty telling white from green since the green appeared to be washed out. The sink-or-swim nature of the test dictated I find a way to practice, so I descended upon a lonely control tower controller in the dead of winter at the Anchorage Lake Hood Seaplane base, which, at the time of day I chose, was virtually deserted.

The bored controller was more than glad to help me and obviously wanted company. I had prepared papers with a hundred blanks on each so he could write down the colors he was going to shoot at me. I then drove to the far end of Lake Hood, flashed my lights, and the tower shot me a hundred signals that I wrote down. When we compared notes, my confusion between green and white was confirmed. The controller said, "You know, since the green light goes through a filter and the white light does not, the white should appear more intense than the green." Armed with this information, we tried again, and I aced all one hundred colors. Just to be sure, we did it again with the same result.

I scheduled the real test and met Kenn Moon, an FAA inspector, at Merrill Field in downtown Anchorage, who emphasized I had to call the colors within two seconds of the flash and even one mistake would be fatal. I passed, thus setting the stage for a whole new career, although at the time I didn't' realize this.

20

1966

A Winter Wonderland Hallucination

Bill Adams flew in from McGrath, and we spent the day at the office developing a lesson plan about how to set up a large fire organization. As we often did, I had invited Bill to dinner at our house so we could enamor Jan all evening with shop talk. I still had a lot to learn about marriage. On the way home we stopped to buy steaks and bourbon. The drive was challenging due to heavy snow that became more intense as we drove up the Anchorage hillside. Eventually we were creeping along the dirt road to our home, which was now very narrow due to the thick, snow-laden alder on both sides. There must have been five inches of fresh snow on every branch. Suddenly, snow started falling off the branches on our left and twenty feet ahead. A baby elephant stepped out in front of us, crossed over in the glare of our headlights, and disappeared into the brush on the right. It was wearing mukluks (leather boots).

The two of us sat for a brief moment, stunned in disbelief. The car was stopped, and the only sounds were that of the engine quietly idling and the repetitive swish of the wipers sweeping snowflakes off the windshield. I asked Bill if he believed what we had just seen. He said no, but confirmed yes by pulling the bourbon bottle out of the bag and removing the cap. We both took a pull and sat silently for another moment, after which discussions began about who to tell, whether to tell, and our immense unbelievability problem. Reporting an elephant-at-large wearing boots to the police would make us look like nutcases. Doing nothing would be tantamount to animal cruelty by ignoring the plight of a poor little elephant lost in the snowy forest.

I was not looking forward to sharing this with Jan since we'd be arriving at the house carrying a liquor bottle with alcohol on our breath, but there was no real alternative, so we proceeded. She had just heard about it from a neighbor. It was rumored to belong to the folks somewhere across O'Malley Road from us who won it in an auction. They were housing it in a barn, and it had wandered off while they were taking it for a stroll through our neighborhood. We discussed calling them to report the sighting but didn't know who to call and decided to do nothing since they already knew the animal was on the loose.

Later we learned the elephant's name was Annabelle, and she had been won in some sort of lottery. Apparently, they wanted to establish a non-profit zoo for kids, at which point Jan announced she was going to spearhead a drive to collect funds. To this end, she, with other artists, designed and produced collection cups adorned with cute animal characters that were circulated around Anchorage in a successful effort to assist with the establishment of a zoo. Years later, Annabelle became prolific with a paint brush and easel. Some of her paintings today are worth thousands of dollars.

The following from Wikipedia is offered to lend creditability to what otherwise would be an improbable story spun by someone prone to fantasy and gross exaggeration:

In 1966, Anchorage grocer Jack Snyder won a contest offering a prize of "$3,000 or a baby elephant." He chose the elephant, a female Asian elephant named Annabelle. Annabelle was initially kept at the Diamond H Horse Ranch, located in the Hillside area of Anchorage and owned by Sammye Seawell, which had the only heated stalls available.

With Annabelle's increasing popularity, Seawell formed a non-profit corporation to build a place "where the public could visit animals and learn about them." It was incorporated on March 28, 1968, as the

Alaska Children's Zoo, which opened in 1969 with Annabelle and other donated animals. The zoo was located on land adjacent to Seawell's ranch. The zoo's name was changed to Alaska Zoo in June 1980.

Fires Y-33 and Y-34

During the summer of 1966 an intense wildfire season developed in the eastern Interior, and I found myself almost equally involved in land management and fire control activities. When serious fires occur, the BLM draws on overhead personnel from throughout the agency, including those in offices out of state. One hot afternoon in July, lightning ignited two fires near the Fortymile River south of the town of Chicken. They were about 30 miles apart and were designated Y-33 and Y-34. The following afternoon, having been drafted to assist with the control effort, I was scouting the leading edge of Y-33 in a Cessna 185 with three fire officials. The fuel was solid mature spruce, the leading fire edge was several miles long, and the flame front was easily 100 feet high above the trees. As we flew parallel to the flames about 100 yards away, I realized that if our engine quit for some reason, and if we managed to walk away from the forced landing, survival from the fire would have been impossible.

Bill Adams had been designated the fire boss, and he set up his headquarters on a rounded dome above timber line. I was reassigned from the airplane to the south flank of the fire to assist the division boss, Carl Johnson, and with about 80 firefighters we commenced construction of a fire line down the valley bottom, burning out as we went. For two days the operation progressed satisfactorily, and we secured perhaps three miles of line. Late the third morning, the terrain we were burning out became fairly steep and was covered with highly flammable caribou moss (which is also known as reindeer lichen). While the breeze in our valley was almost nonexistent, we were unaware that a few hundred feet up a significant breeze was blowing across our line against us.

Our burnout fires rocketed up the slope through an abundance of fuel. Initially we were pleased, however, due to the winds aloft, spot fires started to ignite behind us. Within a few minutes, they were popping up faster than we could beat them out. We now had an out-of-control fire situation downhill from us in the valley bottom, which started working up the valley toward our fire camp, at which point I got on the radio and called for air tanker support. Fortunately, a B-25 tanker was nearby, and I told him to salvo his load on our camp, where we had all congregated. (In those days the retardant in use was borate, a white milky solution that also sterilized the ground and was replaced by the red Phos-Chek a few years later.) The pilot nailed the target with the result that the camp tent collapsed, the fire went around us, and we looked like a bunch of wet snowmen.

Meanwhile, up at Bill Adams's headquarters on the mountain top, a different type of incident developed. Large fires have timekeepers who need a sheltered office to house the hundreds of time slips. An HF radio had been set up in the timekeeper tent with one of the two antenna poles doing double duty as the center pole for the tent. An 88-foot antenna was stretched between the two poles. A food drop was in progress with our DC-3. Personnel, including the timekeeper, were temporarily removed from the drop area for obvious safety reasons. Fresh food was delivered by cargo chutes. Military C-rations were simply pushed out the door to free-fall from very low altitude. During a C-ration free-fall pass, the tail wheel of the DC-3 snagged the radio antenna wire, and Bill Adams's men watched the sudden departure of the timekeeper's tent down the mountainside in a blizzard of time slips. The frustrated timekeeper quit, and administrative efforts were set back several days.

As a result of my stellar success on Y-33, I was transferred 30 miles north to assist Curly Brandt on Fire Y-34 (the West Fork Fire). Curly's fire camp was also on high ground but in the middle of a spruce forest. Curly's troops had already felled the trees which needed to be removed for a cargo drop zone, but the logs still littered the ground. I had only arrived a few minutes earlier by helicopter when our DC-3 suddenly showed up to drop cargo. Curly told him to go ahead and drop anyhow, and the first bundles came out the door. No parachutes opened, and the cargo crashed into the downed logs with devastating effect. It was several bags of radios. Curly called the pilot, but received no response, and the DC-3 made another run. Again, the parachutes failed to open, but this time it was cargo not as fragile as radios. It was gunnysack bags full of steel files to keep axes and Pulaskis sharp—brittle steel files, which on impact became shrapnel! Some files were actually stuck in the surrounding spruce tree trunks. Myself and others were by now sheltering behind trees and under logs.

The dropping continued with no communication aloft. Chainsaws and fire pumps were demolished. Steaks, bread, peanut butter, and jelly were transformed to mush. Bundles of shovels and Pulaskis lost their identity. It was impossible for me to believe that no personnel on board that DC-3 observed the failure of all parachutes to open and the entire loss of cargo. I planned to raise hell about it later when I had the chance. After the last drop streamed in, the pilot finally came on the air and blandly asked if we needed anything else. Curly told him he should make another pass because some of us down here were still living. Later we learned the smokejumpers in Fairbanks were experimenting with a new, innovative way to pack cargo chutes. I fervently hoped they were not going try it on personnel chutes.

Y-34 was a bigger problem than Y-33, and things were chaotic. Days earlier, crews had been positioned around the fire, which had suddenly become huge. Nobody knew how many troops there were, where they were, or their status. Dense smoke, a rapidly expanding fire perimeter, poor radio communications, and the limited availability of helicopters all contributed to what can only be described as a mess. No one knew within several miles where the fire perimeter was. Bill Adams was also transferred from Y-33 as the new fire boss and was setting up the Y-34 Fire headquarters up north in the town of Chicken. Bill decided to organize the fire into two divisions—east and west. Ed Guin from Big Delta was appointed the eastern division boss. He had his back against the Canadian border. I was appointed the western division boss and set up my headquarters on the Taylor Highway where it crosses the Fortymile River.

My first priority was to helicopter-recon the western division to find out how many personnel I had, where they were, and their condition. Fortunately, the smoke lifted enough to make this an achievable objective, and I stumbled across a 40-man crew camped on a small creek. Jim Evans, of Gulkana River fame, was in charge. The fire had run over them several days ago, and with no food, no communication with the outside world, no idea where the fire was, and no direction from higher-ups, Jim correctly decided to hole up near potable water and await developments. Later that day I found more isolated crews in pretty much the same state and requested more helicopters to transport them out to where we could organize an effective fire control force. I never found Curly Brandt again and assumed he probably wound up on the eastern division working for Ed Guin. Bill Adams pushed the right buttons, and the next day several U.S. Air Force H-21 helicopters arrived to start moving these crews to new tactical positions. When Jim Evans arrived at my Taylor Highway assembly point, his comment was, "Damn, I feel like we're trying to organize Chrysler Corporation!"

The western division had the then-prevailing wind to its back, so my plan was to build fire line from south to north, burning out as we went, and eventually tie into the Fortymile River. The line would stretch for miles. The control force was like a snake that had several segments: a scout in the lead with a compass; a D4 bulldozer; crews with hand tools to construct a fire line where the D4 could not; crews to burn out the downwind side of the line; crews for holding the line while the burnout was in close proximity to the line; and crews for mop up and holding. Sal DeLeonardis was my lead scout who would maintain a compass course I provided him direct to the Fortymile River. I cautioned Sal to walk far enough ahead of the bulldozer to avoid magnetic influence on his hand compass. (His normal job was the PR guy for the BLM Alaska state director.) I put Fred Rungee in overall charge of this sector. He ran the BLM operations in Glennallen and had worked with me years ago on the Ophir Fire.

The next two days progressed like an example out of a textbook. With the stiff west winds at our back the burnout fires were super spectacular, progressing eastward into the main fire in what Evans described as, "the white-hot fires of purification." On the third morning at the division fire camp on the Taylor Highway, we woke up to no wind and dense smoke. I wanted to helicopter-recon the fire line building progress, but near zero visibility precluded that wish until early afternoon. By now I had two helicopters, one of which was down for a minor repair, so I climbed aboard an S-55 and headed east for the fire.

Sikorsky S-55 Helicopter.
Courtesy Of A. Hunt. Wikipedia Commons.

There was a well-defined 100-foot smoke ceiling forcing us to skim the treetops on the way out. Ahead, a miles-wide, ill-defined horizontal band of orange materialized and moments later came into focus as a solid wall of flame disappearing 100-feet up into the smoke ceiling. It was moving west— toward us—and in the direction of my fire line construction crews, who were somewhere down there in heavy timber. I couldn't reach Fred Rungee on the radio to warn him, and I was sure they were unaware of the danger, but I did manage to reach Sal, who told me he and the dozer were far ahead of the main work force and he was also out of contact with Rungee. After a short search I found Sal and the dozer. They were in great jeopardy. About a quarter mile ahead of them was a large grassy spot where we could land and pick them up if the fire didn't' get there first. I explained the situation to Sal, emphasizing the need to race as fast as possible to the clearing by raising the blade of the dozer and walking the cat over the timber rather than trying to clear it. I finished the conversation with, "Sal, this is a race you cannot afford to lose!"

Next, I searched farther back up the line for the main crew, but because the terrain increased in altitude, the low smoke ceiling cut me off. I still had no radio contact with Rungee in spite of repeated attempts. Since the grassy spot to which Sal was headed was essentially a flash-fuel area, when the fire encountered it, its speed would increase dramatically, so I contemplated a desperate attempt to burn it out at the last minute if necessary. My thought was that freshly burned smoldering grass would be more survivable than a 5-foot wall of flame moving at high speed, so I detoured back to the fire camp and gathered up a burnout torch, hoping I wouldn't need it. Upon my return, I found the D4 making disappointing progress and told Sal to kick it in the ass. He informed me the cat was overheating and the operator wanted to take it slow. I retorted that they'd both find new meaning to the word "overheating" if they didn't slam it in gear and get the hell out of that timber, so they raised the dozer blade and moved out with renewed enthusiasm.

We set the S-55 down on the edge of the clearing closest to where we expected the dozer to emerge and waited with the engine running. We could observe the main fire flame front getting closer to the other side of the clearing, and it was a truly frightening sight. Both the pilot's voice and hands were shaking, and I could tell he was scared shitless. I was right behind him on that score and kept intoning, "Where's that goddamned bulldozer?" Eventually it broke out of the timber and clattered up to the helicopter with steam coming out of it.

The fire had now broken out onto the grassy open area and was racing toward us. Sal climbed into the helicopter, but the dozer operator was engaged trying to untie his small luggage suitcase from the cat, and in spite of my shouted orders to climb aboard, he kept fiddling with it. I jumped out and, in a storm of profanity, practically yanked his arm out of the socket pulling him off the machine and herding him into the helicopter. Due to the location of several dead snags nearby, our takeoff path was necessarily oriented directly toward the flame front, thereby triggering, as we grew closer before turning, a silent prayer that the engine wouldn't die on us. It didn't, and we returned to the fire camp with me thinking, *"Well, at least we saved two of them, but where the hell are all the others?"*

The day wore on, and the smoke prevented any further reconnaissance. Also, the communications remained inoperative, leaving me to contemplate what was happening or had already happened to my men. During this period, convoys of supply trucks were passing our camp on the highway on the way north to the headquarters at Chicken. Bill Adams had appointed a runt from the BLM property management office to be his supply officer. I'd had many run-ins with this pea-brain over the years in Anchorage, and when he showed up at my headquarters and accused me of high-jacking supply trucks bound for Chicken (which was not true), I gave a nod to my bodyguard, Murphy. Murphy was a huge hulk of a human being who took no shit from anybody. He picked up the poor supply officer, carried him to the edge of the Fortymile River, and threatened to throw him in, following which Murphy forcibly ejected him from the fire camp. The supply officer appeared to turn religious and intoned that the wrath of Bill Adams would soon be upon me, seemingly unaware that Adams was not a god and would most likely find it humorous. This incident was a short, refreshing break from the depression I was sinking into over the unknown fate of eighty of my firefighters.

As the evening progressed, I became more uncommunicative with my staff. I had managed to virtually convince myself I was responsible for the single most disastrous loss of life of firefighters in modern history. Chitchat was not something I wanted to engage in, and I withdrew for a long, drawn-out, sleepless night.

By morning, the smoke had lifted, and I embarked upon a

I'm holding the white coffee cup, waiting for the smoke to lift so I can check on my firefighters.

Photo from Opportunity and Challenge: The Story of the Bureau of Land Management.

helicopter reconnaissance during which I made two noteworthy discoveries: all my people were safe and a rising east wind was pushing the fire back at us and toward the Taylor Highway, threatening to cut off access to our headquarters as well as Adams's domain up in Chicken. Later that day, the fire breached the highway, and my men were starting to describe "ten-thousand-acre slop-overs." Chartered bus drivers negotiating the Taylor Highway told of running gauntlets of flames. John McCormick flew over in the P-51 Mustang and made the unforgettable pronouncement: "Today, we are going to burn Chicken." Chaos reigned again.

As if things couldn't get any worse, Ed Guin's entire eastern division unexpectedly emerged out of the Fortymile River riding military amphibious vehicles with Ed in the lead looking like Erwin Rommel riding his tank. They resembled a defeated army and described being completely overrun by the fire. Guin was furious and blamed me for causing it all with my burnout fires. I had never seen him so angry and for a while thought he might physically attack me. I had difficulty comprehending how he could blame me for fires that overran him more than thirty miles from our location since there were already fires between our divisions even before we ever started burning. There had never been any radio communication or coordination between us throughout the week because none was possible. Also there had been no communication from Adams's headquarters to the two of us because they didn't know what was happening either. We had been two independent operations at the mercy of the winds.

As often happens, the rains suddenly moved in, and the fires lay down. A new fire overhead team arrived to replace Adams, Guin, myself, and other key overhead. I returned to Anchorage bitter over the whole affair—it had been a debacle in which I had participated. When I arrived home, my loving wife provided comfort, understanding, and suggested that maybe we should have another baby. I happily submitted to the idea, and the conception of our forthcoming son, J.T. Thurston,

was undertaken. It was a refreshing change of pace from the West Fork
Fire Y-34.

21

1967 - Part 1

The Aircraft Division

In Alaska, due to its far-flung field operations, the Bureau of Land Management maintained a division of aircraft that was headquartered at Merrill Field in downtown Anchorage. It was headed by John "Mac" McCormick, who, due to his mustache, people on the sidewalk occasionally mistook for Tennessee Ernie Ford, the famous country singer. Mac supervised a small fleet of government aircraft plus many contracted, leased, and chartered aircraft.

The 1966 fires had served to accentuate an ongoing dispute between fire control managers and the division of aircraft over who called the shots during aerial firefighting operations. Traditionally, the fire managers made both strategic and tactical decisions, such as whether air tankers were to be used at all and, if so, on what area of the fire. On large fire operations, tanker drops were often supervised over the fire by an air attack boss who detailed the requirements for individual drops to the tanker pilots. During the 1960's in Alaska, the air attack boss was usually an Aircraft Division pilot who doubled as the "chase plane pilot" who flew immediately behind the tanker while providing flight path corrections and drop-gate sequencing instructions. The fire personnel maintained that pilots were not fire behavior or fire control experts, and therefore fire personnel should be guiding these drops. The pilots maintained that over the years, they had accrued more air tanker firefighting exposure and experience than all the fire managers put together and since flight performance knowledge was necessary for safety, pilots should guide the drops. The dispute produced numerous shouting matches at fire control staff meetings during the period.

One evening after work and over martinis, McCormick broached the subject, suggesting that a person with both aviation and fire control experience could solve his problem since, if the pilot also had fire control experience, nobody could complain. Indeed, I had always harbored an aviation interest, and this, coupled with the fact that the lands work I was currently doing was boring and made me feel like just another government bureaucrat, led me to agree that if he could arrange it, I would consent to being transferred to the division of aircraft. Both my boss, Jim Scott, and the Alaska State Director, Burt Silcock, tried to talk me out of it, saying I was throwing away a promising career. I felt I was throwing away a boring life behind a desk being just another bureaucrat and held firm. They reluctantly allowed me to transfer.

The division was comprised of the chief John McCormick, his secretary, a dispatcher, pilots, mechanics, and an avionics technician. An administrative staff between the chief and his troops on the line did not exist. I served as that staff along with the taking on of various special projects, such as the air tanker program. Before long I checked out in the Aero Commander twin-engine chase plane and started training for air tanker operations.

The Red Devil Incident

An early introduction to my new job occurred when I was dispatched to fly a Cessna 185 from Anchorage to Pilot Station 400 miles due west on the Yukon River to deliver aviation case gas in 5-gallon cans for a gas cache. The rear and right-front seats of the airplane had been removed, and case gas occupied the entire cabin space behind me and to my right. The day was crystal clear, and after departing Anchorage, I climbed to 10,500 feet to cross the Alaska Range. This was the life I had always dreamed about: viewing some of the most spectacular country in the world; flying on a beautiful day in a well-maintained aircraft cared for at the expense of someone else; traveling to a remote outpost in the wilderness; and being paid to do it. My heart swelled with gratitude, and I breathed in deeply.

Gasoline! I could smell gasoline in the cabin! Then I felt a dampness on the back of my head and shoulders. The gas can immediately behind my head had sprung a pinhole leak, and due to our reduced pressure at high altitude, the gas was spewing out in a very fine spray. I was a flying bomb, hovering on the fringes of detonation, at high altitude in the middle of nowhere! There could be no electricity allowed, so I instantly killed the electrical master switch. Now the only electrical source (except the static type from exterior air flow) was the engine ignition system, which was isolated from the problem area way forward.

I had to separate myself from this airplane in a hurry, and while shedding altitude as fast as possible, I vectored in on the nearest landing strip, which was Red Devil on the Kuskokwim River. It was a remote gravel strip, and I dove straight in on it. As the wheels rolled along the gravel, I cut the engine, opened my door, and after slowing down some, dove out of the airplane, sustaining only minor scrapes. The airplane coasted to a stop while still on the runway, for which I was very thankful. As I stood there recovering my composure, I felt significant discomfort to my back and shoulders and realized the gas in my gasoline-soaked upper clothing was irritating my skin, so I stripped my shirt off.

Fortunately, the day was bright and sunny and above freezing so I spread my clothes out to dry and embarked upon a series of exercises to stay warm. I was hoping on one hand that another airplane would show up and have something on board to help me clean my skin, and on the other hand, since my airplane had the runway blocked near the halfway mark, if one showed up, I hoped he was proficient at short-field landings. As it turned out, after two hours, nobody showed up, I was getting cold, so stifling my apprehension, I unloaded the airplane to let things air out. While halfway expecting to blow up any second, I was nevertheless surprised how much the fumes had dissipated, and after two hours I loaded back up and headed for Pilot Station, leaving the leaky gas can behind. Shortly after, the aircraft division implemented a new policy prohibiting the carriage of case gas in aircraft cabins. Guess who wrote it.

A Log Cabin Winter

Back at our home on Our Road, we were planning two significant events: getting rid of the dog and moving to a larger house. The dog wore out his welcome by barking under our open bedroom window all night long. Then, the next day, he really upset me. After a frazzled day at work, I stopped on the way home and bought a six-pack of Olympia beer. Jan had let the dog out, and as I entered our driveway, it was jumping up and down, overjoyed at my arrival. Just as the car stopped, the right front of the vehicle dropped off, making a loud sound. Exiting the car, I walked forward and discovered the right-front wheel horizontal on the ground under the bumper. It had come completely off. Highly pissed, I opened the rear door to recover my six-pack from the back seat. The dog was all over me, and as I extracted the beer, he knocked it out of my hand. All six bottles broke on the ground.

Furious, I slammed the rear door shut, accidentally mashing the tip of my right index finger. Holding the wounded finger, which was dripping blood, in my mouth and with the dog continuing to jump all over me, I stumbled through the front door into the house. Jan, at the kitchen sink, turned, observed her pathetic husband, and cooed, "Oh, did little Jimmy hurt his little, itty-bitty finger?" The dog's days with me were numbered. Several days later we gave him to an acquaintance who regarded the dog as a wonderful gift.

Also, our tiny home became too tiny, and with the forthcoming advent of another child, we explored our options and before long convinced ourselves we should build a house of our own design. In the Brookwood Subdivision, on the foot of the lower Anchorage hillside, we purchased two lots in a stand of 40-foot birch. Next, we hired a designer (not an architect) to produce a plan that could be handed to the building contractor for execution and then presented it to the bank with our loan request. Due to my status as a "stable" federal employee, the loan was approved, and we searched for a contractor. The firm we found was managed by Lee Cabe whose name alone should have scared me, but we signed him up and put our home on Our Road for sale for a nominal profit.

Unexpectedly, our little house sold quickly, so we decided to spend a few weeks in our Girdwood log cabin during the fall transition. We moved out during an early September Indian summer with the un-realistic expectation we would be in the new "Brookwood House" by Thanksgiving. All was warm and serene as we visualized our life in our new dream home. Overlooking the fact that we had two kids in diapers and the cabin had no running water, we thought our log cabin life would be an adventure!

It was, but not in the manner I anticipated. As the golden Indian summer transformed itself into to a cold, wet, dismal fall, my almost daily checks on the house construction progress were depressing be-cause often little or no activity was observed. One evening after dark in late October, I drove by and witnessed an outdoor party in progress with loud music and empty beer cans littering the grounds. The work-ers were uncommunicative, and the structure was not yet even fully enclosed. The next day I tried to visit Lee Cabe and found his office vacated with no forwarding address or way to contact him. Later we received a notice from the court notifying us they were going to auction the house off on the west steps of the Anchorage Courthouse on a certain date at 10:00 a.m. We retained an attorney.

The attorney blocked the sale and other arrangements (which I can't remember) were made to continue construction. Completion before early next year was in doubt, and the weather transitioned from rain to freezing rain. I was driving the Seward Highway to work daily on a road surfaced with water over ice, at times in high winds after dark. One morning I spun out halfway up Bird Hill and wound up broadside in the road. A large truck appeared over the crest of the hill, and it was obvious there was no way he could stop. For a moment I thought about bailing out of the car so I could get out of the middle of the road but realized it was far too slippery to stand up and there was not enough time to crawl away. The truck's loud horn was blaring, and I lapsed into a full panic! The demise of Bill Smith flashed through my mind, and somehow, I got the car pointed downhill, at which point I raced to stay ahead of the truck that was now breathing down my neck. Since you are reading this, it's obvious that I made it, but I'll never forget the front grill of that truck in my rearview mirror and the sound of his horn.

The short road to our cabin rose steeply about twenty feet at its very beginning off Glacier Creek Road, thus presenting a challenge when things were slippery. At times, when our car couldn't get up the rise, we'd leave it at the bottom and carry our stuff to the cabin. One dark evening the road surface was rain on ice. We had no ice cleats. On the steep slope, there were no hand holds as we attempted to crawl uphill from the car, holding flashlights. Jan was clutching our baby, little Jimmy, and I carried the groceries. Near the top of the rise, she slipped and lost Jimmy, who tobogganed down the slope and completely disappeared under the car. This triggered a level of hysteria from Jan I had never before encountered, and against a background of loud, continuous wailing, I slid down on my backside amongst an avalanche of groceries and collided with left front tire of the car. More high-pitched wailing was emanating from under the vehicle, and reaching under it, I extracted my son, who was less than pleased with these developments. When we finally reached the cabin, we determined the baby was OK, and I returned to the car to retrieve our daughter. I then settled down for a long discussion about why we were living here in the first place.

Two weeks later I rose from bed, boiled some water, shaved, and dressed for work by my accustomed candlelight, taking great care not to wake anyone, especially the babies. This day, meetings at work required a tie so I was more formally dressed than usual. I opened the door to depart, and my flashlight illuminated a 3-foot wall of fresh snow on our entry deck with heavy snow still falling. After changing into more suitable garb, I waded out into the snow wearing a headlamp and clutching a snow shovel and broom. The car had been left at the foot of our hill along the edge of Glacier Creek Road two hundred feet away, and I struggled to get there, resembling a scene out of *Doctor Zhivago*. The snowplow had already gone by, leaving a 6-foot-high wall of snow on the edge of the road. I slithered off it onto the road and observed no sign of the car. It was embedded in that wall of snow somewhere, so I walked along the road poking the snowbank with my broom handle. Before long I heard a metallic thump and started uncovering the car. Arriving at my meeting late, I suffered a disapproving look from Mac, who greeted me with, "Where the hell you been all morning, Thurston?"

By late December our cabin fever rose to unacceptable heights, and we departed the cabin for a two-week vacation in Hawaii, leaving our children with relatives in Seattle. We had been assured that by the time we returned, the house would be ready, and surprisingly enough, it was.

22

1967 - Part 2

Lightning Storm Detection

By 1967 we had been operating the P-51 Mustang for ten years, primarily for lightning fire detection. In order to find lightning fires, it was first necessary to locate the storms causing them. Often, on warm sunny days, a layer of fair-weather cumulus clouds at 4,000 to 5,000 feet would prohibit spotting a thunderstorm's towering structure, even if relatively nearby. On clear days, the curvature of the earth and haze still limited distant visibility. In the 1960s, fire weather forecasting was an art still in its infancy with frequent botched forecasts of lightning activity. This resulted in the P-51 being dispatched hundreds of miles to non-problem areas while active lightning areas remained undetected. John McCormick, having flown numerous lightning fire detection patrols over the years, had been, for some time, contemplating the viability of using jet aircraft to locate the storms, but this resource was financially out of reach to us, and he didn't speak of it. Even I was unaware of his idea.

During the 1967 fire season I was preoccupied fighting fires with the air tanker fleet. A series of lightning fires in the Yukon-Kuskokwim Deltas prompted the BLM to set up a fire staging area on the Red Devil Airstrip. Fire crews were arriving by fixed-wing transport aircraft and being transported from there to fires by helicopter. Up to now, only small helicopters had been available to work on fires in Alaska. This season, a larger Bell 204B Huey materialized on the scene and confusion developed over how to best utilize it. The pilot was becoming frustrated with the inefficient operation. I happened to drop into Red Devil for an unrelated reason and after landing was introduced to the Huey pilot— Harry Barr from Duncan Aviation in Lincoln, Nebraska. After some discussion with Harry and the on-site fire manager, the problem was resolved, and I departed to harass more fires with the air tankers. Harry Barr was destined to become a significant factor in my life, but of course I was unaware of this at the time.

Air Tanker Operations

In 1967, the air tanker fleet was primarily made up of B-25s and a B-26 operated by Denny Lynch. The B-25 pilots I remember included Bob Schlaefli, Paul Hanson, Ed Thorsrud, and Don Gilbertson. Our aircraft headquarters was located on Fairbanks International Airport just south of the terminal building in a run-down house trailer. One of our seasonal Cessna 185 pilots requisitioned a bedroom in it for the summer, and the women he dragged back from the seedy 2nd Avenue bars in Fairbanks usually hung out there, making Bob Johnson and I somewhat uncomfortable. Airline terminal passengers were frequently treated to the spectacle of our antique WWII bombers departing our ramshackle trailer and lumbering by in clouds of engine smoke and dripping oil to arrive at their pre-takeoff positions. On a fire call, I generally got off ahead of them because the smaller engines on my Aero Commander didn't take as long to warm up. This also gave me a few minutes to size up the fire situation and get organized prior to the first tanker showing up.

Early season lightning fires southeast of Fairbanks materialized, and George Kitson wound up managing the Ketchumstuk Fire, which was the largest in that area. Bob Johnson and I were both engaged providing air tanker support to George for several days, during which his firefighter population steadily increased as did transportation backlogs around the fire. Harry Barr showed up with his large Huey helicopter, and this was a new thing to George, who constantly addressed it on the radio as "big chopper." Having something that could carry more than two passengers was new to us.

Farther west, near the Salcha River, lightning started a new fire in heavy timber. Smokejumpers were dispatched, and I took a temporary leave of absence from George's fire to assist in the initial attack effort. The fire was very intense, and smokejumpers were still parachuting when I arrived over it. To my horror, I watched as a jumper descended into the smoke convection column directly over a towering column of flame and disappear. It took over ten minutes to contact the jumpers on the ground, at which point I learned he was not injured, and all were OK. I had been almost certain he was a fatality.

One day while at home in Anchorage during a presumed day off, Jan volunteered to give me a haircut, which was long overdue. She had never cut a man's hair before but felt it couldn't be all that complicated, and with great reluctance I submitted. The scissors seemed to be snipping for an inordinate amount of time as she kept working back and forth on both sides of my head. An occasional "oops" was making me feel antsy, but I hung in there until she finished. Finally, she suggested I check it out with the bathroom mirror. When I saw myself, I let out an involuntary, "Jesus H. Mahogany Christ! What did you do to me?" and returned to the site of the massacre.

My poor wife was sobbing, and as I tried to console her, the phone rang. The dispatcher wanted me in Fairbanks ASAP to chase air tankers around, and I departed home immediately. Arriving at Fairbanks I walked over to the fire dispatch office and found several tanker pilots perched on the front steps. Strangely, instead of their usual joking and bantering when they saw me, they appeared solemn, and I feared there had been an accident or something. When I inquired, it turned out they thought *I had been in an accident* and were simply being respectful. Upon learning the truth, they couldn't stop laughing.

JIM THURSTON

Antique 2 Crash

On the afternoon of June 26, fire number Z-02, thirty-three miles west of Livengood (north of Fairbanks) requested air tanker support, and I responded with several air tankers behind me. On its north side, the fire was burning in spruce and backing down slope. There was light wind, good visibility, and the slope was reasonably unbroken with a few gullies. A bombing run crosswise to the ridge and parallel to the advancing line of fire offered an easy approach with no obstacles, so I briefed the first arrivals, who were Paul Hanson and Donald Block in Antique 2, a B-25. The briefing was conducted while I flew a simulated bombing run in my Aero Commander at treetop level, indicating the intended release point for the drop while crossing a gully. Hanson began his approach, and I fell in behind him and slightly higher. During the approach I had him make a minor lineup correction, turning right slightly and then left for a better lineup. After the correction Hanson asked how the lineup looked, and I replied it was good.

As he crossed the small gulley, he tripped his gates, and the retardant began flowing out of the aircraft in a normal drop pattern. About two seconds later I observed that the wings of the B-25 were plowing through the tops of spruce trees. The left wing gradually lifted, and to my horror, the bomber commenced a cartwheeling maneuver with the wings almost vertical and the right wing tip touching the treetops. At the peak of the cartwheel, the nose of the aircraft was pointed straight down, the fuselage broke in half at the waist-gunner turret locations, and large chunks of bomber were ejected skyward on my starboard side as I passed by. The cartwheel completed when the fuselage entered the timber tail first, with the aircraft disintegrating violently as it sluiced its way down the slope.

I came around, made a pass, and observed that what was left of the wreckage was unrecognizable. At that moment, Bob Schlaefli (in another B-25 overhead) called and proclaimed, "Jim Thurston—Paul Hanson just crashed!" After acknowledging the obvious to Schlaefli, I summoned the fire's helicopter and told him to check for survivors.

There were none, and since the fire was burning just uphill of the crash site with several hundred gallons of spilled gasoline on the ground, I ordered extraction of the bodies to a nearby creek.

I felt dazed, and the moment seemed surreal. Denny Lynch was next in line to drop with his B-26 and voiced his concern about possible air turbulence in the drop area. To reassure him—as well as myself—I made another low pass and found the going smooth, after which Denny made his drop and the others followed. The fire progress on that portion of the perimeter was eventually halted, and during the return flight to Fairbanks I began critiquing my actions. News travels fast, and before I could reach a phone at Fairbanks to call and assure my wife I was OK, an Anchorage dispatcher called her and lead off with, "Did ya hear about the crash?" at which point she collapsed in shock and became hysterical. (Sometimes common sense can be elusive.)

To this day, I contemplate whether or not I somehow contributed to this accident and am confounded by the fact that this was a comparatively easy drop since the run was slightly downhill over fairly gentle terrain in light wind. My prevailing best guess is that the aircraft "got behind the power curve" during the final stage of its approach, and the descent rate surpassed the aircraft's ability to recover in time to avoid contact with the trees.

The next day the FAA demanded a meeting during which they criticized me for moving the bodies, saying I should not have messed with an accident site until after the investigation. I responded that because of the gasoline hazard, I wanted to preserve the remains for the crew's families and if the fire ignited all that gas there would be nothing left to inspect. I also pointed out to them that under the Federal Aviation Act of 1958, they had no jurisdiction since we were a government agency, and thus, they could go buzz off. The discussion served to further darken what was already my black mood, and it took some effort for me to refrain from ripping into them further.

23 |

1967 - 1969

The "Shit!" Button

One day the Aero Commander was down for maintenance, and Mac rounded up a Cessna 210 for me to use chasing retardant bombers. The 210 is a high-wing, single-engine airplane with retractable landing gear. Its relatively high cruise speed made it acceptable for my operations on a temporary basis. I headed out of Fairbanks to take on a fire in the Nation River drainage next to the Canadian border. It was a long flight from Fairbanks, and one or two bombers were also down for maintenance, which resulted in prolonged time periods between drops. The hours passed by in agonizing slow motion as I orbited endlessly over the fire, waiting for the next bomber.

Eventually I had to pee—badly—so right after a long-awaited drop, I bugged out for the community of Eagle on the Yukon River. Having never been there before, the first thing I spotted was the grass parade ground (which had also served as an airstrip on my charts), and I instantly decided to land on it post haste. Due to the rapidly increasing bladder pressure, my landing approach to the east was abbreviated, and I touched down too fast. At its far end the parade ground abruptly terminated with a high cliff overlooking the great, wide, fast-flowing Yukon River. I had been confident I could stop without going over it— until I realized the runway was sloped downhill and I was committed to land on slippery grass. The airplane stopped without going over the cliff—barely, and the incident ended happily as well as memorably. I don't know what the people of Eagle may have thought, if anything, because after completing my "mission" semi-publicly, I immediately departed with as little fanfare as possible and headed out intercept the next bomber, which was a four- engine, 2,000-gallon PB4Y-2 air tanker.

During their flight to the fire, the tanker captain was indoctrinating a new pilot to the intricacies of this particular aircraft and had swapped the pilot and copilot seats. When they entered the fire area, I fell in behind him to provide the usual pre-drop approach guidance and radioed that I was on his tail. An instant later a 500-gallon red blob of fire retardant fell out of the bomber's belly, and there was no radio response. I asked what the hell they were doing, upon which a second 500-gallon blob emerged, followed by the word, "shit" from the bomber. I asked if they were alright because I was worried that something was seriously wrong in that cockpit. The tanker assured me everything was OK, that he still had 1,000 gallons remaining, and he'd explain what happened after we all returned to Fairbanks. I had been counting on the whole 2,000 gallons to pinch off a critical point on the fire and had to make do with half as much. I was tired and pissed, but in the end, we pinched the fire off and headed home.

In Fairbanks they explained what had happened. The pilot and co-pilot control yokes both had radio buttons and a tanker gate release button on opposite sides of the yokes. The radio button was on the left side of the left yoke and the right side of the right yoke. Upon my first call, the captain (who was now in the right seat but accustomed to the radio button on the left) pushed it to answer me and dumped 500 gallons. When I called again, he pushed the left button a second time and dumped another 500 gallons before realizing what was happening. He finally responded on the radio by pushing the right button (now known as the "Shit!" button). It had been a long day.

Introduction to High Altitudes

One day the next season, still assigned to the dilapidated house trailer on Fairbanks International Airport with my tiny flock of air tankers, and in the heat of the summer sun, I was killing time by cleaning the bug-splattered windshield of my Aero Commander airplane. This was done in a state of semi-boredom, waiting for the next fire call and while contemplating heavy decisions such as whether to take a nap or run over for lunch at the airport cafeteria. These deep thoughts were interrupted when a type of airplane I had never before seen landed, taxied up, and parked next to me. It was a Learjet piloted by Harry Barr, whom I had met at the Red Devil Airstrip last year. Almost immediately, and before I really had the chance to chat with Harry, several well-dressed BLM officials arrived in an SUV, piled out, and boarded the Lear, while at the same time indicating I had important fire duties at the airport and didn't need to join them. The Lear taxied out, took off with an impressive roar, and climbed steeply skyward, disappearing from view. I shuffled over to the airport cafeteria amazed that my boss, John McCormick, had actually wired together some sort of deal with Harry Barr to acquire the use of a Learjet. It was the first business-class jet I had ever seen, even from a distance, as was the case with almost all us Alaskans.

When I returned from lunch, the Learjet was back, and the officials had disappeared. McCormick had arrived from somewhere and was in an intense conversation with Harry about spotting thunderstorms from high altitude. As I walked up to them, McCormick said he wanted me to come with the two of them to get a feel for how a high-altitude lightning fire detection program might work, indicating that we would be able operate up to 44,000 feet and see much more from up there than we had from the P-51 Mustang.

Startled, I asked if he meant right now.

Slightly peeved, he responded, "Yes, right now. There are supposed to be lightning storms in progress out west somewhere between Tanana and Galena, and there is no reason not to go have a look. So get into the airplane Thurston, and let's go."

As we taxied into position for takeoff, McCormick was in the left seat, Harry in the right, and I was ensconced on the jump seat behind Harry. (Now remember this was half a century ago, and a chance to ride in a Learjet was a big deal for a hayseed pilot like me whose primary experience was limited to tooling around the Alaskan treetops in slow airplanes!) The takeoff and fighter-like climb-out was a new, exhilarating experience, and upon reaching the high cruising altitude, I noticed that when you looked straight up, the sky was black, not blue. We immediately spotted several mature lightning storms perhaps 200 to 250 miles westward and roughly estimated their locations, such as 40 miles southeast of Galena, etc. Upon arriving over them we determined that our rough estimates were close enough for government work.

The flight instantly demonstrated that we would be able to locate these storms effectively enough to assign low-level search aircraft, dispatched from around the country, to meaningful missions underneath them. Further, because of its high speed, we realized we would be able to sweep-search the entire thunderstorm-prone areas of Interior Alaska in less than three hours. This was a brand-new, never-before-tried concept of John McCormick's that triggered the end of the P-51 Mustang era. Since I had never actually flown the P-51 and had only been scared half to death in it one day ten years earlier with Bob Johnson, replacing it didn't bother me all that much, although I knew several pilots would miss it.

That evening while having dinner at a Fairbanks restaurant, McCormick informed me that he needed someone to develop and run the high-altitude thunderstorm patrol program, and I was it. This coming winter he and I would both go to the factory in Wichita, Kansas, and attend the Learjet ground school. This season, Harry would start my flight training while on patrols—*beginning tomorrow*. Next spring, I would do the FAA check ride for the Lear type rating and wind up as the primary Lear pilot. I had not seen this coming and was in shock. I thought McCormick or someone else was going to drive this chariot— not me. Mentally I was still back on a slow day scrubbing bugs off my airplane's windshield, and I spent the night tossing and turning, questioning my ability and mired in apprehension.

The next day was my introduction to flying a Learjet, or any other jet, for that manner. Harry tucked me into the left seat, and we commenced taxiing. We had an immediate problem. Because Harry didn't like to burn fuel unnecessarily, he would save fuel by taxiing on only one engine and light off the other just before initiating takeoff. The nose gear steering apparatus was totally different from anything I had ever encountered, and the asymmetrical thrust of only one engine initially had me veering left and right on the taxiway like I was on something.

Harry's demeanor as a flight instructor was not something I had expected. I quickly came to realize that while Harry was one of the most polite, considerate person I had ever met in day-to-day life, he was adept at hammering on you during flight instruction. This was not through any drill-sergeant approach; rather it was by gently expressing his disappointment with my performance, especially if it involved my failure to correct a deficiency he had just pointed out. During the course of the summer, it became apparent that Harry was an extraordinary airman, unlike any others with whom I had flown. When the season ended, I could fly a Learjet, but knew little about its systems and inner workings because I had yet to attend the factory school scheduled for the coming winter in Wichita, Kansas.

Next spring, Harry returned with a vintage Lear Jet Model 23, which we used for the check ride with the FAA for my type rating. The Lear (N613W) was Serial 13—the 13th Learjet ever made. A part of the ride was to have me demonstrate (or fail to demonstrate) my proficiency at handling unexpected engine failures at the early stages of takeoff and during missed approaches. The entire ride was performed while wearing a hood to block outside references, thereby simulating instrument flight conditions. The Anchorage control tower cleared us for the approach, and we commenced descent on the runway 6 approach glide slope over Fire Island.

At this point we began to hear a lot of chatter between the control tower and an airplane on the ground. Under my hood I could see the FAA inspector's rear end rising off the seat, apparently to observe something happening ahead. He said it was one of our airplanes on the runway tilted to one side, like maybe a landing gear malfunction had occurred. About that time the control tower rescinded our landing clearance with instructions to "go around." With the runway blocked, we were now limited to doing only low instrument approaches with simulated engine failures at the missed-approach point, and we completed several before transitioning to our home base across town at Merrill Field.

After completing the FAA check ride paperwork, I returned to our airport hangar and while parking saw my boss, John McCormick, getting out of his car. Mac came over and asked if I had passed the check ride and if we'd done any V1 simulated engine failures during takeoff. I responded that I passed but couldn't simulate any takeoff engine failures because some asshole had landed with his wheels up and had the runway blocked. Two steely eyes bored in on me, and McCormick said, "That asshole was me!", (Which, of course, I already knew).

He had been doing a test flight in a Grumman Goose turboprop with an FAA maintenance inspector and had forgotten to lower the landing gear. I said, "Oops!"

Thunderstorm Patrols

During the summer of 1969 we implemented the "High Altitude Thunderstorm Patrol" program. To plot storms, we made a 4-foot-wide map board with World Aeronautical Charts (WACs) that covered most of the flammable Interior of Alaska. The board was located in back and covered with cellulose. With a grease pencil, the person doing the plotting would mark storm locations by latitude and longitude utilizing estimated relative bearing and distance called out by me. Initially, we operated at 41,000 feet and later at 44,000 under block altitude assignment from FAA Air Traffic Control Center.

At these altitudes, we were above most civilian and military aircraft, assigned a special radar transponder code for the season, and free to wander around without respect to the normal instrument flight altitude requirements. Because we were out of the way in our own airspace, FAA paid us little attention, except for one

Learjet in Flight

Courtesy of Jim Ross NASA Dryden Flight Research Center.

instance when air force fighters started an intercept run on us because someone had accidentally assigned a target drone radar transponder code to us for the season.

I felt we could locate storms within 200 nautical miles on either side of the aircraft, sufficiently close to establish search areas for low-level aircraft assigned to patrol for lightning fires under the clouds. Usually, in Alaska the troposphere limits thunderstorm height to approximately 40,000 feet MSL, which is about 20,000 feet higher than the usual Interior Alaska cloud, so they were easy to spot. A fire weather meteorologist often rode with us to help estimate the character and likely lightning potential of each storm.

Patrols would often originate at Merrill Field in Anchorage around 11:00 a.m. as the result of a fire weather forecast prediction, especially for dry lightning storms. A typical route could be from Anchorage west to Aniak, north to Selawick, southeast to Lake Minchumina, northeast to Fort Yukon, and south to Fairbanks for fuel. Since a patrol could cut a 400 nautical mile swath through Interior Alaska, patrols would generally last two and a half to three hours. If there was activity, we would dispatch low-level patrol aircraft from McGrath, Galena, Fairbanks, and other bases to their assigned areas under the storms. After fueling we would depart Fairbanks, emerge again to high altitude, and contact the various low-level patrols to see what was happening. Depending on that information we would either reassign patrols, terminate them, or dispatch more of them. Usually, we would arrive back in Anchorage in time to join the 5 o'clock going-home traffic and happy hour. Fresh back from flying 500mph all afternoon, one day a teenager in a loud jalopy pulled up next to me at an intersection while I waited for the red light. He repeatedly looked over at me while revving his engine. When the light turned green, he burned rubber taking off through the intersection. I was "impressed."

During the years of plotting thunderstorms, we started correlating our data with the occurrence of holdover fires, which are lightning fires that don't flare up and become active until two or more days after ignition. These are "sleepers" that can pop up under very adverse conditions. A typical situation involves a storm that ignites a fire but rains on it enough to prevent immediate spread. The lasting ability of the smoldering fire depends upon its immediate surrounding fuel, which if under the protection of a spruce tree, improves its chances since conifers tend to shed water away from their stem or truck. Also, red squirrels frequently store their spruce cones in great numbers directly under the stem underground. If a lightning bolt traveling up or down the tree stem ignites a stash of pitch-laden cones, and if the storm puts out significant rain, these cones can smolder in their cozy protected habitat for days.

So now let's say a dry spell begins and lasts for days. Surface fuel temperatures can push 100 degrees during hot days in the Interior. Eventually the smoldering fire comes out of its hole and takes off across the country during conditions of high temperatures, low relative humidity, low fuel moisture, and gusty afternoon breezes. To compound the problem, the storm that started it (days ago) has long since been forgotten. I've seen this scenario result in over 100,000 acres burned just the first day. So, it has become obvious to me: *the most significant wildfire threat in Alaska, next to human beings, is the red squirrel!*

But on a serious note, eventually we began to predict (with occasional accuracy) where holdover fires might pop up during a dry period days after thunderstorms. Years later we teamed up with researchers from the U.S. Forest Service Fire Sciences Laboratory in Missoula, Montana, who were charged with developing lightning detection equipment. In retrospect, I think this study may have been a forerunner for the development of today's system that pinpoints lightning strikes with great accuracy across the globe.

24

1969

The Swanson River Fire

On the afternoon of August 3,1969, a request for retardant bomber support was received for a new fire just broken out on the Kenai Peninsula, and I responded out of Anchorage in our Aero Commander chase plane. The weather was hot and windy; flames were spreading northeast in grassy flash fuels toward a road upon which were gathered a collection of firefighters, tanker trucks, bulldozers, and other equipment. They were not in a position to observe the fire and asked me for a report. I told them the fire would be on top of them in a few minutes and to get the hell out of there. They did. This marked the beginning of the largest wildfire control effort ever mounted in Alaska, culminating in late fall with over 4,000 civilian and military personnel deployed at the peak of the effort.

After the failure of several initial attack control attempts, the BLM pulled Bill Adams out of McGrath and appointed him fire boss (known these days as "Incident Commander"), and a fire headquarters was established at a motel in Kenai. During the days following, numerous fire control assets flooded into the area as the fire continued to grow. In addition to hundreds of firefighters and out-of-state overhead, there were fleets of helicopters, bulldozers, and some ground water tankers. Most of Alaska's fixed-wing air tanker fleet was relocated to Kenai Municipal Airport where a retardant mixing plant was installed. I was placed in charge of the air attack efforts for the fixed-wing air tankers and water-dropping helicopters.

During the weeks that followed we experienced one defeat after another as the fire inexorably worked its way south toward Soldotna and Kenai in spite of our efforts. Smoke was often thick, during which the Kenai Municipal Airport had to operate under instrument flight conditions, which complicated the fire aviation effort. The terminal area was clogged with numerous fire aircraft including DC-3s, B-25s, PB4Y-2s, B-26s, various light twins, Cessna 185s, a large fleet of helicopters, and a C-119. There were also private aircraft rubbernecking the fire while not announcing their presence.

In those days we were simply not prepared to handle the air operations for a fire of this complexity. With only one exception, no policies or procedures had been developed for managing air traffic. You simply flew in the fire area practicing visual separation and hoped not to collide with anything. The exception was the requirement for air tankers to stack themselves at 1,000-foot intervals when more than one tanker was in a holding pattern waiting their turn. To this day, I am amazed we had no midair collisions because I alone experienced numerous near misses. This was reflected in my steadily diminishing supply of gin, vermouth, and olives for evenings on the home front during the six-week period of intense low-level flight activity in restricted visibility conditions. I was coming home each night with clothes reeking of smoke but thankful for getting through the day and contemplating my odds for surviving the next.

One morning, a cold front roared through the area, and the south end of the fire broke out making a major run south toward Soldotna and Kenai. An existing road running east–west could have provided a control line, however a 40-knot north wind made this highly improbable. Bill Adams was in a Cessna 185 scouting the breakout and contacted me in my Aero Commander at the north end of the fire. Bill wanted me to bomb the south head of the fire in an attempt to prevent it from crossing the road and moving into Soldotna's nearby subdivisions. I resisted the idea because in this wind I felt the retardant would be ineffective, but Bill urged me to check it out, which I did. After checking, my opinion was unchanged, and Bill started pleading to at least try it. He believed we could lose a lot of homes and businesses if we didn't stop this breakout.

Against my better judgement I dispatched a 2,000-gallon PB4Y-2 air tanker from the Kenai base, intercepted him, and told him to fall in about 100 yards on my tail. This was going to be a salvo bomb run near treetop level directly on the head of the fire to knock it down and give the ground troops on the road a chance to control it. In this area the terrain was flat, and due to the wind, the smoke was fanned out ahead of the flames. Moments prior to reaching the drop point, visibility in smoke abruptly went to zero, and I—and the tanker following my ass— went on instruments. The Cessna 185 with Bill Adams was overhead, and the pilot called to warn us that a military Huey helicopter had just entered the same smoke going the opposite direction!

A second later embers from the head of the fire were bouncing off my windscreen, and I told the tanker to salvo his load. Seconds later we popped out into the open, and it took little time to discern that we had accomplished nothing since the fire was already crossing the road. I never saw the Huey, so we must have passed each other in dense smoke. However, at the moment I had been preoccupied with flying at tree-top level on instruments. Returning to land at Kenai I contemplated meeting Adams's Cessna 185 when he landed, pulling him out of it, and strangling his scrawny ass for everyone to see, but then realized the real idiot was me—I should have never let him talk me into it.

That afternoon, the winds subsided, but we were now selectively making retardant drops in subdivisions. A motel near the river was threatened, and we alternated between drops from air tankers and a Huey scooping buckets of water out of the Kenai River to keep the flames from the structure. For a time, spectators gathered in clumps too close to the drop zone and forced us to abort runs, which in turn probably also forced my blood pressure up toward outer limits. Unknown to me, a B-25 tanker descended prematurely to my altitude, breaking the 1,000-foot rule. He flew out of my sight in tight formation just slightly behind and on my left side. When I abruptly turned left, we passed so close I could hear the roar of his engines over that of my own! On the radio, I heard the pilot say, "Uh-oh." Later at the airport we had words.

Several days later as I was preparing to depart on a mission, Bill Adams intercepted me on the Kenai tarmac with two men who he introduced as state civil defense executives. They wanted to go with me to see what the operation looked like. I told them they really didn't because the experience would trash them. One of them authoritatively proclaimed that they were both commercial pilots who absolutely knew what they were getting into and demanded to go. All the seats in the airplane had been removed except the pilot's seat and the rear divan, upon which the two would sit. Knowing the forthcoming gyrations of the mission, even I would never have sat back there; but these guys eagerly jumped in, self-assured of their knowledge and experience. The mission lasted over three hours as I herded air tankers around to combat numerous breakouts.

For each tanker, I did treetop level passes to designate the precise drop area for the tanker pilot observing overhead, often in smoke and turbulence. Sitting in the rear of an airplane cabin doing tight turns at treetop level in thick smoke would be a challenge to any gastrointestinal system, and these guys were no exception. For three hours they sat back there barfing into their T-shirts, which amounted to cruel and unusual punishment, but I couldn't interrupt the fire operations on the basis of barfing privileges. When we landed at Kenai Airport, they staggered off the airplane and never said thank you. I later told Bill it probably had not been one of his best PR moves.

That fall, McCormick marched into my office one day and told me to get rated in our DC-3. I argued that it would be a waste of time because I probably wouldn't be flying one that often, given my entanglement with the Lear and air tanker programs. After losing the argument and after getting checked out by Bob Johnson, I called the FAA to schedule a DC-3 type-rating ride. The only air carrier inspector available was in Fairbanks, so I scheduled the ride with him the next day.

The AW-650 Argosy Turboprop Freighter

Yet another major problem involved the undependability of the radial engines on our cargo aircraft fleet, which included DC-3s and a C-119, both owned and under contract. This was the backbone of our logistical support for the Swanson River Fire, and the radial engine breakdowns fractured it. I wished we had had a C-130 Hercules at our disposal, but during a normal fire year, the expense would have been way too extravagant. Still, I felt we needed to somehow acquire turboprop engine dependability, and the opportunity presented itself late fall of 1969.

After the check ride, the inspector and I had a meal in the airport cafe during which the subject of our aircraft problems arose. I expressed my frustration with radial engines in general and my desire to go turboprop, and he asked me if I was at all familiar with the Argosy. I said I had never heard of one, and he described it as a four-engine pressurized turboprop cargo plane manufactured in England. In the United States they had been used by Universal Airlines under air force contract to haul freight between bases; the inspector had been an Argosy captain. He said there was a small fleet of them mothballed Marana, Arizona, and agreed to mail me data on the airplane.

I returned to Anchorage's Merrill Field as a spanking new DC-3 driver after dark in the middle of a hefty Anchorage snowstorm. After reviewing the Argosy data, McCormick flew down to look over the Marana fleet and eventually decided we should lease one through Harry Barr for the next season. Harry made arrangements, and found an ex-Argosy captain named Lee Svoboda and a flight engineer/mechanic named Richard Hoag. 1970 was the start of the Argosy program, which ran for 20 years in Alaska. It was triggered by our cargo aircraft problems during the Swanson River Fire.

25

1970

The Reeder Air Crash

It was Friday afternoon, July 3, and since our aviation activities were semi-quiet, I was home to grab at least one day off during the 4th of July holidays. McCormick was out of contact in Juneau, so I was the acting aircraft chief. The phone rang, and Charlotte Daniels, the McGrath dispatcher, greeted me with, "Jim, Reeder's DC-3 just crashed on take-off with 27 people on board. It's on the other side of the Kuskokwim River on fire!" A half hour later I was taxiing for takeoff at Merrill Field in the turboprop Aero Commander headed for McGrath.

At McGrath, the station's lawn was a scene of multiple bloody, bandaged people on cots receiving first aid while waiting to be loaded onto a National Guard C-130 Hercules. I could still see smoke rising from the crash site next to the Kuskokwim River. At that point there were five known fatalities and fourteen serious injuries. The airplane, which was under contract to the BLM, was transporting a Stebbins Village native firefighting crew to Galena. Charlotte Daniels told me it looked like the airplane might have lost power just as it became airborne because it staggered along at a very low height the entire remaining length of the runway, barely crossed the river, and crashed.

Later, Bob Johnson and I walked out onto the runway and found the DC-3 propeller assembly off to one side and a series of concentric gouges in the runway tarmac where the takeoff area would have been.

It appeared that upon contacting the runway, the propeller separated from the aircraft and spun off to the side. For the propeller to contact the runway, the landing gear had to be retracted or in the process of retracting. There would be a big investigation.

That fall, I felt sorry for Jim Scott, the Anchorage District Manager. Jim made a special trip to Stebbins Village and apologized for the accident and loss of their people. It was a tough trip.

The Brookwood Subdivision Debacle

Home life had its memorable instances as well. One morning while backing out of my driveway to head for work, I noticed water in the roadside ditch along our property. There had been no rain for some time, and even when it did rain, I never noticed any water in the ditch. The subdivision had its own water distribution system, and its line ran under the ditches, so I suspected that might be the source and decided to keep an eye on it.

That evening, the subdivider who also owned the water system called to announce that there was a leak between his distribution line and our house which meant it was our problem to fix. I asked how he could be sure of that, and he said that when he shut the underground valve off to our house, the leak stopped, so it had to be between his line and our house. The idea of paying through the nose for a contractor to remedy this problem made me decide to do it myself because, hey, it can't be all that difficult to dig a hole and replace a valve—can it? The next morning, I returned to the house with a rented backhoe tractor, enthused with the thought that in a few hours' time I could dig a hole ten feet deep, swap out a simple valve, return the tractor, and call it a money-saving day. This was my first experience operating a backhoe, and I had to learn what each lever did by trial and error.

As I tried to dig, the backhoe behaved as though it had been bitten by some horrible monster-spider and was thrashing in agonized spasms, almost totally out of control. I accidentally knocked over several of the small birch trees next to the hole. About six feet down, I began to encounter water. The soil was almost completely sand and gravel, and the sides of the hole were unstable. As I continued digging, the sides began collapsing into the hole that was steadily becoming bigger and bigger, with small birch trees cascading into it. The water seemed to be coming in faster, so I dug faster with the result that I now had a ten-foot-deep hole filled with nine feet of water and lots of small floating trees. The situation was hopeless, so I jumped into my pickup truck and came back with a rented 1½-inch Pacific Marine water pump and 100-feet of hose, which was the shortest length available. After throwing in the suction hose, I started the pump, which ran for maybe one minute before quitting. It was totally clogged with sand and gravel, which filled the whole length of the 100-foot hose, making it almost too heavy to pick up.

Back at the rental shop they advised me to instead rent a 3-inch trash pump, which sure looked ornery enough to get the job done, so I hauled it back to my ever-widening hole. When I fired that sucker up, the water in the hole was gone in a few minutes, so I jumped on the backhoe and, because the hole was filling with water again, resumed digging like crazy. All of a sudden, the bucket emerged out of the bottom of the pit with the main water line plus the line to our house stuck between its teeth, twisted and broken. Water was spurting out of the main line, which meant I had just interrupted the water supply for the entire subdivision.

Normally this would be the time to pause for a bit and reflect upon the actions taken to get into this mess, however, with the Brookwood Subdivision water world crashing down on me, I retreated to the house and called a contractor. He appeared shortly and after appraising the situation summoned a barricade supply firm that erected barriers around the hole's perimeter. The barriers all had warning signs and flashing lights since the water had already refilled the hole and was a danger, especially to curious children (who actually were attracted to them). Since the hole's walls were still collapsing, as its diameter increased, it was steadily eating into the subdivision's main road.

With nothing left to do except fret, I called a friend and invited our family over to dinner at their house to escape the horrible scene while the contractor did whatever he was going to do. A few hours later we returned, and upon entering the subdivision, I observed people in their yards and driveways pushing brown water into the street and gutters half a mile from our house. Some who recognized me shook their fist and cussed at me as we drove by. When we rounded a corner, the site of my catastrophe came into view and blocking the road was the largest backhoe I had ever seen with a fleet of pickup trucks. Driving up to them I found that my "hole" was now more like an impact crater with flashing lights, spectators, and half a dozen workmen in the bottom. The authoritative roar of the backhoe's massive diesel engine provided a soothing backdrop for the whole scene.

The contractor approached smiling. They had the problem fixed. The packing of the valve on the main water line had been burned as the result of thawing the line during the winter—something I had never done. Evidently the handle to our valve was used as one of the electrical contacts to thaw a line for the house across the street. Thus, the original problem all along was not of our making. It could probably be successfully argued, however, that the spectacular park-worthy topographic feature just created in the Brookwood Subdivision was indeed my problem. Both the subdivision manager and the people across the street never agreed that they were in any way responsible. Thus, my "money-saving day" became my "let's go bankrupt day" with minimal fanfare and no need to dwell on this touchy subject any further.

Argosy Operations

The first Argosy arrived in the spring of 1970 with Lee Svoboda, John McCormick, Harry Barr, and the flight engineer/mechanic, Richard Hoag. After a week or so of ground school taught by Svoboda, flight training commenced. Eventually Harry and I took the FAA check ride and acquired our type ratings. Due to confusion over similar sounding acronyms, the check ride had a hilarious moment when, reacting to a simulated engine failure, Harry told the flight engineer to feather the flight director instead of the props. Powered by four Rolls-Royce Dart turboprop engines, the airplane received substantial use during the season, and McCormick arranged for two Argosy's for the next year.

The airplane grossed 88,000 pounds and could carry 25,000 pounds of cargo, which often had to be unloaded by the crew in horrendous clouds of mosquitoes when there was no one around at the landing site.

During active fire operations, due to constantly changing situations, we often were unsure of our next destination and, even more

AW-650 Argosy.
Courtesy of Axel J., World of Wings Photography.

importantly, where, when, or if we might get our next chance to eat. For that reason, we practiced "defensive eating" and would gorge ourselves at mess halls at every opportunity. When times were busy, we worked shifts up to eighteen hours flying and humping freight. Pilot duty limitations and unions did not exist. Such was life on the last frontier.

Locked Out

During this period, Wally Hickel was the secretary of the interior under President Nixon. Hickel was a longtime Alaskan and tended to be a no-nonsense, hands-on guy, especially with respect to construction and development issues. My impression was that he might be a little short-tempered,

LOOKING BACK Model 681 "Hawk" and "681B Propjet"
Courtesy of San Diego Air & Space Museum.

and staying on his good side would probably be a smart move. During the summer of 1970, the plan to build an 800-mile trans-Alaskan pipeline from Alaska's North Slope oil fields to Valdez on the Prince William Sound was a hot national issue, and Hickel was intimately involved. To this end, a trip was scheduled for me to fly him and several staff from Fairbanks to Prudhoe Bay along the proposed pipeline route in a twin turboprop, pressurized Aero Commander.

It was a hot summer day in Fairbanks. Ten minutes before our planned departure time (and before Hickel arrived), I managed to lock myself out of the airplane. Because the cabin door is immediately in front of the left propeller, the door is automatically locked by the master switch, the electrical system is energized to prevent the possibility of someone disembarking into a still-moving propeller. Since I wanted to check one of the exterior anti-collision lights, I turned on the master switch but forgot to hit an override button, so when I stepped out and closed the door, I was locked out. Since this was one of my first VIP flights, I was already very nervous, so when I discovered this predicament, I started to panic.

There was a small access panel just large enough to squeeze through on the left rear fuselage that can be unfastened without tools, so I removed it and crawled in. My hope was that if I could reach the battery and disconnect a cable, it would de-energize the door lock. I squirmed forward, found the battery, and disconnected the cable, upon which I heard the door lock up forward go "click." Because I couldn't reconnect until after I had opened the door, I had to crawl back out, open it, and crawl in once again to reconnect the battery. I crawled out, opened the door and noticed, thank God, there was still no sign of Hickel. I reconnected the battery on my second trip, crawled out, replaced the side panel and took measure of myself. I was a wreck. The airplane had been baking in the sun several hours, and the heat inside had been excruciating. I was disheveled, drenched with perspiration with clothes matted to my body, and wearing a few grease smudges as accent makeup. I figured they would wonder why a mechanic was flying the airplane. When they arrived, Hickel asked where the pilot was, and I had to tell him it was me. I got some curious looks, but nobody said anything else, and we departed for Deadhorse at Prudhoe Bay.

Years later when the pipeline was under construction, Bob Johnson had a winter trip in the same airplane with VIPs to a pipeline camp on Galbraith Lake in the Brooks Range. In those days, we landed on the pipeline road and taxied up to park in the equipment yard. It was 42 degrees below zero. To keep the engines warm while the VIPs visited, Bob broke out the thermal engine covers and decided to leave the starboard engine running so it would not cold soak while he attended to the port engine. With the port engine covered, he went to get the other cover out of the cabin and found the door locked. The generator on the running engine was energizing the door lock even though he had turned the master switch off. So, this was a classic: locked out of a turboprop airplane at 42 below zero with one engine running!

Bob immediately thought about me getting locked out and disconnecting the battery but realized that since the generator was producing the electricity and not the battery, disconnecting it probably would not work. The nearest building with electricity was a hundred feet away so Bob borrowed a 1/4-inch drill and half a dozen extension cords (no battery drills manufactured yet) and drilled a hole through a small plexiglass window vent next to the pilot seat. Through this hole he inserted a coat hanger wire bent in such a configuration as to allow flipping off the starboard generator switch on the overhead panel with the result that the door unlocked. The VIPs never learned there had been a problem.

Bill Adams

Alaska has many colorful characters, and one the most memorable was famed fire boss and my good friend Bill Adams. I am writing this as a brief special section which spans the period of 1958 to 1970 and is all about Bill. I first really became acquainted with Bill and his wife, Betty, when Joe Kastelic and I drove to Tanacross as their guests for

Thanksgiving in 1958. We played poker for three straight days without stopping and consumed a gargantuan quantity of booze. Toward the end, Bill kept sliding under the table, but Betty would catch him by the collar and pull him back up to play another hand.

For the most challenging fires, the BLM turned to Bill due to his often-successful strategies for controlling large wildfires. Because he often employed burnout fires, he was known as "Backfire Bill." Some of his feats were so spectacular that I occasionally wondered if perhaps he possessed a small streak of pyromania. By 1959 Bill was running the BLM McGrath station where he had recently been transferred. McGrath is located in the west-central Interior. During my fire training indoctrination earlier that spring, Bill had hammered into me the niceties of backfiring (really, burning out) that I later employed on several large fires.

During that period my supervisor was Jim Scott, another colorful character who was the BLM Anchorage District Manager. One summer, the BLM Washington office organized a surprise inspection of all the Alaska BLM field offices to evaluate the extent to which various EEO and other personnel-related policies were being followed. Scott was one of the Alaska-based people assigned to the group, which was comprised mostly of Potomac River paper shufflers unfamiliar with the wilds of Alaska. They were traveling in a BLM Grumman Goose amphibian and eventually plopped down unannounced at McGrath airport. When Scott returned to Anchorage, he told me the following story:

Since the BLM aircraft parking ramp was adjacent to the BLM station house, it only took the inspection team a few minutes to descend on Bill's office. The station also served as the Adams's residence and was a well-built, handsome log structure. At this time, the McGrath district was overrun with fires, and numerous native crews were being assembled and dispatched into the field. Controlling so many people in the tiny McGrath village erupted into a major problem due to the introduction of alcohol from some unknown source. A couple of firefighters actually fell into the fast-flowing Kuskokwim River and nearly drowned, prompting the need for immediate command action. Because there was no facility adequate to forcefully retain numerous people in the village, Bill had implemented a unique solution. The front yard of his facility was a well-groomed grass lawn bisected with a walkway leading to the house entrance. He had his fire control aids dig holes in the lawn and plant 3-foot-high posts unto which those personnel most inebriated were secured by ropes. It was this scene that greeted our inspection team as they strolled down the walkway flanked on both sides with flashbacks from some B-grade movie about the Roman Empire.

Jim Scott told me this story and later elaborated that the Washington team was so shocked, they decided to eliminate any mention of the McGrath station from their report. As far as they were concerned, McGrath did not exist and what happened in McGrath was going to stay in McGrath.

Years later, Bill came up with the idea that a more efficient way to start backfires would be through the use of aerial-dropped thermite grenades. A plane load of them were procured from the Lower 48, and carry racks were attached under both wings of a BLM Cessna 185 single-engine airplane. An electrical drop mechanism permitted sequential release of "the little darlings," as Bill called them, so that a mile-long line of fire could be ignited in under 20 seconds. The pilot assigned to this mission was something less than wildly enthusiastic as he contemplated the chances of one of "the little darlings" getting hung up in the rack and staying with the airplane instead of dropping.

The first test was on a large fire that was merrily crunching its way toward a creek that could provide a natural break if widened a bit by a burned-out area. Firefighters were on the ground next to the creek to back up the effort. The Cessna made its drop pass, and within minutes there evolved a raging inferno. Firefighters were observed jumping into the creek. The episode scared everybody involved so badly that the decision was made to abandon the project. Bill reluctantly concurred, and the first test was the last test.

Bill told me another story: One year in October, the village of Unalakleet called the BLM McGrath station to request help fighting a fire. Bill and a helper loaded a fire pump, hose, and other hardware into a chartered aircraft and headed for the fire scene. Upon arrival it was almost dark, and the temperature was somewhere below freezing. The village is located on Norton Sound at the mouth of the Old Woman River on the west coast of Alaska. As told to me by Bill, the fresh river water next to the village was frozen, and upon it he noticed a large water tank lying on its side, the weight of which had depressed the ice enough that cracks had allowed a pool of water to form around it on the surface.

After throwing the pump suction hose into the pool, and deploying the fire hose into position for hosing down nearby structures, he fired up the pump, which started on the first pull. The fire hose quickly filled, and almost immediately Bill smelled he was pumping heating oil instead of water. He shut the pump down. The tank had been rolled out onto the ice earlier to keep it away from the fire and was leaking. In the darkness and in the confusion, nobody had noticed Bill's activities, and disaster had been averted only by seconds. Bill told me later that a village official politely asked him to have a safe flight back to McGrath and assured him that in the future, they would probably refrain from bothering BLM for any further calls for assistance.

26

1971 - Part 1

81 Below Zero?

Each winter, one of us pilots would attend the air force winter survival course for airmen at Eielson Air Force Base south of Fairbanks. The course consisted of two days of class plus three days in the field. The pilots who attended in the years before me had varying degrees of luck. Whereas some would encounter mild, chinook conditions, others would experience forty below zero or colder. Students were expected to survive individually in coffin-size burrows in the snow, constructed so as to trap body heat and permit as much heat as possible to radiate upward through the moss from the earth below. Except for a 4-inch candle (for light), this was the only other heat source in your self-made tomb. The entrance hole diameter was the width of one's shoulders, and after crawling in, it was plugged with your snow-filled rubberized survival bag. Apparently, claustrophobics had to choose between either freezing to death or going wacko.

One of our pilots woke up in the middle of a particularly cold night and had to pee. The thought of losing all his precious heat (after all, it was probably a toasty 10 below zero in there) was more than he was willing to do, and he decided to void into a condom. So, he filled one up lying on his back in the sleeping bag and proceeded to snake it out over his chest and under his chin. The condom caught on the sleeping bag zipper and tore open—a catastrophe! He bolted out of his burrow to an umpire's shack and was disqualified.

In 1971 I was armed with this knowledge when I arrived at Eielson to start class. It was 50 below, and I was not exactly jumping up and down with unbridled enthusiasm. The military had a cold temperature limit for the exercise. If it was colder than 50 below, they did not require survival in individually constructed shelters. Although they had to be constructed for training purposes, for safety concerns the students instead spent the night in a cozy 10-man shelter built by the military. When we arrived in the field to begin the exercise, it was not colder than 50 below. It *was* 50 below, and so we had to survive individually. This year there was about three feet of snow on the ground, so we had plenty of material with which to construct our individual "tombs." Walking was a challenge with no snowshoes, and it took forever to gather spruce branches for a bed, roof construction, and the campfire, given the rudimentary survival kit cutting tools.

There were thirty students total, broken into three 10-man groups, spaced a half mile apart, which were to compete with each other for the construction of the best ground-to-air signal for search aircraft. My group contained army helicopter pilots, air force fighter jocks, a couple of B-52 drivers, and of course the lone outlier—me. We constructed a campfire that quickly became the focal point for all of us, and it immediately became a factor that tended to slow the construction of our individual digs—nobody wanted to get more than eighteen inches from the fire. Gathering fuel for the fire and completing our shelters competed with warmth from the fire, which could not continue if we didn't wade through deep snow to service it. I remember the toes of some rubberized "bunny boots" starting to visibly melt from standing too close to the fire.

The night was something to endure. I am slightly claustrophobic, and the act of sealing myself into a tomb with only a 20-inch ceiling, barely enough room to spread my arms, and a short flickering candle for light is still memorable. The next morning it felt colder, and the instructor team confirmed it was 62 below zero.

It was time for the ground-to-air contest between our three teams. I was surprised the air force would still fly. One team laboriously stamped out a huge SOS in the 3-foot-deep snow and filled it with spruce branches while we harvested spruce limbs and built a large pile to torch off for smoke. I don't know what the third team did. Before long a helicopter could be heard in the distance, and we lit our fire. As our fire grew, we could see the helicopter a few miles away—for some reason it was a big one—milling around like he was lost. I had been designated the fire bug (due to my extensive fire experience that I had bragged about around the campfire), and utilizing an orange flare from the survival kit, I held it over the fire's convection column, and the orange color rose skyward with the smoke. The helicopter turned straight for us, and I could see he was dangling something on a string below. We had been told there was going to be a prize for the best signal, and it appeared that might be it.

A large helicopter hovering 50 feet directly above a person, blowing down 100-mph winds in minus 60-something temperatures, tends to create what I like to think of as a lasting memory. He dropped the item, which turned out to be a can of real coffee grounds instead of the military MRE (meals ready to eat) equivalent we had been tolerating that morning, and it was quickly put to use. There was one little problem— it was a big snowshoe rabbit year. A cross section cut through the snow revealed multiple layers of rabbit turds, dropped after each successive snow. Gathering snow to boil for water poised challenges. While the rest of the group hung around the fire and brewed the fresh coffee, I was gathering firewood. When I returned it was all gone except the last cup, which they had saved for me. A B-52 pilot graciously poured it out into my cup, and a good-sized rabbit turd rolled out with the last drops. The shocked looks on the faces surrounding the fire told me this was no practical joke—they all realized they had been drinking stewed rabbit turd soup. I politely said, "No thanks, I think I'll pass," and poured it on the ground.

The second night was spent in the community shelter thanks to the dropping temperature, which the cadre said was somewhere in the minus mid-sixties. At the end of the exercise during the bus ride back to the main base, we passed through the small community of North Pole. A large sign at the specialty Santa Claus store on Santa Claus Lane said it was minus 81 degrees, and although it probably wasn't that cold, it sure felt like it.

Helicopter Training

Similar to my DC-3 experience, one day Mac walked into my office and decreed that it was now time for me to get a helicopter rating. Again, similar to the DC-3 situation, I asked why, and once again lost the argument. We were operating a leased Hiller FH-1100 jet helicopter, mainly in support of the cadastral engineer's land survey program, and it was sitting on our ramp available for training. Years later it became apparent that Mac was trying to round out my aviation credentials, but at the time I was too dumb to realize that.

Another of our pilots, Jim Deam and I were going to receive flight instruction. Trading back and forth, we were each going to fly both a morning and afternoon session. We each had to accumulate a minimum of 25 hours' time in order to get a commercial helicopter rating. My introductory flights with the instructor were uneventful, and I launched into the various time-building solo exercises after a couple of hours in the machine. The practice area was Campbell Airstrip in Anchorage (under BLM jurisdiction) and the peaks of the Chugach Mountains overlooking town. At the airstrip the menu called for simulated auto-rotation's and practice hovering. I augmented this with observations of moose and other wildlife, following which I would run up the Anchorage hillside to the mountains for pinnacle landing practice on craggy mountain peaks `and return to do more maneuvers and check out more wildlife. After a few days of this I started getting bored.

One morning while grinding my way up the hillside to the mountain peaks, my attention was caught by a friend's hillside home with its large flying deck overlooking Anchorage, and I thought I'd have some fun. Louanne used to be our neighbor, and I figured she was probably home, so I moved down and positioned the helicopter skids just above her flying bridge deck railing. (Louanne wasn't all that bad looking, either.) The expansive deck windows were blocked on the inside with closed drapes, but the sliding glass door slid open and from behind the drapes, just like Johnny Carson, out stepped my wife Jan. Looking to my left for the first time I noticed her car in Louanne's driveway. After a few smiles, etc. I got out of there and headed for the mountains. In what later turned out to be an extraordinary display of idiocy, instead of commenting that I had stopped because I had noticed her car in the driveway, I instead commented that I was surprised to see her emerge from behind the drapes! This in turn generated her question about *why* I had stopped, which was awkward to handle.

Just east of Campbell Airstrip were a handful of small lakes and ponds. Landing on one, I created a line 50 yards long in the snow by dragging through it with the helicopter skids. Next, I created a second one parallel and about 25 yards distant. After doing the same thing perpendicularly, I had a tic-tac-toe board and initiated it by scratching a rectangular O into one of the squares. Back at Merrill Field I told Jim Deam it was his move, and the game began.

With 25 hours under my belt, I showed up at the FAA to meet my check ride examiner. I found myself across the desk from John Schommer, of military bearing complete with crew cut, no smile, and set jaw line. His first question was whether or not my helicopter had SAS. Deciding to lighten the conversation, I confessed that the only ways I had ever heard "SAS" used were for Scandinavian Airlines System and sex, alcohol, and skiing—therefore, I'll say no. Being intuitive, I could read the look on Schommer's face: "Why do they always have to select me to handle the smart-ass oddballs?"

After completing an otherwise successful oral exam, we departed Merrill Field in the helicopter for the mountains. As we approached the lake with my tic-tac-toe board, I told Schommer I had a job to finish that would only take a moment. Dropping down, I scratched in the (prearranged) winning O and drew the line through all three in a row. The check ride was uneventful with Schommer commenting, while handing me my completed paperwork, "You know, for only 25 hours, you're not all that bad a helicopter pilot." Neither he nor I were aware that in the not-too-distant future our careers would intertwine.

Juneau Kamikaze Instrument Approach

One July afternoon at Merrill Field in Anchorage, the Learjet was sitting idle because of the lack of thunderstorm activity around the state. McCormick walked up to me and said we had a high-priority trip in thirty minutes to Juneau with two BLM employees and announced that he was going to be the captain. This surprised me because I had been flying the Lear almost exclusively all summer and couldn't remember offhand the last time he had been in the aircraft. My concern over his state of currency increased when I checked Juneau weather, which was down to minimums, meaning if ceiling and/or visibility were lower, a landing would be illegal. Because of the rugged mountainous terrain, the Juneau instrument approach was generally regarded by pilots as "hairy." In fact, I remembered a conversation over a beer one day with Red Dodge, the senior captain for Western Airlines, in which he stated, "You don't f**k around in Juneau—it's the worst instrument approach in North America!"

I went into the office and tried to talk Mac into letting me fly the leg down and him flying the leg back, but to no avail, and before long we were airborne. During the flight south, Juneau weather remained unchanged. At the time, the FAA Juneau approach consisted of a localizer, the Sisters VOR, and low-frequency radio beacons, but no glide slope or distance measuring equipment (DME). With no glide slope or DME information, the pilot had to rely on the localizer beam to stay on the approach track and use intersecting radials from the Sistors VOR and other radio beacons for cross-track information, which would allow for doing descent step-downs to ever-lower safe altitudes. Keeping track of intersecting radials along the approach track in such unfriendly terrain would keep a copilot busy changing frequencies whilst descending amongst the rugged inhospitable terrain.

Having been cleared for the approach by air traffic control, Mac turned in toward Juneau, intercepted the localizer beam, and started a descent. He did not reduce power and pretty soon our airspeed reached 300 knots. I started chanting, "Reduce speed! Reduce speed!" and there was no reaction, although he was glued to the localizer beacon. The cross-fixes on our approach course were now racing by like a picket fence —the moment I tuned into the next one we had just past it, and I was shouting, "Slow down! Slow down!" with no response out of Mac.

The last radio beacon on the approach course was Coghlan Island, and just as I tuned it in on it, its needle reversed itself, signifying we had just passed over the station that was only six miles short of the runway threshold and we were still doing 300 knots! I started chanting, "Coghlan Island! Missed approach! Coghlan Island! Missed approach!" at which point Mac abruptly pulled the nose straight up, tumbling both of our primary flight display gyros with only a third backup battery gyro still operable. The G-forces were trying to hold my lower jawbone against my chest, which complicated talking to the Juneau tower who was wondering where the hell we were! I told them we were executing a missed approach, and suddenly, like a sky rocket, we popped out of the clouds into brilliant sunshine at about 10,000 feet.

Mac decided to try it again, and at this point I gave my strong-willed boss a stern lecture: "We're not going to do that shit again! No more warp five approaches! If you can't manage your approach speed, I'm going to do this approach!" Mac then executed a flawless approach with no surprises. As I look back, I should have taken over when speed became a factor on the first approach, but fear of how my superior would physically react, along with the fact that I totally owed my aviation career to him, had been major factors. To this day, I have no idea what was going on with him since I had never observed similar behavior before. We had pulled up only seconds before catastrophic impact with the Juneau runway! This was the low point of my aviation career, and I don't recall Mac ever flying the Lear after that.

About three months later, on September 4, 1971, Alaska Airlines Flight 1866 (a Boeing 727) was conducting an instrument approach into Juneau in foul weather when it impacted a mountainside at the 2,500-foot level, killing all 111 people onboard. As of that date, it was Alaska's worst air disaster.

Two Near Disasters

One day that summer our DC-3 was somewhere west of McGrath preparing to drop smokejumpers on a fire. A jumper was poised in the open doorway as the airplane approached the drop point. Unexpectedly the jumper's chest chute (reserve chute) opened and caught the slipstream. The open parachute served as a mammoth drag chute and for a few seconds the jumper was caught inside serving as an anchor. Up in the cockpit, the pilot's airspeed indicator plummeted toward zero, and the pilot fought to prevent a stall by jamming the aircraft nose down. The jumper was pulled out through the aft door frame, and the other jumpers observed in horror as the jumper's head appeared to have been severed and was falling separately from the jumper.

Regaining control of the aircraft, the pilot circled to observe the descending jumper, who wound up lying on his back on open tundra, but not moving. His head was still attached although there was no helmet, which had fallen separately. It was decided not to perform a rescue jump due to the condition of the doorway frame that had been torn apart, and instead a helicopter was dispatched out of McGrath. I remember the jumper had injuries but do not know how severe.

Due to its questionable airworthiness, the DC-3 disembarked the smokejumper contingent at McGrath and proceeded to Merrill Field in Anchorage where the pilot parked it on our gravel ramp behind the hangar building. It was now late at night, and the pilot went home after setting the aircraft brakes and wheel chocks. He could not shut the damaged door, so the airplane was left unsecured. Sometime that evening kids got into the DC-3 cockpit and started twisting knobs and throwing switches at random. Our DC-3 was unique because it had an emergency jet-assisted-takeoff (JATO) rocket mounted under the belly, which the children somehow managed to fire off. The racket woke up most of downtown Anchorage while the rocket dug a 2-foot-deep trench in the gravel. So many Anchorage emergency services responded —it seemed the only organization missing were the Daughters of the American Revolution. Amazingly, the set brakes prevented the airplane from literally being launched into our hangar/office building and the subsequent demise of both.

27

1971 - Part 2

A New Sheriff in Town

President Richard Nixon fired Secretary of the Interior Wally Hickel in late 1970 and replaced him with Rogers C. B. Morton, a congressman from Maryland. I had never heard of him. In early July, Morton arrived in Alaska to survey his Interior Department domain, and I, having oozed into the VIP pilot slot, met him and his wife as we loaded into the turboprop Aero Commander for our first flight together. For the next several days we circuited the state with lots of attention of course being paid to the Alyeska Pipeline and North Slope activities. Morton, I was told, was also a pilot who used to fly a Beech Baron. Also, when chairman of the Republican National Committee, they had a turboprop Aero Commander just like ours, and he felt right at home—that is until we started landing at several out-of-the-way bush strips that were eye-openers for him and his staff.

The last evening of his Alaska visit was at Kodiak where over dinner he told me he had a five-week western tour of the United States planned to visit Interior Department field offices and asked if I would be willing to bring the airplane down and do the flying. This was way over my pay grade. My boss was John McCormick, whose boss was Burt Silcock, the BLM Alaska State director, who was sitting next to me. Through eye contact, I tossed the ball to Burt, who knew he really had no decision in the matter and responded positively. I then asked the secretary if he was stuck on the Aero Commander or would he maybe prefer a Learjet. (The lightning fire season was about over, and the jet would be available.) Morton's eyes lit up, and he asked about the pros and cons. I responded that instead of flying through the weather, you flew over it, and it took only slightly more than half the time. Since the Aero Commander cost was about half that of the jet, it was almost a wash, depending upon variables (and PR risks). By the time the trip ended, I had decided I actually liked the secretary because he was affable, a gentleman, and had a good sense of humor.

Operation West

A couple of weeks later McCormick told me I was to fly the Operation West project and the departure point would be Dallas, Texas, for a direct trip to the LBJ Ranch for the secretary to meet with LBJ. I was told to wear a suit. I didn't own a suit, having dribbled mustard on the only one I had, which was the one in which I had been married. I knew that the southern states had high temperatures and humid environments, which after years in Alaska I hated. I began to kick myself for being such a blabbermouth in Kodiak. My saving grace was that Harry Barr would be riding with me to hold my hand—he had flown Richard Nixon and many other dignitaries over the years.

For the trip, Harry switched the Learjet from the Model 24 I was currently flying to a stretched Model 25 canary yellow jet that his firm had recently repossessed from the prime minister of the Bahama Islands. It seemed Duncan Aviation had leased the Lear to the government, but making the lease payments wasn't in their plan. Meanwhile the prime minister's pilot had had a falling out with the prime minister and had surfaced in the U.S. looking for a job. Because the prime minister wouldn't return the jet, Harry hired the pilot to repossess the airplane by getting onto the premises and somehow bluffing his way to access the Lear.

| 208 |

The pilot returned and approached the prime minister's hangar guards. In response to the guards telling him he could not access the hangar, he said, "Yes, the prime minister and I had an argument, but it's all patched up now, and he has to go on a trip, so let me in." The guards bought the story, the pilot taxied out without out any clearance and turned onto the active runway for takeoff. The control tower challenged him for trying to depart without any clearance, and he turned the radio off, took off, and snuck into Fort Lauderdale where an associate of Harry's had a fleet of executive jets. Now, just a few days later, I found myself flying the secretary of the interior in a canary yellow airplane stolen from the Bahamian Government on the way to meet LBJ! (You can't make up this shit!)

Glenn Wheeler

During the early 1970s I often had lunch at Peggy's Airport Cafe in Anchorage across 5th Avenue from Merrill Field. They were well known for their pies. Frequently my lunch companion was Glenn Wheeler, who worked for several companies and usually flew the larger helicopters. On occasion I had interfaced with him during wildfire air attack operations. I enjoyed chatting with Glenn because he would have been Central Casting's choice for a rough-and-tumble Alaskan helicopter pilot with a wild disposition. Glenn was a stocky, bearded single guy who was the life of the bar-scene parties. He had a reputation as a hell of a helicopter pilot as well as a bandit (one who ignored FAA rules when convenient).

One day while working for Era Helicopters, Glenn was ferrying a Sikorsky S-55 helicopter across the north edge of Prince William Sound on the way to Anchorage. This country is very rugged with many glaciers draining into small fjords along the coast. Near the head of one of the fjords he spotted a Cessna 170 floatplane upside down in shallow water with the pilot standing on one of the floats. The S-55 was on pontoons, and Glenn sat down on the water next to the Cessna, following which he discussed with the distraught pilot how the Cessna could be salvaged using ropes he had on board. Eventually they jerry-rigged a sling with the intent of lifting the airplane onto a nearby gravel beach where the sling rigging could be improved.

Both men climbed into the helicopter, and Wheeler hovered the S-55 above the Cessna, attempting to lift it out of the water. Abruptly, one of the lines broke and the helicopter inverted, landing upside down in the 4-foot-deep water next to the Cessna. Neither were hurt, and Glenn found himself standing on one float trying to console the sobbing Cessna pilot standing on the other.

Before long, a Cessna 185 flew overhead and took note of the scene below with great wonderment. It was one of our airplanes on wheels piloted by Keith Caldwell, and he landed on the beach. After shutting down the airplane, Keith and Glenn communicated by shouting over the water. Glenn asked Keith if his airplane had HF radio, and it did, so he waded ashore to use it and called the ERA office at Merrill Field. After getting the owner, Carl Brady, on the radio, he told him he needed some parts for his S-55 helicopter, but it would be a short list. Brady said, "OK. What parts do you need?"

Wheeler, knowing that on HF radio the whole state can hear you, and not wishing to reveal to the world that he had just wrecked a helicopter, replied, "All the parts!" (e.g., send me another helicopter).

Department-Wide Aircraft Survey

At some point we learned that the department had commissioned a fellow named Ruby to conduct a nationwide survey of the department's aircraft operations and make recommendations for improvement. He was from the airline industry and was a past president of the Airline Pilots Association. Alaska was his last stop, and after a short discussion, he confessed to being totally bewildered about what to recommend because there were so many specialized and unique aircraft operations involved that were totally foreign to his experience. I felt a little sorry for him because he was on the spot to come up with something intelligent and was totally clueless. Comparing Interior's highly diverse aviation programs to the rigid, inflexible, union-infused airline industry was like trying to compare a zebra to anteater. They had little in common.

We never did hear what message Ruby carried back to Washington and some months later figured the effort had probably died a quiet death. This relieved us since the common fear we all had was that some jerk would try to fashion our various aviation programs after the General Services Administration's motor pool model, which would have been a disaster.

Anchorage Hillside Fire

Having lived on the Anchorage hillside for many years, we gradually transitioned to homes higher up the hillside with better views. When Kasilof Hills, a new subdivision, was created even higher than we already were, we purchased a unique five-acre lot with a breathtaking view of all of Anchorage, Sleeping Lady Mountain, Cook Inlet, and the Alaska Range. The lot was a mini-dome within a hairpin turn of the main road and had lots of tall grass, some alder, and one spruce tree on the dome summit. Looking to the future, I built an elaborate balsa wood model of what I envisioned could be constructed. It had great detail, including an elevator and a circular staircase surrounding a four-story plexiglass saltwater aquarium full of dazzling tropical sea creatures. Using surveying tools, I also surveyed and constructed a detailed 3D model of the entire five acres. (I dreamed big and sometimes unrealistically.)

On a Saturday morning in May, I was running around town checking off my honey-do list and stopped to pick up art supplies for Jan at Blaine's Art Supply in Spenard. Exiting the store, I noticed a small smoke had popped up way above the Alpenglow Subdivision on the upper hillside, and the smoke column was lying flat due to being pushed by a southeast wind. While driving to the next store, I contemplated that this could be a big problem due to the fuel conditions up there.

Between the time the snow cover melts and green grass takes over, the previous year's grass remains thick, dries out fast, and becomes a highly flammable flash fuel. A fire in this fuel with a healthy wind behind it is virtually unstoppable, and this area is famous for its southeast hillside winds. Those conditions existed now.

Exiting Montgomery Ward 20 minutes later, it was obvious this fire was embarking on a run toward hillside homes, and I called the BLM Fire Control Office in the Cordova Building to see if they were getting on it. The response was, "What fire?" I told them to look out the god-damned window and asked to speak to the on-duty fire control officer. They said it was George Kitson, but he wasn't scheduled in until noon.

I called his home and asked George about the fire that was almost directly up the mountain from his Oceanview house. His drapes were closed and when he opened them, I heard, "Holy shit!" at which point I hung up and drove home satisfied my Paul Revere mission had been a success.

When I walked into my house the phone rang, and it was McCormick telling me the fire guys wanted to get the air tankers mobilized, so back down the hill I went to Merrill Field. By the time I arrived, from down there I could see the fire was probably going to start encountering hillside homes within an hour or so, and the wind was increasing. A fire guy named Jack Lewis joined me in the right seat, and we took off to size up the situation in the Aero Commander. Up at the fire some structures were being threatened and the wind turbulence was almost extreme. There was no way a retardant bomber operation up here could be either safe or effective, and I gave the order to stand down their mobilization.

As time went by, the fire swept through many subdivisions including Kasilof Hills. When the fire reached our dome lot, it came up three sides simultaneously and took everything with it. (Later we found that even an old 2-foot diameter log on the ground had completely disappeared.) Due to the turbulence I decided to return to the airport, and as I started descent, an updraft hit so hard, I chipped a tooth on the microphone

I was using to tell the Merrill control tower I was five southeast—landing. With both flaps and landing gear down, engines pulled back to idle, and the nose pointed down, we were going up over 3,000 feet per minute! The tower said they couldn't see me, and I replied "You're not looking high enough!" Only five miles away at Merrill Field the winds were almost calm.

Now, almost a half a century later, in my view the Anchorage hillside is even more vulnerable than it was in 1971. Flammable capital investment has significantly increased so losses will be significantly higher. The much higher population has produced many more potential fire-starters, especially in the younger crowd during 4th of July, etc., so the frequency of ignitions will also be higher. Jan and I lived on the hillside for many, many years, and we loved it, but as our time there increased, so did my fear of being burned out of house and home. One of these years there will be another huge fire event, most probably during a hillside wind. I would not want to be there.

28

1972 - Part 1

The Nordale Hotel Fire

Because of the reasonable rates, the Nordale Hotel in downtown Fairbanks was the spot where most of us stayed when flying out of Fairbanks. It was simple but clean—nothing fancy and very old. It had a fire escape for each floor, and many rooms had ropes coiled under the windows so, if needed, one could open the window, throw out the rope, and slither down. The walls of the building were insulated with sawdust. It was known by all to be a fire trap, but the price was right. I spent many nights there over the years.

On the night of February 2, 1972, it burned to the ground and killed eleven people. The temperature was 19 degrees below zero. One of our pilots, Jim Deam, was there and barely escaped, falling into the street with hardly any clothes on. He lay there on his back in the freezing cold gasping with serious smoke-inhalation damage to his lungs while spectators stood gaping nearby but not lending a hand. Eventually he was taken to the Fairbanks Hospital and survived. Several days later I flew the turbo Commander up, retrieved him from the hospital, and returned him to his family in Anchorage. I was appalled at the sight of what remained of the Nordale—a smoldering heap of rubble.

The Headhunter

Late fall, a character from the Office of Management Consulting at the Department of the Interior in Washington materialized on our doorstep to talk with McCormick and me. He informed us that the secretary of the interior was not happy with the state of the department's aircraft programs and wanted our opinions about it. We both had similar views: there were too many accidents, too much loss of life, too many inefficiencies, too many unqualified people making aviation management decisions, and the government's financial management systems were not tailored to aircraft fleet management. We assumed he had been making the rounds of the other agencies in our department, but he didn't say and drifted off into the darkness. Mac and I both felt something was going to happen with the new sheriff in town, but we had no idea what. Very mysterious.

Stinky Meyer

Carol "Stinky" Meyer was an Anchorage FAA flight examiner who we got to know in the normal course of FAA pilot certification activities. One day I asked him how he got that nickname, and he told me his story. It seems that back in the old days, Carol was working for a fellow named Carl Brady somewhere in Washington State spraying crops with a small helicopter. Brady had a truck and a trailer upon which the helicopter sat while they transferred from farm to farm.

At some point they arrived at a "T" in the road and had to decide whether to go right or left. Carol thought left, and Brady thought right. They got into a healthy argument, and Brady finally told Carol to go left if he must, but by God if he was right, he'd kiss Carol's ass. They turned left, and a couple of miles later it was obvious Carol had been right, upon which he stopped on the deserted road. Carol got out of the truck, pulled down his pants, bent over and pointed at his butt. Brady made good on the wager and kissed it. Hence the nickname thereafter of "Stinky." Carl Brady later became the founder of Era Helicopters, which operated in several areas of the United States with headquarters at Merrill Field in Anchorage. Eventually he also created ERA Aviation which later morphed into Ravn Alaska, a local Alaskan airline.

Aviation Task Force

McCormick walked into my office one day and announced that the Department of the Interior was going to commission its own internal aviation study, and I had been designated to chair it. It would be comprised of aviation representatives from each of the bureaus having aviation programs around the country. I would have to visit and later organize a task force effort utilizing office space at the Bureau of Reclamation's Headquarters in Denver, Colorado. Apparently, the Ruby study had, for whatever reason, bombed. Furthermore, he had been told that Secretary Morton felt that due to the very nature of aviation, a centralized management structure overseen by aviation professionals may make more sense than the current defused arrangement often overseen by foresters, geologists, wildlife biologists, etc. For this project, I would receive guidance and support from Dick Hite, a deputy assistant secretary in Washington, D.C.

I was stunned. I was tucked away up here in Alaska, which was as far from Washington as I could get, and wound up being fingered for this? I wasn't completely blind and felt that this may possibly be leading to my relocation from Alaska—in effect being kicked out of my nest. Subsequent rumors were confirming this. While I wouldn't have turned down an order to conduct the task force study, I figured that if I was told I had to move to Washington, I would have refused and quit if necessary. But I could see there were pros and cons to this opportunity. Since we were concerned about where this operation may be headed under some unknown entity, being in the driver's seat might not be so bad. Also, I had been starting to feel that my luck as a pilot might run out if I continued on the same track. There had been too many close calls (many of which have not been touched upon in this memoir), and the odds were that eventually I would pay a price. On the other hand, the thought of having to leave Alaska once again depressed me.

So, I embarked upon a visit to the various Interior Department aviation operations throughout the western United States and met with the managers, aviators, and maintenance supervisors involved. At Boise, Idaho, the director of the then Boise Interagency Fire Center (now the National Interagency Fire Center) indicated he had office space available should a national aviation program wish to locate there. The various organizations had mixed reactions to what was in the wind, varying from "foaming-at-the-mouth" against to cautiously supportive. At Portland I met with Don Hodel, the Bonneville Power Administration administrator who voiced that he was opposed to the idea of any department-level involvement in his aviation program. His aircraft chief, Harry Windus, was silent on the subject.

Sometime later, after assembling the task force members in Denver, a schedule was developed and assignments were made to gather information about aircraft inventories, personnel, finances, accident histories, unique mission requirements, and problems to be addressed. Subsequent meetings organized the data and recommendations were proposed to consolidate aviation management efforts and, where practical, aircraft services. It was well recognized, however, that setting up a pool of government aircraft across the board (for instance similar to the Government Services Administration [GSA] vehicle pooling arrangement) was impractical due to the many unique operations, in some instances this might work, like in Alaska. The task force members had obviously been programmed to guard the parochial interest of their various bosses, and efforts to reach objective viewpoints became a challenge.

During the proceedings, I noticed that, almost exclusively, the energy and interests of the group were centered on their government-owned aircraft. I was aware that the dollars spent on the in-house, government-owned operations in Alaska were minuscule compared to those spent on aircraft contracted from the private sector; I figured this to be true for all the western states and the Gulf of Mexico. Yet there was little preoccupation or interest with the privately contracted or charter aspects of our operations. I did not discern any group (outside of John McCormick) who was responsible for contracting and who had technical experience—for everyone else, contract writing and administrative support was usually performed by contracting officers who had virtually no expertise in aviation matters and tended to be omnipotent over management, citing their special procurement authorities. Aircraft services contracts were considered just another contract (along with building construction or cattle-grazing leases) and, as a result, were fraught with problems, some of which laid the groundwork for fatal accidents. Because of this dynamic, the aviation management concerns of most of the task force centered on their own government-owned aircraft and not the big picture.

As I recall, the government-owned aircraft fleet was only about 115 aircraft, while contracted and chartered aircraft were over a thousand. Although many serious and fatal accidents happened in the contract and charter sector, I was largely unable to generate much interest in this subject with the task force because, unlike McCormick and myself, they had very little exposure to it.

When the time came to make the fundamental recommendation about the structure of aviation management in the Department of the Interior, and confronted with an assembly of bureau representatives programmed to protect their own turf, I pulled the trigger and announced, "Gentlemen, the Secretary of the Interior wants to consolidate his department's aircraft programs. We are not going to continue sitting here debating whether or not to do it. We are going to debate how to do it!" My effort to get them to see past their immediate parochial concerns began to bear fruit. With much reluctance they endorsed the consolidation recommendation but most likely immediately ran home to voice their reservations to their bosses. Somehow, I had the feeling I'd been herding sheep and tough sledding was ahead with Interior's Bureaus.

29

1972 - Part 2

The Search for Boggs and Begich

On October 16, 1972, a Cessna 310 disappeared with four men on a flight from Anchorage to Juneau. The weather was terrible with very low ceilings, fog, freezing rain, and turbulence. The passengers were Alaska Congressman Nick Begich, his aide Russell Brown, and Louisiana Congressman Hale Boggs, the U.S. House majority leader. The VFR flight plan stated they planned to fly through Portage Pass (at the head of Turnagain Arm), over Prince William Sound to Johnstone Point, and then via Yakutat to Juneau. Their failure to arrive triggered the largest search-and-rescue effort ever undertaken in the United States, reported to involve 40 military and 50 civilian aircraft for 39 days. On October 20, the day was clear and an Air Force SAR-71 spy plane searched the area from 80,000 feet with no results. As of this writing, no sign of the aircraft was ever found. I was in one of the civilian government aircraft and was flying the Aero Commander with five Civil Air Patrol observers on daily assigned search areas.

During that sunny clear day, I was searching our assigned area just north of Prince William Sound in exceedingly rough terrain when another of our search aircraft piloted by Gary Candee called me to announce he had spotted a small oil slick in calm waters just off Gravina Point. He was running low on fuel, had to return to Anchorage, and requested I come over and do a follow-up investigation. Upon arriving at Gravina Point I spotted the oil slick immediately about 150 yards offshore; it appeared to be about what one might expect oozing out of two small aircraft engines, so I notified the Coast Guard. When they arrived in their Sikorsky Search and Rescue (SAR) helicopter, they flew directly to the oil slick (with no guidance from me), and as I orbited above them, they hovered about ten feet over it and lowered a container to acquire an oil sample. It appeared to me that the severe downwash of the rotor blades was dissipating the slick, but the helicopter flew off to deliver its oil sample for analysis.

Courtesy Wikipedia Commons.

That evening when I called the 5040th Air Rescue Coordination Center in Anchorage to find out the test result, a major informed me there was no oil in the sample. I responded that wasn't surprising since the rotor downwash had dispersed it, to which the major said they were not going to do more follow-up and wouldn't provide rationale as to why. This amazed me because between myself, Gary Candee, and our total of ten observers, plus the coast guard flight crew, a total of at least 15 people had seen the slick!

After expressing my frustration to Mac, he acquired permission from the Anchorage Police Department to use their dive team for our own search. I trotted down to the USGS map office and purchased a marine chart for the area around Gravina Point, which indicated the depth around the oil slick was shallow—only about 30 feet deep. A plausible scenario of the flight that my mind envisioned was that the Cessna started picking up a load of ice after squeezing through Portage Pass into Prince William Sound and was unable to squeeze back. Assuming that the Whittier Airstrip was fogged in, the next available airport was the Johnstone Point Airstrip, which was only 15 miles from the oil slick. Crashing into the sea while maneuvering to land in low visibility only

15 miles away from the intended airport is not an unusual scenario, especially if loaded down with ice.

Gary Candee and I flew out with three divers and their equipment in one of our turbine gooses and anchored at the spot offshore that Gary and I agreed had been the approximate location of the slick. The first hint that something was not quite right was when I threw the airplane anchor overboard. I kept letting more and more anchor line out and when it stopped, we were out about two hundred feet! This was ridiculous—the marine chart couldn't be that far off, so I scrutinized it once more. Then I found it. The depth numbers on the chart represented fathoms and not feet. A 30 on the chart was actually 180 feet! Not being a mariner and having zero boat experience, this never occurred to me, and having to explain myself to the divers was quite embarrassing. They gave it a try anyhow by going down the anchor line, but deep down the visibility without lights was almost zero. We returned to Anchorage with me being frustrated at myself and disillusioned. Candee was pissed. The cops enjoyed the trip.

The White Paper

Later that fall I spent most of my time holed up in my office at Merrill Field writing what would become known around the Interior Department as the "white paper." At the time, I envisioned our mission would be to "raise the safety standards, increase the efficiency, and promote the economical operation of aircraft activities in the Department of the Interior." Eventually I returned to Denver to get help preparing a presentation for Secretary Morton. The BLM's National Operations Center in Denver was familiar to me from various past administrative encounters, and they possessed capabilities I required. At the time, the acting director was Harry Starkey, whom I knew, and he was very supportive of my effort.

Starkey believed a management consultant, who was under contract with the center, would be a great asset and introduced me to Larry

Stevens, who later provided critical help through the preparation process. One day, Starkey approached me and said that if it were at all possible, he would like to work for me. This was a pleasant surprise. Starkey had an excellent reputation around the department. He was known as something of a financial wizard in both the Bureau of Reclamation and the Bureau of Land Management. He also knew my present overseer, Deputy-Assistant Secretary Dick Hite in Washington, D.C.

One evening in the Ramada Foothills Motel, I lay in bed staring at the ceiling. I was going to propose the creation of an aviation management entity and was contemplating what to name it and settled upon "Office of Aircraft Services," or "OAS." I was aware this might cause confusion by some with the "Organization of American States," but figured if they were that dumb, they couldn't be much of a problem.

The Ugashik Narrows Incident

Early in the year I had traveled down to Napa Valley in California to get acquainted with a Grumman turbine Mallard that had been converted by Fred Frakes. Fred had operated the airplane in its standard engine configuration in Alaska for a while but had had a landing mishap at the Swanson River Airstrip on the Kenai Peninsula. The passenger in the right-front seat was Dick Crick, a geologist for Atlantic Richfield Oil Co. who is credited for the first significant Alaskan oil discovery in Cook Inlet. Dick was one of my skiing friends and told me that when the airplane rolled out, it suddenly veered into the timber, and a good-sized log pierced the bow (a Mallard is a flying boat) and then the cockpit where it stopped short just before crushing his chest. Fred then transported the Mallard to California and engineered the conversion to turbine engines. He painted it a distinctive red, white, and blue. In recent years I've noticed the same plane featured in Michelob beer ads.

In Alaska a Federal/State Land Use Planning Commission was going to be flying all over the state for months on end determining which lands under the Alaska Native Claims Settlement Act should be set aside for additional national parks, wildlife refuges, and other uses. They had many millions of acres with which to play. Because the Mallard could accommodate the commission's headcount, we leased it from Fred for that purpose. It was also a hell of a VIP fishing airplane. Fred and I brought it to Anchorage where I took and passed a type check ride from FAA's Stinky Meyer. Small world.

That summer I was flying Secretary Rogers Morton around the state in a Learjet but transferred to the Mallard to visit a cabin owned by a Fish and Wildlife Service (FWS) guide near the Ugashik Narrows on Lower Ugashik Lake on the Alaska Peninsula. This was an event sponsored by Gordon Watson, a wildlife biologist and the head of FWS in Alaska. Several of his staff were also attending. Gordon and I had been sparring for some time over the pros and cons of consolidation. He was dead set against it and saw this visit as a chance to impress upon the secretary why it should not happen. FWS had an extensive aviation program in Alaska, which included their biologist-pilot program. He was afraid I would eliminate this program if things went the way he was afraid they would under me. The program allowed biologists to pilot government aircraft in the course of their duties and had established minimal flight experience and training for them to qualify. Over the years there had been numerous accidents and criticisms of the program, and FWS personnel were paranoid over what I might do. In fact, I was not so disposed but felt that flight standards, training, and experience requirements all should be improved. I think Gordon was probably less than happy that I was the pilot flying the Mallard on this visit, but to his credit, he was amiable.

We splashed onto Ugashik Lake, lowered the gear, taxied up onto the beach in front of the cabin, and shut down the Mallard. Before long everybody was settled inside the cabin (which was of good size), and happy hour commenced. Gordon and the other FWS guys were intently briefing the secretary about their various Alaska activities while I sat out of the way on a chair near a window. Before long an airplane buzzed the cabin, and out the window, I saw a Cessna 206 go by, turn, come back, and buzz us again. Gordon Watson said it must be one of their biologist-pilots who had been out looking for the good fishing spots and must want to talk to us. He turned on a radio and the pilot who started asking advice about the wind conditions for landing. At this point I quietly slipped out of the cabin onto the beach. It was my opinion that a floatplane pilot who didn't know how to read wind on the water probably should not been flying a floatplane, and I wanted to see how he handled it.

Standing on the beach I watched the airplane going away from me over the lake on what was apparently his downwind leg for landing. He kept going and going, didn't turn back for several miles, and then proceeded straight at us perpendicular to our shoreline and low over the water. When I heard a crunch of beach gravel underfoot, I realized I had just been joined by Secretary Morton and Gordon Watson, at which point Gordon said to the secretary, "Now here's an example of our biologist pilot program, Mr. Secretary. This fellow is a low-time pilot but has sat in the right seat for hundreds of hours watching how it is done." Before long, the airplane was about ten feet above the water with no flaps down, obviously coming at us too fast and perpendicular to the shore. He had to be going at least 70 mph when his floats contacted the water only about 40 feet from the shore and approximately 80 feet from where we stood. The airplane slid up the beach onto flat grassland and completely disappeared—about 150 to 200 feet—into the dense alder brush. People were pouring out of the cabin to check on the airplane as the three of us stood in stunned disbelief. Gordon then uttered a sentence I'll never forget: "Well, there goes the biologist-pilot program!"

I turned on my heel, headed into the cabin, seized hold of a bottle of Early Times that was on the counter, and poured me a stiff one. A second later the secretary came in, saw me holding the glass, and said

"Would you pour one for me too? That's the damnedest thing I've ever seen. He didn't even have his flaps down!"

The FWS host put on a banquet-like dinner for us all, and the secretary asked where the unfortunate pilot was. He was told he was basically hiding, too embarrassed to show his face. Morton said to go get him and bring him to join us. When the pilot walked in with a scarlet red face, he asked the secretary to please forgive him—he had only been trying to crash the party. This generated some needed levity. Later the group employed "people power" to drag the airplane back into the water. If there was any damage, it was probably limited to the bottom of the floats, which were not leaking.

30

1973

OAS Is Signed into Existence

Eventually it became time to go to Washington, D.C., and present my white paper masterpiece to the secretary of the interior. Had it not been for Larry Stevens, it would have been a disaster. We had been working closely through a difficult process, and Larry had repeatedly kicked the soap box out from under me and reacquainted me with the realities of performing concise presentations to executives with short attention spans. We figured we had 45 minutes maximum. My first presentation rehearsal rolled on for almost two hours before we cut it off, realizing that drastic trimming was necessary because it was hopeless in its existing form. We restructured it.

The time finally arrived for me to perform my dog and pony show for the secretary, and we traveled to Washington. Eventually, Larry and I were escorted to the PCC room, which was for executive briefings. It was equipped with visual aid equipment and various other gadgets. I never knew just what PCC stood for because I never asked. I was too uptight to give a damn. Just after getting set up, the secretary of the interior and several others unknown to me strolled in, and the show began.

Forty-five minutes later I wrapped it up and the secretary turned to a person next to him and told him to run this by the White House Office of Management and Budget (OMB), Senator Ted Stevens, and Congresswoman Julia Butler Hansen, who were both chairs of the Interior Appropriations Committees. This person was Dick Hite, whom, over the years, I would come to know very well. His title was Principal Deputy Assistant Secretary for Program, Budget, and Administration—a real mouthful. Years later he told me that after the briefing he asked the secretary, "Where the hell did you find this guy?" Thanks to Larry Stevens, he thought I was some sort of professional management consultant pitch man—not the hayseed from Alaska I really was.

After the presentation I responded to an invitation from Burt Silcock, who was the director of the BLM, to join him for lunch in the executive cafeteria. During his tenure as the BLM Alaska State director, I knew I had his confidence and respect, but Burt was very concerned with where all this was going. He expressed to me that while he would have no problem with me being in charge of the department's (and thus the BLM's) aviation programs, he knew I would not be around forever. And when I was replaced, he was fearful it would be with some political appointee whose primary interest was climbing the political power ladder and who had no real concern for the aviation requirements of Interior Department programs, which had taken decades to evolve.

Burt had a valid point, and I shared his concern because I had been having the same reservations for several weeks. At the same time, I was aware that critical management decisions for the department's aviation programs were traditionally being made by personnel often not technically equipped with necessary knowledge and background in such matters, and in many instances, this had resulted in severe consequences. So, in spite of my fears of the risk of institutionalized political mismanagement, I had just recommended to the secretary of the interior the creation of OAS, and I told Burt I believed in what I was doing. Burt and I were friends, and this was painful. In the back of my mind, I wondered if this was the right thing to do. I walked away from our discussion with a heavy heart under a cloak of uncertainty of what the future might bring. My hope was that with time, the common sense of what I had proposed would become obvious to all, even my friends. It was difficult for me to believe I was carrying these burdens around as a lowly GS-13-nobody from the hinterlands of Alaska.

On July 1, 1973, OAS was signed into existence. The Washington people wanted me to move to the Interior Building. I said I would rather be unemployed in Anchorage than work in D.C. and held my ground. I proposed the Boise Interagency Fire Center facility for OAS Headquarters since they had space available, and that was where it was going to be if I was to be involved. Interior's aviation programs were predominantly in the western states and Alaska. It made little sense to have the OAS director remote from the real-world activities in those areas, and I was not going to cave on that issue. I also had experienced that Washington tended to serve as a toilet for new, innovative thought, which was often flushed down the drain by political appointees whose primary interest was avoiding anything controversial. Thus, I believed that locating there would be a direct path to the sewer. Dick Hite disagreed. He was a career Washington operative—the senior career official in the entire department, but for the moment I had the power, and he didn't, even though he was now my boss. (Actually, Rogers Morton was.) I won, but as the result I was going to have to move to Boise, Idaho, and I was very sad at the prospect of leaving Alaska once again.

Back in Alaska, it was decided that my family and I would move to Boise early the next year. I hired Larry Stevens as the deputy OAS director and Jim Starkey as my administrative officer and financial advisor. The three of us worked endlessly on the phone during the winter setting up the OAS organization. Starkey handled the conversion of office space at the Fire Center to accommodate OAS Headquarters and found a secretary for me, named Bev Williams, who stayed with me my entire tenure as OAS director. Recruitment efforts were undertaken to attract qualified aviation personnel from various Interior aviation organizations to join us. The plan was to consolidate the aircraft operations in Alaska first, digest this, and then consolidate the Lower 48's fleet.

Senator Stevens made it clear that if we consolidated Alaska, we damn well better also consolidate the Lower 48. The commercial aircraft

| 228 |

operators in Alaska were very sensitive to the Interior Department's aviation activities and particularly resented government-owned-aircraft competition with their available private-sector services. Stevens generally supported the OAS concept, however, it had become increasingly clear to me that both his political concerns and the Interior bureaus' paranoia were entirely concentrated upon the government-owned aircraft fleet, but for different reasons. The senator did not want to catch flak from the commercial aircraft operators for unwarranted government competition with the private sector. The bureaus did not want to lose control of their fleet aircraft. Nobody was voicing concern about the management of contracted or chartered commercial aircraft except for one bureau component—the USGS Alaska Branch of Geology, which was deeply involved with seasonal helicopter services contracting. We knew the size of the contracted and chartered aircraft activities far exceeded that of government-owned aircraft, but hard information was lacking and would continue to be unknown until OAS got a handle on it.

Trips back and forth from Anchorage to Washington, D.C., began to take place about every other week to extinguish brush fires generated by various bureaus paranoid about OAS. Occasionally, it was necessary for me to "wet nurse" some directors who actually supported OAS but were fearful of losing the confidence of their employees if they didn't at least appear to stand up to this perceived outrageous intrusion into their aviation affairs. Other directors genuinely resented OAS and were not afraid to show it. It got back to me that alarms were beginning to sound even outside of the Interior Department over at the U.S. Forest Service under the Agriculture Department. In the Interior Building, hallway glaring was intensifying. Also, some bureaus were voicing concerns underground to their congressional overseers, while at the same time, the likewise paranoid commercial aviation industry was registering concern to their representatives on the Hill because they didn't know what to expect.

Meanwhile, Secretary Morton temporarily relocated to the West Coast for cancer treatment, leaving day-to-day operations of the Interior Department to Undersecretary John Whitaker, about whom I knew almost nothing. In effect, Morton's absence put me in the position of a lone sheep surrounded by a pack of wolves. Under Whitaker, the department had six assistant secretaries, one of which was a cynical critic, another a big supporter, and four others with neutral or unknown positions.

As time progressed, I became more and more discouraged. During my morning walks to the department, as I approached, I would gaze up at the huge, monolithic, block-sized Interior Building and fantasize that there were probably 6,000 people in there and most of them hated me! By any measure of both Interior Department and congressional politics, I believed the wheels were coming off my wagon. It was becoming difficult to get an audience with departmental operatives I needed to meet, and I was actually "stood up" on several occasions. To say I was uptight would have been a gargantuan understatement. When strolling down the hallowed halls of the Interior Department building, my imagination told me that everybody's eyes were on me, that they were hostile eyes, and that they believed I posed an existential threat to their bureaucracy's fundamental creed, which was (and still is) "Don't gore my ox!" In one instance, a couple of bureau directors and an assistant secretary of interior indulged in some intense glaring and borderline snarling as we passed each other walking those ancient halls.

While in Washington, I often dined at Blackie's House of Beef, just a few blocks from the department. It was dark and lonely, but the food was good, and it was a decent place to lurk in a corner and kill time while clutching a beer. It was here that I decided that with no support this whole exercise was hopeless and the next morning I would inform Dick Hite that I was bailing out and would be returning to Alaska immediately.

About then, a lone figure wearing woodsman clothes, boots, and a backpack slid behind the table next to me and ordered a beer. Moments later, he said, "Is that you, Jim?" and I turned to see Jack Horton, one of the assistant secretaries who had been with Morton during his Alaska trips. Jack was an ex-naval aircraft carrier pilot, and we had hit it off during those trips. Eventually he made the mistake of asking me how it was going, and I told him I was bailing out and going back to Alaska tomorrow.

Jack was shocked and said that the secretary was depending on me—I couldn't leave. To which I said, "I'm sorry, Jack—I'm out of here. These people aren't real, and I'm fed up." Horton begged me to give him a chance to help out. He had a 10:00 a.m. meeting the next day with Roy Hughes, the secretary's executive assistant, and would hand the time off to me, if I would stay long enough. So, I reluctantly agreed, in part because I was feeling guilty abandoning Morton, and I could always leave tomorrow afternoon instead of morning.

Roy Hughes was an intimidating figure, but I was in no mood to be intimidated. I knew I held some cards and figured I couldn't lose—the prospect of returning to Alaska and not having to tolerate this bull-shit was, to me, not a losing proposition. Thus, I resolved that it was going to be my way or the highway. After I explained my grievances, Hughes asked me what it would take to keep me from abandoning the program. I told him I wanted to brief Undersecretary Whitaker and all the assistant secretaries in the PCC room within 48 hours to solicit their support—across the board—and if I didn't get it, I'd be gone. Hughes set it up for the next day, and I marched out of the Interior Building only halfway believing that all this was happening.

The next day I held the briefing. The departmental hierarchy all gave me lip-service support, and I naively departed thinking I had really accomplished something. Years later, Secretary of the Interior Cecil Andrus commented to me that when he took over, he found that the Interior Department was a shark tank, and he was right. The longknives eventually reappeared, but I managed to hold them off for several years during which OAS became institutionalized after a couple more near-death experiences.

31

1974

1974 in General

The year 1974 developed to be the worst start possible for OAS. In summary, we lost one government-owned and three leased aircraft with a total of eight fatalities and one minor injury. My good friend, George Kitson, was comparing us to Amtrak, which had been having " multiple accidents during the same period.

The Baron Crash

In the early spring, a leased Beech Baron flown by Glenn Waits with three passengers flew head-on into the side of a steep snow-covered mountain in Thompson Pass enroute to Valdez. The weather was good except for flat-light situations due to a high overcast. Flat light can obscure the difference between snow-covered terrain and the sky, a phenomenon well known to skiers. It appeared that due to the flat light, the pilot never saw the mountain, and the Baron impacted in deep snow on a very steep slope, setting off its emergency locator transmitter.

Upon locating the wreckage, search aircraft initially attempted to recover the bodies but called off the attempt due to a severe threat of avalanche. It was decided to wait until spring until after the mountain slope avalanched into the valley a half mile below for recovery of the victims. I called the families of the victims and had torturous conversations with them trying to explain why their loved ones could not be returned for a couple of months while at the same time trying to console them. I thought it would be appropriate to notify my Washington, D.C., boss, Dick Hite, and left him a message about it. He never acknowledged my message.

The Point Hope Pool Hall

Due to ongoing controversy in the Interior Department over OAS, Dick Hite figured he probably ought to find out what the hell Thurston was up to in Alaska and came up for a visit. The morning of June 7, McCormick and I were briefing Hite in Mac's office about the Alaska operation when we received information that an Argosy piloted by Harry Barr

Thurston, Hite, and McCormick
(I may look happy, but I'm not.)

had crashed on landing at Point Hope on the extreme northwestern Alaska coast. During the rollout, there had been a structural failure in the starboard landing gear, which collapsed. There were no injuries. Later that day, Harry Barr returned to Anchorage to acquire some salvage equipment and provided us the details. Since Harry would be returning to Point Hope, Hite said he wanted to ride along and visit the site.

The details Harry had provided us were inscribed in the Point Hope runway. When the landing gear collapsed, the starboard wing tip started dragging through the tundra bordering the runway and provided resistance that made the airplane veer to the right. To offset this, he turned the hydraulic nosewheel steering full left. With the nosewheel cocked almost ninety degrees to the path of momentum, it excavated a sizable trench in the gravel runway curving off into the tundra. Damage was visible to the number four engine propeller blades and the wing tip. Also there probably was some significant damage to the underbelly. Eventually Harry salvaged the engines and some avionics, after which he deeded the Argosy to the Point Hope Village. The villagers cut off both wings with chainsaws and salvaged the fuselage, which they dragged into town. I was told that later they converted it into a pool hall, and for a while it was one of the largest structures in Point Hope.

Campbell Airstrip Crash

One Saturday morning in Boise, and not very long after the Point Hope incident, I was enjoying the domestic activity of planting some ornamental vegetation around our new home. Just as I was about to plop a cute little flowering shrub into its freshly dug hole, the phone rang, and John McCormick, in his usual gentle way said, "Thurston, we just put an Argosy into the trees at Campbell Airstrip. It's on fire, and I can see the smoke from here. I'm headed out there now!" There was no "goodbye"—no nothing.

I stood there for a moment—the phone in one hand and the plant in the other—thinking, *"This can't be real. I'm having a bad dream!"*

By the time I arrived in Anchorage, it was early evening. I surveyed the wreckage and was briefed with the information known so far. The flight engineer had failed to remove the elevator chocks and the locked elevator went unnoticed during the control check in the cockpit. The Argosy had initiated a takeoff to the south with zero chance of leaving the ground. When it didn't lift off the runway, the pilot froze on the controls in disbelief and never attempted to abort the takeoff, running out of runway and into the forest at perhaps 120 miles per hour and under full takeoff power. The resulting logging operation caused the aircraft to partially disintegrate and catch on fire. Amazingly, all five crewmembers escaped with no injuries except the copilot who broke an ankle jumping out of his window.

Lost at Sea

As a pilot, Bob Johnson had been my aviator's idol ever since we met in 1956. In my eyes, if I ever knew a pilot who would not lose his life in an airplane, it was he. OAS acquired a G-73 Grumman Mallard amphibian from the U.S. Army Corps of Engineers and put it to use for offshore bird surveys conducted by the U.S. Fish and Wildlife Service. On Septem-

OAS G-73 Mallard
*Courtesy of Dustin Clesi,
US Corps of Engineers*

ber 30, 1974, Johnson and three FWS biologists departed Anchorage departed Anchorage enroute to a bird survey area in the western Gulf of Alaska, east of Kodiak Island under excellent visual flight conditions. The next day, McCormick called me in Boise with the news that the airplane never showed up in Kodiak, which was the planned destination for the evening, and he was initiating a search.

The next two days yielded no search results. McCormick called to express his frustration and broke down sobbing. They were longtime friends. After composing himself, he suggested that having the air force do a high altitude run with a SR-71 from their base in Beale, California, would be worth trying since the forecast called for the end of searchable weather in two days. I needed more information and called the air force SR-71 commander at Beale Air Force Base.

I asked if such a mission to the Gulf of Alaska would be practical, and if so, could they do it tomorrow. The answer was yes. I then called Dick Hite, who in turn contacted Undersecretary John Whitaker. Two hours later my phone rang, and it was the White House switch board, which had assembled a small telephonic round table of officials to query me about why I thought the SR-71 should be deployed. In addition to Undersecretary Whitaker, there were a couple of generals from the Pentagon, two more from the Strategic Air Command in Omaha, a colonel from the Alaska Air Command, a colonel at Beale Air Force Base, and some unknown person in the White House proper. One of the generals asked me to explain why a SR-71 mission would be appropriate. I responded with three bullet points:

1. It's our last chance. The forecast says tomorrow will be our only search weather opportunity for almost a week.
2. Your people at Beale say the mission is doable and the aircraft is available.
3. SR-71 searches must have some merit because you did one for Boggs and Begich, who were on a political fundraising trip, two years ago. This trip involves the same number of people, except they were on official government business and not engaged in trying to solicit money from others.

The SR-71B Blackbird
Courtesy of Armstrong Flight Research Center of the United States National Aeronautics and Space Administration (NASA).

Bob Johnson Lake.
Courtesy of Google Earth.

I sensed the group was not prepared for my response, but they said they would take the matter under consideration. From their tone, I felt they would probably maneuver for any way possible to get out of doing it since it could open the door for other similar requests. So, I slammed down a couple of beers and went to bed.

At three in the morning Undersecretary Whitaker called to say I did an excellent briefing, but the military nevertheless declined. I passed the word on to McCormick that morning, and the search aircraft took off on the last good day with no results. For a week thereafter, the weather prevented searching, and the odds that Bob Johnson and his three passengers were still alive declined to about zero. They had simply vanished. Years later, Carl Jeglum, an associate, managed to have a lake in the Brooks Range dedicated to Bob. You can google "Bob Johnson Lake" and view it. I haven't seen Carl in over sixty years and don't even know if he is still with us, but either way—thanks, Carl.

Senator Ted Stevens

One day I was summoned to Capitol Hill to meet with Senator Stevens, who was the chairman of the Senate Appropriations Committee. Upon entering his office, I was escorted into the senator's private office and ushered into a chair positioned directly in front of the senator's desk. The only things missing were a glaring spot light over the chair and the senator. The staff member left, and I thought I was the only one there until I heard some rustling noises coming out of a closet in the back right corner of the room. A moment later the senator emerged, clutching a collection of folders against his chest. He did not look at me or acknowledge my presence. He plunked the bundle down on his desktop, sat down, and started thumbing through the folders. A moment later he looked up at me and said that he was receiving nothing but complaints about OAS from his constituents in the Alaska commercial aircraft sector and asked for an explanation.

For the next hour, I explained the OAS program and objectives in Alaska, ongoing problems, and plans to deal with them. I also elaborated upon my views about government competition with private-sector commercial aviation activities. At the end of the meeting, he came out from behind the desk, was congenial, and put his arm around my shoulder as we strolled out. I figured I probably did OK and got the hell out of there.

32

1975

Ice Island T-3

Ice Island T-3 (otherwise known as Fletcher's Ice Island) was a floating outpost for scientific study in the Arctic Ocean from 1946 to 1974. One day in October 1974, I was wakened from sleep at my desk in OAS Headquarters by an urgent phone call from Lou Menen at the U.S. Geological Survey Headquarters in Reston, Virginia. I had been involved with USGS and Lou in several of their projects around the country, and they were appreciative of the services OAS had provided.

This time they wanted me to provide them with a set of eyes and ears by sending someone up to Ice Island T-3 to find out what the hell was going on up there. The U.S. Geological Survey had a cadre of scientists on the island along with other agencies. They somehow received word that the island had started breaking up suddenly and without warning, and they had been unable to receive any further word about it. Nor were they able, through their own bureaucracy, to arrange for any quick follow-up action, so they called me. I assigned Bill Rainey, the OAS safety officer, to the project, and he departed Boise a few hours later for Alaska. Eventually he arrived at Barrow, the northernmost community on the North American continent, via local airlines. He was incredulous to see passenger luggage unloaded into a backhoe bucket that then turned and dumped the contents into a nearby snow berm for the passengers to sort through. This was Bill's first visit to Alaska, and he was quite impressed with the difference between this and, for example, Boise Airport's luggage handling procedures.

Ice Island T-3.
Courtesy Wikipedia Commons.

The Naval Arctic Research Laboratory (NARL) is located nearby at Point Barrow and was heavily involved with the T-3 project, so Bill caught a ride to the ice island on one of their aircraft. Bill reported to me that upon his arrival, the situation was semi-chaotic because the island was continuing to break up as new fractures kept appearing with unpredictable results. Much effort was being given to dragging various structures back and forth with a small bulldozer as new open-water channels continued to appear between widening cracks. The scene reminded him of what you see after kicking an anthill.

Bill tracked down the USGS contingent to verify how they were doing so he could report back to the officials in Virginia. One of the scientists he spoke with told the story of how he had been having lunch in the Jamesway hut dining hall when the breakup started. Initially there had been no noise. After eating, he opened the door to depart and found himself looking down at open water. His end of the structure was actually cantilevered out over the water, and for a moment he was the only person inside who was aware of it. Moments later everybody left the Jamesway through the door at the other end. T-3 was evacuated as the result of this breakup in 1974, was last visited in 1979, and eventually drifted through the Fram Strait (between Greenland and Iceland) in 1983 after being monitored for over 30 years. Rainey returned to Boise after only two days.

Dick Hite

Dick Hite was my direct supervisor, and although this short background may be a little boring, it is important from the standpoint of understanding future events that are far more colorful. He was also the principal assistant secretary for the Office of Policy, Budget, and Administration and held the highest career (non-political) position in the entire department. During political changes of the guard, it was Hite who was standing at the entrance of the Department of the Interior Building to welcome incoming new secretaries. It was also Hite who served as the anchor at congressional hearings for the Office of the Secretary since he knew more about its workings than anyone else, including the secretaries proper. The Office of the Secretary was the collection of administrative, budget, OAS, and legal offices operating at the departmental level above the various bureaus. For many of the politicians on Capitol Hill, if they really wanted to know what was going on in Interior, they asked Dick Hite.

Dick was easygoing, perhaps ten years older than me, a sharp but not flashy dresser who oozed knowledge about the inner workings of the Interior Department, had a great sense of humor, and loved martinis. He also headed up the Departmental Ethics Office and was supposedly the most ethical person in the department.

OAS was one of the many organizations under Hite's responsibilities, but relationship-wise, he seemed to treat me as special. Early on, this was completely understandable since it was known to all that OAS was a pet project for the then Secretary Rogers Morton, and it would not be to anybody's benefit to overtly f**k with me—a process that was instead conducted behind the scenes. Also, because I lived faraway, I was not around Dick frequently enough to become "boring." In a few years we would not have this backstop, but thankfully by that time OAS would be accepted enough within the department to survive, primarily because we had proven to be of some benefit in the eyes of most (but not all) bureaus.

Working for Hite was a different experience compared to other supervisors. I came to realize Dick had little interest in OAS programs, indeed he was unaware of most of the OAS activities and machinations described herein because his interests lay primarily with the intrigues of Washington, and I didn't want to bore him. Even my occasional reports to him about fatal air crashes generated hardly any reaction. In one respect this was a good thing because, with the Potomac River people out of my hair, I was essentially left as a free operator. Getting him to return a phone call was a different matter. Even when I needed some policy guidance urgently, I occasionally waited for over two months. I pictured myself as the cobweb-covered skeleton waiting by the phone in the famous cartoon, but at least I was virtually independent.

John "Mac" McCormick

Were it not for John McCormick, I would not have had an aviation career. The first I ever heard of him was in late September 1956 when I heard his voice on the HF radio in our Fairbanks dispatch office. He was in Anchorage, talking to someone else somewhere, and I thought his voice sounded a little like Donald Duck. BLM Alaska had an aircraft division, and Mac was in charge of it.

At its start around the late 1940s, BLM aviation in Alaska had one Cessna 170, and Mac was the pilot. A few years later he heard there were some surplus Grumman Goose aircraft available in Long Island, New York, so he and Bob Johnson went down, took possession of two of them, and flew them back to Anchorage. The navy guy had offered to give them some checkout training, but Mac refused, telling him they could figure it out, but asked him to at least show them how to start it. He then flew off with one hand on the control column while reading the airplane manual with the other. Over the years they developed into highly proficient bush pilots, performing feats that are unthinkable today.

Their primary mission was to support the then fledgling Alaska Fire Control Service under the command of its founder, Roger R. Robinson, who many years later became the founder of the Boise Interagency Fire Center (now the National Interagency Fire Center) as well. In those early days there was no VHF radio navigational system (no omniranges)—only low-frequency beacons and four-course non-directional radio ranges. During bad fire years, the smoke throughout Interior Alaska would at times top off at twenty thousand feet above sea level with ground-level visibilities less than a half mile. Flying in this environment, these pilots often had to dead reckon off the nearest radio beacon for many miles to locate fire crews earlier deposited on remote, smokey, wilderness lakes.

Mac also handled the arrangements to procure contract aircraft services and became an expert at it. He was known in the Alaskan aviation community as a straight shooter who you could always depend on, and many deals were consummated with a handshake. He was well respected. Later, when he was driving a P-51 Mustang around the country chasing lightning storms, the only thing missing was a white scarf to complement his Tennessee Ernie Ford mustache. I learned a hell-of-a-lot from him.

With the advent of OAS, we swapped roles, and I became his boss—an uncomfortable situation that I felt was upside down from what it should have been. Mac had so much more experience, it was ridiculous. Earlier, when the Interior Department headhunter came by, I had recommended Mac as their man. As director of OAS, I could see a role for Mac in our Boise headquarters as a special projects guy, so I moved him to Boise and hired John Schommer from the FAA to replace him as Regional Director. There had been a constant stream of rumors that a sizable government amphibious aircraft fleet was operating in Micronesia, and I needed someone with time available to check it out. After moving to Boise and before the project got off the ground, Mac died of a heart attack, and I lost my mentor. Over time the Micronesia concerns gradually faded away as the odds of its existence became less and less probable.

The Rat-Chokers

OAS dreamed up special names for the various programs it was involved with. For instance, geologists were the "Rock-Pickers"; foresters were the "Tree-Huggers"; drug enforcement agents were the "Door-Kickers"; and the airborne coyote gunners were the "Rat-Chokers."

Out west, there was a war between ranchers and coyotes, which were killing sheep. The Fish and Wildlife Service found itself pressed into this problem by politicians and established programs to deplete the coyote population on public lands leased to ranchers. The Rat-Choker program involved shooting coyotes from slow, low-flying aircraft like the Piper Super Cub. This required a pilot in front with a gunner in back shooting a shotgun out the right side of the Super Cub. The top and lower halves of the side door would be open, thus providing ample space for a shotgun to be maneuvered in quest of an unfortunate coyote. Shooting passes were often quite low, only 40 or 50 feet above the ground, and sometimes lower. A Super Cub is a simple, easy-to-fly airplane, but it can spin into the ground under the right circumstances. If the airplane stalls at very low altitude, the resultant vertical spin is unrecoverable, and the result is often a fiery death.

Because the very nature of the Rat-Choker program involved the hazardous flying techniques described above, the accident rate was high and often fatal. Aircraft employed were usually chartered or contracted. OAS tightened up the flight experience requirements, and our flight inspectors conducted rigorous slow-flight maneuvering drills.

The Door-Kickers

As a result of our working-capital funding basis, OAS was able to provide services outside of the Interior Department to other agencies, as long as it did not compromise our in-house responsibilities. An official from the Drug Enforcement Administration (DEA) Washington Headquarters contacted us because they were uncomfortable with their Chicago office aerial drug tracking program. Essentially, they requested an evaluation of the best way to conduct the ongoing program. Because he possessed a sharp, analytical mind coupled with aviation experience, I dispatched Randy Smith to Chicago, where he sat down with the Door-Kickers and reviewed their aircraft activity.

That evening, he called me on the phone at home and started out with, "You won't believe this!" at which point I felt there might be an unforgettable moment coming. There was. Apparently, to keep track of drug movement within the vast Chicago Midway Airport complex, a Door-Kicker with less than 50 hours of flight experience was flying a Cessna 150 with tracking equipment at low altitudes directly over the center of the airport, chasing drug shipments! Early the next morning I called our Washington contact at DEA and warned him that our recommendation about their Chicago aircraft operation was short and to the point: shut it down!

Later, Randy worked with the DEA on various aviation planning efforts and won admiration from that agency. This was expressed by Peter Bensinger, the drug enforcement administrator, in a personal letter to me in 1976.

NOAA and the P-2V Neptune

In the late 1970s OAS acquired a surplus P-2V Neptune for extended overwater wildlife surveys in Alaska. During this period, the National Oceanic and Atmospheric Administration (NOAA) found itself involved with the tuna industry's discontent over porpoises, which had an appetite for tuna. To define the extent of the problem, NOAA's Bureau of Fisheries, which had jurisdiction over both tuna and porpoises, needed to somehow quantify the extent of the porpoise population off the South American, Central American, Mexican, and

Southern California coasts. Since this would require survey flights 800 hundred miles out to sea, NOAA said that they could utilize the OAS P-2V for that purpose when the Alaska survey program ended, but I was reluctant to commit. To send a complex aircraft off on such an extended, remote mission for weeks on end with maintenance support thousands of miles away was begging for problems, and I sure didn't want to get wrapped around the axle on this operation, but NOAA put the pressure on, and I finally relented.

The planning for this mission had several quirks, one of which was the requirement for bundles of cash to pay for fuel costs up and down the coast from sources that didn't honor credit cards. To solve that problem, we provided a safe that was welded to the cockpit floor with the combination lock code known only by the captain.

Courtesy of Naval Air Station Jacksonville.

I then signed for fifty thousand U.S. dollars' worth of pesos, which were stuffed into the safe, and admonished the captain about how important it was to his career that I personally would not have to pay back any of it out of my own pocket.

Courtesy of Sr. Airman Dennis Sloan, USAF.

Another problem was that the pilot and copilot didn't get along well, but they were the only two pilots we had who were qualified in the Neptune. Over the phone, I admonished them to put their differences aside for the mission, and they agreed they would. A little guy in the back of my mind, called "reservations," was now excitedly jumping up and down, but nevertheless, the Neptune departed for Southern California with their biologists, all apparently in high spirits. I then adopted an out-of-sight, out-of-mind approach to the mission and fervently hoped that over the coming weeks I would hear very little from them.

Periodically the NOAA supervisory biologist called in with progress reports. Initially, things were purring right along with no significant glitches. Almost daily they were running transect lines up to 800 miles offshore and collecting good data. Then one day the supervisor mentioned that he was getting the impression the pilots perhaps weren't all that fond of each other. "No big problem though, just thought you should know." I hate that kind of message and began stewing about it, but there was nothing I could do in the near term.

Eventually the big one happened. One of the engines trashed itself, and they needed a replacement. This wasn't just any engine—it was a Wright R-3350, 18-cylinder, 3,700 horsepower monster that, when mounted on a stand for transport, was too big to fit in anything except an Air Force C-5 Galaxy strategic transport aircraft so I had to buy space on one. At the time the Galaxy was the largest aircraft in the air force inventory, and I was coming unglued because we were going through all this crap on behalf of some f**king porpoises!

Following the engine replacement, the project continued for several weeks without serious problem, except that the supervisor, upon checking in one day, mentioned that the pilots really don't get along well. He said one pilot had told him the other pilot had a personality like a shit sandwich. Not long after, while operating out of Panama, the second engine failed, and they managed to park the airplane at Howard Air Force Base in the Canal Zone. Since their project was almost completed, I told them to jump on the airlines and come home. We were finished too.

A couple of months later, a major at Howard Air Force Base called and asked what in the hell should they do "with this f**king airplane." I thought for a moment and asked if they could use it for target practice, to which he responded with an enthusiastic "You bet!" That was the concluding episode of what had been a difficult, but overall successful, venture into NOAA's south-of-the-border porpoise survey.

33

1976

U.S. Navy Combat-Readiness Training

Someone in the Chief of Naval Operations (CNO) office came up with an idea about how to save lots of money on their aerial combat-readiness training programs. The idea was that rather than use expensive navy fighter jets as radar targets for these exercises, why not use much less expensive civilian business jets? Indeed, why not?

Around Thanksgiving they pitched the idea to Congress, which jumped at it hook, line, and sinker. The savings would be huge, and the navy told Congress that they could put a contract in place and have the new operation start next October 1. Then they visited their Naval Air Systems Command (NAVAIR) procurement division and told them they needed the system up and running by next October 1, approximately 11 months distant, to which NAVAIR responded that they could have it ready in four years—maybe. They had no experience contracting out to the private sector for civilian aircraft services. Since they were now on the record with Congress, the navy started a frantic search for people who did this kind of procurement and discovered OAS.

In Boise, I met with Captain Murray, the deputy chief of air warfare from the Pentagon's CNO office, who explained their problem and implored me to take the project on. I responded I would, if the navy gave us a million dollars up front to get the ball rolling. They did, and we went to work, eventually awarding a competitive contract to Flight

International Aviation for services utilizing two fleets of Learjets, one in San Diego and the other in Jacksonville, Florida. I was informed a pool had been established at NAVAIR to bet on whether or not OAS could pull it off by the start date. The Lear fleets took off on schedule the morning of October 1 from both U.S. coasts, and my staff said the navy guys were so pleased they almost peed themselves.

The Seeds of Our Potential Destruction

The seeds for our forthcoming near-death experience were sown one day when Bob Salazar, the chief procurement officer for the Bonneville Power Administration paid me an office visit. He carried a message from Don Hodel, the administrator, that they planned to purchase an aircraft, and because they had working-capital funding, they didn't need to go through OAS. He was surprised when I informed him that since OAS also operated under a working-capital fund, our involvement should be no problem.

Salazar indicated that Hodel was intent on Bonneville doing their own thing, so I dictated a memo to Dick Hite stating Hodel's position and gave a copy to Salazar that he could show Hodel. My pay grade was not high enough to take on the Bonneville Power Administrator so, summoning up my best Pontius Pilate act, I had placed the ball in Hite's court. My expectations were that I would probably hear nothing further about it. I was mistaken.

Al Zapanta

In late 1976, President Ford appointed Al Zapanta to the position of assistant secretary of the interior for Program, Budget, and Administration, thereby providing Dick Hite with a new boss. My headquarters' "spy team" found that Zapanta was closely involved with Ford on many issues and that he had been a highly decorated special forces (Green Berets) general in Vietnam. Translation: "You don't f**k around with this guy!" After his arrival, our village tom-toms went silent regarding the goings-on back east, and I was unable to pry much information out of Hite. I expected that eventually Zapanta would want to meet with me, however for two months, there was only silence.

Showdown at Bonneville Power

Then one evening at my Boise home, I was relaxed watching TV when the phone rang. It was Dick Hite, and his greeting was, "Thurston, where the f**k are you?" Taken aback, I said I was home, of course, and asked what was going on.

Dick told me he was sitting at the bar in the Portland Marriott Hotel with Zapanta who was extraordinarily pissed that I wasn't there to meet him. I responded that I was unaware that any of you were coming out west because nobody had told me. Hite told me his secretary had notified me, and I told him she had not. Dick then insisted she had, and I said, "Dick, do you really think that I would sit home and intentionally stand up your boss? That's ludicrous. And what are you doing in Portland?" Hite said we had a ten o'clock meeting the next morning with Bonneville Power and I had better find a way to be in attendance. He threw in that Zapanta was fit to be tied. So I decided not to finish to not finish my TV show and instead went to work getting airline reservations. Luckily, I latched on to a Hughes Air West Boise-to-Portland flight with a 9:00 a.m. arrival.

I had been told to meet them in front of the Bonneville Power building. Hite and Zapanta were waiting on the sidewalk for me as my taxi pulled up. Dick then made the introduction. I said, "Glad to meet you."

I shook hands with Zapanta under a glaring scowl accompanied by an unfriendly, "Yeah, let's get going." It was a "doghouse" greeting, and inside we rode the elevator to an upper floor in complete silence. The spacious BPA conference room windows overlooked Portland and contained a large assembly of BPA executives with Don Hodel sitting at the head of the table. I found myself seated next to Harry Windus, BPA's aircraft chief, whom I had met and come to respect during my task force study days.

After roundtable introductions, Zapanta launched into a variety of topics unrelated to OAS, and I was wondering why he wanted me here in the first place. His delivery was authoritative, brisk, to the point, with no antagonism, and about what you would expect from a general. Suddenly that all changed when he brought up OAS and BPA's end-running OAS for their airplane purchase. At that point, Salazar, the BPA chief procurement officer, spoke up to his fellow Hispanic to justify their action. Zapanta ignored him, and turning to Hodel, virtually ripped him a new one in front of his own troops, emphasizing that if he ever tried that again, he would have his butt. As the tirade continued, Windus and I started slowly sliding under the table in shock. The only thing missing was that we were not holding hands.

Zapanta then announced he was running late for a flight to Los Angeles, terminated the meeting, and departed. As the shell-shocked BPA staff filed out of the room, only three people remained: Hodel, Hite, and myself, at which point Hite suggested we go somewhere and have lunch. In my mind, there was no way Hodel could think I hadn't orchestrated this, and having lunch with him would cast the word *awkward* into an entirely new dimension. I could have shot Hite, but before long the "awkward threesome" was seated in a nearby restaurant booth where I sincerely apologized for the debacle, stressing that I had only just met Zapanta on his front steps and we had barely spoken.

Surprisingly, Don Hodel was somewhat cordial, something I would not have been, were I he. I was upset with the way Zapanta conducted the meeting. I had undertaken a lot of bridge-building to gain OAS acceptance, and in my opinion, that day a bridge was not only destroyed —it fell into the Columbia River. When I returned to Boise, Larry Stevens, my deputy director asked how it went, and I struggled for adjectives to describe it.

The Bureaucracy Closes In—Too Much Authority

In late 1977, Zapanta decided he had to get a handle on OAS and Thurston's delegated authorities. These were cited in complex bureaucratic legalese by my finance guy, Harry Starkey, at the inception of OAS. That these authorities were virtually indecipherable was by design. Hite's domain in Washington also had a procurement office, personnel office, finance office, etc. Left to their own devices, they would have loved to absorb OAS offices with similar functions into their own domains and "streamline" us, thereby adding to their importance and influence. The problems were that procurement expertise in aviation required specialized experience and expertise, as did the financial aspects, and these offices—especially the personnel office—were renowned for taking forever to do anything, even within their "expertise". Nevertheless, Al sent Dick Hite to Boise to look into it.

After a couple of days talking to Harry Starkey and Larry Stevens, Hite sat down in my office and dictated a memo to Zapanta which stated in part, "After careful review of the OAS delegated authorities, it appears that Thurston has more administrative authority than you, and possibly even the secretary of the interior." He seemed to have a professional admiration for the wisdom of his old friend Harry Starkey, who had pulled a good one off on this bureaucracy years prior, but now felt he had to blow the whistle. This was not helpful, and the fact was that, were it not for these authorities, OAS would not have survived coming out of the gate in 1973.

For the next six months, Zapanta required that OAS submit all personnel action requests through Hite's office as a test to gauge their efficiency. Of the numerous requests submitted during that period, and in accordance with our expectations, they failed to process even one. In view of this, Zapanta appeared to become more supportive of OAS, although he was apparently unaware that in Portland several weeks ago, he had planted the seeds with BPA's Don Hodel that were destined to eventually challenge our institutional survival.

About that time, Gerald Ford lost the election, Zapanta departed, and a whole new crew of political appointees moved in. The authority issue faded away, and I remained intact with authorities undiminished.

34

1977 - 1980

The Idaho Mafia

One day in February, 1977, standing at the entrance of the Department of the Interior Building, Dick Hite (who was about to leave the Interior Department) welcomed new Secretary of the Interior Cecil Andrus to his domain. Andrus was the ex-governor of Idaho, and prior to his arrival, the rumor mill had been buzzing about all the Idaho people he was planning to bring with him, hence the "Idaho Mafia." One of them was appointed as assistant secretary for Program, Budget, and Administration and thus became Dick Hite's new boss. His name was Larry Meierotto and the only information I could dig up on him was that he once was Seattle's deputy mayor.

Shortly thereafter, Dick Hite moved over to the White House Office of Management and Budget OMB) and I was concerned that, to date, my superiors had not approved the OAS consolidation of government aircraft in the Lower 48, in spite of my numerous pleadings over the years. Each year in the spring I had testified at the Senate Interior Appropriations hearings, which were chaired by Senator Ted Stevens from Alaska, and I was worried about being clueless on the new regime's position on this matter, especially because I had heard Uncle Ted was getting antsy about it.

The Congressional Hearing Disaster

On the day of the 1977 hearing, I arrived at the department office anxious to check out Meierotto's position on the consolidation issue for the congressional hearing. Along with the other office directors, I was ushered into his office where we sat down around a conference table, and he immediately announced that we all would have to leave in a moment because we were running late. He then went around the table machine-gun style firing questions. To me, he asked what issues does Senator Stevens have with OAS, if any. I responded that he will want to know why we haven't consolidated the Lower 48 aircraft, which we promised to do in 1973. He then asked if there was anything else, and I said no, at which point he terminated the meeting, and we all went up to Capitol Hill.

At that moment I realized that if attacked by Stevens, the only defense at my disposal would amount to little more than blaming my own superiors for their fear of making a decision over the years, but luckily, as we filed into the hearing chamber, Meierotto, who knew virtually nothing about OAS, told me he would do the testifying for OAS and I should sit with the audience. I gratefully found a seat in the very back row and awaited developments because I figured things were going to get hot.

Uncle Ted slid into his command chair and opened the proceedings. He was frowning. Larry Meierotto read his prepared opening statement for the Office of the Secretary and then stated he was ready for questions. Stevens shouted, "OAS! I want to talk about OAS!" I pictured a large eagle swooping out of a tree toward a terrified rabbit as Larry recoiled, turned in his chair, and summoned me forward with a great swoop of his arm. This had to be the worst of the worst for me. Stevens was highly pissed, and the boss of my boss, whom I was now sitting next to, had his head down and appeared to be studying his shoes. The only things I had going for me were that Stevens and I were both Alaskans, and several years ago he had actually put his arm around my shoulder. The chairman then launched into his attack: "Years ago you sat in that chair and told me you were going to consolidate Interior's aircraft nationwide, and you haven't done it, and I want to know why!"

For a nanosecond I contemplated standing up, spreading my arms out, and saying in a classic Steve Martin gesture, "Why Mister Chairman, I forgot!" but I chickened out. Instead, I gave a rambling, unconvincing, milquetoast answer that obviously provided Uncle Ted no satisfaction, and he eventually gave up on me and moved on to other targets. I was white-hot furious, stood up, grabbed my briefcase, muttered, "Thanks a lot, Larry," to the person I had only met 45 minutes earlier, and stormed out of the hearing chamber bound for National Airport.

The Move to Decapitate OAS

Not long after the disastrous Senate hearing, I woke up to a glorious, sunny, spring Saturday morning at home in Boise. I was sitting comfortably outside on my deck with a cup of coffee enjoying the sound of twittering birds while preparing to read the morning edition of the *Idaho Statesman* newspaper. When I opened it up, it featured a major article about Senator Ted Stevens's intent to abolish the OAS presence throughout the Lower 48 and retain only the Alaska contingent. As chairman of the Senate Appropriations Committee, he possessed the power to make that happen. I felt like I had just stuck my foot into a boot and encountered a scorpion.

Monday morning, I arrived at my office and was told the OAS flight operations dispatcher had scheduled a trip in the Midwest the next day for Secretary Andrus in a Learjet chartered from Duncan Aviation in Lincoln, Nebraska. Harry Barr was to be the pilot, and I arranged to join him on the flight. The secretary was the only passenger, and so, armed with a General Accounting Office (GAO) report that praised us for our efficiencies and cost effectiveness plus several other briefing papers, I brought Andrus up to speed on what was happening in the real world. He appeared receptive to my sales pitch, and we had a warm-handshake departure at Kansas City.

The next morning, I received a call from the Boise office of Democratic Senator Frank Church. They were upset that the Republican senator from Alaska was trying to undermine an organization on their Idaho home turf and were going to fight it. Later I found out that the Interior secretary's press secretary, Chris Carlson, had been the one to plant the story in the *Idaho Statesman* to generate local support but had never bothered to inform me, so I called him up and dumped on him. Now we had a dispute centered on the wrong issue—political turf—instead of OAS worthiness, but it apparently worked because I never heard anything more from Senator Stevens about it.

The Close of 1980

As the year drew to a close, my assessment of OAS progress (with the exception of the still outstanding Lower 48 aircraft consolidation issue) was good because our operating procedures were now streamlined and efficient. We had acquired a handle on the contract and charter aircraft programs, which turned out to be considerably more extensive than initially realized, and had mandated viable aviation safety measures throughout the department. OAS personnel were continuously in the field nationwide performing aircraft inspections, pilot flight evaluations, safety inspections, rotary-wing manager training, and customer-requested transportation studies. Things were going fairly smoothly, and we were enjoying good working relationships with most of our customers in the bureaus. Our favorable performance was about to be validated by the U.S. General Accounting Office (GAO).

In November, Jimmy Carter lost, and Ronald Reagan won the election. The hierarchy of the department (i.e., all the political appointees) disappeared up to the sixth floor of the Interior building and started writing job resumes (at the taxpayers' expense). Reagan's advanced teams were circulating around "measuring the drapes" and sizing up who was to get which office. Jim Watt, who had a reputation of being an anti-environmentalist, was designated the next secretary of the interior, and grounding rods were installed around the building to handle the incoming barrage of lightning strikes he was due to attract. Cecil Andrus packed his bags and headed back to Boise. I wondered what was coming next.

35

1981 - Part 1

The Beginning of the End

When Jim Watt came to the department, I'm not sure Hite was standing on the front steps to welcome him, but early on, Hite did materialize on the scene, kind of like a resurrection, and took over his old office. Not long after, there were televised Senate nomination hearings, and low and behold, they were interrogating Don Hodel for the position of undersecretary of the interior. Since he had been smiling after Hite and I had parted company with him in Portland four years earlier, I was unsure what to expect but felt it was definitely time to hold on to my shorts.

The OAS Abolishment Order

While at home on a sunny weekend afternoon on March 16, an excited Len Small from our Atlanta office called and told me the National Park Service in Atlanta had received a faxed copy of a departmental order abolishing OAS effective next September 30, the end of the fiscal year. It was signed by Undersecretary Donald Hodel. The reason given was that decentralized aviation programs operated by the bureaus would be more efficient and economical than OAS. No data was offered to support this contention. I called Dick Hite at home and asked what he knew about it, and he informed me it was news to him because, after all, it was Sunday, and he was home. I had difficulty believing he could have been unaware of this, since all departmental manuals and directives were distributed from his Office of Policy Directives, and an order to abolish one of his own organizations would necessarily have to have flowed through his hands.

The next day, Larry Stevens and I mapped out our actions to be undertaken. First, we would send notices of our abolishment directly to all our government customers so they could undertake planning for the new arrangement come October 1. Next, we would similarly notify all the private-sector contractors that as of October they would be contracting to whomever, but not OAS. Finally, we arranged to notify all OAS personnel of the order and promised to keep them updated with more clarification from Washington if and when we received any. OAS morale disintegrated, and our people were craving more information regarding their fate. As of the close of Monday, there had been zero communication from Hite or anyone else in Washington.

From all the incredulous phone calls from our bureau customers, we figured that by now the entire Interior Department world have probably received faxed copies of the abolishment order, but OAS had not, and it began to appear that we had been purposely left out of the information loop. We had been left dangling in the wind. Days later, having still not received word from Washington, we requested and received the formal notification. I finally heard from Hite, who claimed to not have much information except he planned that shortly he would come to Boise and meet with the OAS employees regarding their futures. I asked for an audience with Hodel and Hite said he was virtually unapproachable on OAS matters. Hodel's smile in Portland four years ago had been a charade.

Several days later, Hite arrived in Boise, and all Boise OAS employees were gathered in the Fire Center auditorium. Dick stood on the stage and informed us that as of October 1, all of us would be out on the street, with no rights to move into other agencies, i.e., there would be no "bumping" rights. In effect, the department was preparing to completely abolish all personnel with specialized aviation knowledge and experience and have the bureaus, which now had no such resources, take over their own aviation management responsibilities. This was patently insane and born out of the fact that Hodel (and Hite, for that matter) had no real knowledge about what OAS actually did, and had an apparent need for retribution. Many of our people with long careers were going to be pushed out the door without any retirement, including myself after 28 years of service. Given Hodel's rigid stance toward us, it was going to be almost impossible for me to sugarcoat this to the OAS employees who would almost certainly start hunting for other job opportunities.

The U.S. Navy

Upon receiving notice of our forthcoming demise, Captain Murray, the deputy chief of air warfare in the Chief of Naval Operations office, came to visit me again. He asked what I was going to do after the abolishment, and I told him I didn't know; we were in effect being thrown out into the street, and I hadn't had the time to think about it. Murray said there was no way the navy could jump into managing this operation, and asked if I would consider forming a corporation to take over management of the program next October under a sole-source contract. I responded positively but cautioned that since this could be tickling the edges of the conflict-of-interest laws, I would first have to get some legal advice.

After Captain Murray departed, I called Dick Hite, who was not only my boss, but the top official in the department responsible for assuring compliance for all personnel to the conflict-of-interest laws. I told him about the navy's proposal and asked what he thought about it, to which he responded he saw nothing wrong with it under the circumstances. I also told him I would necessarily have to create a corporation before October 1 in order to be ready to take over the navy contract by that date and would start providing him supplemental disclosure statements as this matter progressed. I asked if he had a duty to disclose this to Hodel, since it now appeared he was on a vendetta and would probably try to squash any opportunity I might have with the navy. Also, it was my impression the employee conflict-of-interest disclosures were subject to the Privacy Act. Hite agreed with that and said he was not going to run to Hodel.

A few days later, Burt Stanley, our OAS attorney from the Interior Department's Office of the Solicitor in Sacramento, was in Boise on OAS business. After work we met to discuss the navy's proposal and potential conflict-of-interest considerations. The following week we received a formal written opinion from the Office of the Solicitor stating that since, come the next October, OAS would not exist, there would be nothing to conflict with, and therefore no problem. However, Stanley recommended that since I would still be the OAS director until October 1, I should play no active role or take any income from the corporation until that time. I then called the navy and told them I would accept their proposal.

Aviation Management Services Co.

At this point Larry Stevens resigned from his job as OAS deputy director and went to work forming Aviation Management Services (AMS) and establishing an office in Boise. Myself and handful of others planned to join AMS after OAS was abolished. For now, I remained at OAS and avoided any activity with the corporation, although I faced a big dilemma: whether or not to "save" OAS. Larry had correctly pointed out that if OAS survived, it potentially could become a competitor with AMS at the Defense Department because, in the realm of contracted aircraft services, we would both be in the same business. On the other hand, even though it appeared the chances of OAS surviving were close to zero, I could not in good conscience stand by while the government deliberately trashed the careers of dedicated, competent employees over a vendetta against me.

Government employees are prohibited from lobbying, but I didn't have to. Phone calls were avalanching in from both our federal customers and private-sector contractors who were incredulous about our abolishment. Many stated they were contacting their congressional representatives to express their opposition. Before long a congressional staffer with the House Interior and Insular Affairs Committee called and started mining data about OAS. I answered all his questions honestly. He then asked how I would feel if they had the U.S. General Accounting Office come in and perform a critical audit on OAS. I said I would welcome an independent audit and would cooperate with them. Before long, over 16 GAO auditors were scattered across the country interviewing people from Florida to Alaska and crunching numbers.

36

1981 - Part 2

A Meeting with Hodel

Eventually Hite told Larry Stevens and me to come to Washington because Hodel wanted to meet with us. In the meeting, Hodel did most of the talking, which consisted of listing all the information we should gather to bring back to him in a week. I was given no opportunity to voice any concerns about his abolishment decision. In passing he said I had a pretty good lobbying team, to which I remained silent. To Larry and me, it was obvious that with Congress and the GAO breathing down his neck, he probably felt he needed to gather a few actual facts to back up his contentions that OAS was worthless.

A week later we both returned and were given a vacant office to hang out in until Hodel summoned us. Enduring terminal boredom, we occupied the office the entire week with no summons. Late Friday afternoon Hite called us and declared that this amounted to cruel and unusual punishment—that it appeared Hodel would be too busy to see us until next week; we should return to Boise, and he would call us when Hodel was ready. We left a wheelbarrow-load of documents for Hodel in Hite's office. Just over an hour later, Larry and I boarded an airliner at Washington National and left town.

A Heated Conversation

Monday morning Hite called me and said 20 minutes after we departed, Hodel called down and wanted to meet Saturday morning. In a panic, Hite had dispatched a person to Dulles International Airport to track us down because he thought that was our departure point. Actually, it had been, but we had found a much earlier flight out of National and switched. When Hite told Hodel we had returned to Boise, Hodel exploded. I said, "Dick, you *did* tell him that we departed as the result of your suggestion, didn't you?"

Hite said he couldn't because Hodel had been unapproachably furious and was ranting. He went on to inform me that Hodel said I was insubordinate, untrustworthy, and disloyal. Furthermore, Congress had scheduled a hearing about the OAS abolishment, and I was not to testify at government expense. If I did testify, I would have to be on annual leave and travel at my own expense.

I responded that I felt he was throwing me under the bus, and as far as I could see, Hodel apparently was unable to grasp the fact that true loyalty has to be earned in life—it cannot be decreed—that's what tinhorn dictators do. I said to Dick that I had a message for him to give to Hodel: "Tell him I said he can go f**k himself!" and slammed the phone down in disgust.

The OAS Hearing

Eventually the GAO reported in draft form, and it was circulated. It would not please Hodel. As the date of the congressional hearing neared, the GAO auditors were still floating around OAS offices, and we gleaned several observations from them. One commented that from their interviews at the department with Hite and Hodel, Hite had largely been "shooting from the hip" in response to their questions, and Hodel had virtually no factual responses—just opinions that contradicted facts they had already ascertained. He appeared to be largely unaware of actual OAS functions, its impacts on aviation safety, operational efficiencies, and cost savings. Some viewed it as a vendetta at taxpayer expense. Later I heard the hearing did not, however, go well for Hodel. Another official in the department had commented that he couldn't understand why they were trying to abolish the only agency that had received a favorable GAO report in the department's then 101-year history.

Dangling in the Wind

Summer was waning, and the September 30 abolishment date was relentlessly approaching without word from anybody about our forthcoming demise. I had a feeling that most of my people still didn't believe our abolishment would really happen, and our operations were still trucking along like everything was hunky-dory. The department had yet to put forth how its aviation program would be implemented after OAS, and bureaus had been expressing concern that they were neither equipped nor ready for a transition. Also, I had yet to receive a contract from the navy, and it appeared that NAVAIR contracting division was moving at its legendary glacial pace. I continued, however, to faithfully submit updated conflict-of-interest reports to Dick Hite, the departmental ethics officer, with no feedback from him of any problems he might feel over the creation of AMS.

Meanwhile, the GAO showed up again because they wanted to do a government-wide aviation study using OAS as a model of how the government should operate. The thought stunned me. I couldn't imagine any person trying to implement such a plan being capable of withstanding the heat across the board from all the pissed-off government bureaucracies, each with their own congressional oversight constituencies. I really didn't think it would be a doable objective, and told them so, but was inwardly proud they thought OAS was hot stuff.

September 30, 1981

Abolishment day. It was to be a day of high drama. There was still no word from Washington. I called in but was told Hite was unavailable. My employees were asking what to do at the end of the day if no word arrived. I put out a directive that essentially stated to remove all personal belongings from offices, secure all government aircraft and vehicles, leave all government keys in appropriate places, and go home. It was difficult to realize this was not a dream. I could not believe Hodel was vindictively inflicting so much anguish on my people and their families, but I put it in my perspective: he was a typical politician and apparently didn't care.

At 4:45 p.m. the navy called and said AMS had been awarded the contract with an October 1 effective start date (tomorrow). At 4:50 p.m. the employees were packing up when Hite's Office of Policy Directives called to say the OAS abolishment order had been rescinded. The bastards had waited until literally the last minute! As of the next morning I would still be the OAS director and at the same time be under contract to the U.S. Navy. I called Burt Stanley, the Interior department attorney in Sacramento, and asked what I should do. He said to be sure to update my conflict-of-interest statement and stay away from AMS activities and salary, so I did. I tried one last time to call Hite, but no answer.

37

1981 - 1982

Miranda Rights

A week or two later two investigators from the Office of Inspector General marched in and informed me I was under investigation by a federal grand jury and read me my Miranda rights. They then read the charges, which involved conflict of interest over AMS, misuse of government and contracted aircraft, animal cruelty, and anything else they could think of, following which they handed me a subpoena. They also had a directive from Hite reassigning me from the position of OAS director to some sort of assistant in the Boise Office of the Solicitor. They informed me that I was being replaced by Fire Center Director Jack Wilson, one of the most antagonistic enemies of OAS. Indeed, the GAO audit portrayed several instances where Wilson had launched criticisms at OAS that were later verified as patently false.

They asked if I had any questions. I asked why this was of any surprise to Hite because I had been sending him conflict-of-interest statements for months about the navy contract as well as discussing it with him, and he had seen no problem with it. They responded that they had talked to Hite, and he had maintained he knew nothing about my conflict-of-interest statements about a navy contract. With that, I realized that the only person who could testify that I had submitted statements to Hite was my secretary, Bev Williams, who had both typed them up and mailed them. I felt it was probably certain the statements that had been sent to Hite were now gone—either shredded, burned, or buried in Hite's backyard. The chief of the Interior Department's Ethics Office was covering his ass, and I had been assigned the role of a piñata in his grand scheme. I was being thrown under the bus.

I called Larry Stevens at the AMS office and told him to look out—the Redcoats were coming—and half an hour later the investigators descended on him. That evening the local TV news showed up in my driveway, and I refused to dialogue with the bloodthirsty asshole known for chasing scandalous news. Instead, I read a prepared statement condemning the Interior Department's actions, extolling my innocence, and telling them to vamoose.

With the GAO auditors underfoot, I had to tell them what was going on, so we convened in my office, and I briefed them. They, as much as anybody, felt this was a Hodel vendetta but realized that, politically, using OAS as a great example probably wouldn't play in Peoria. Later they met with the White House Ethics Officer who provided his opinion that there probably was no conflict. After briefing the auditors, I walked out of OAS for the last time.

Two days later I managed to connect with Hite on the phone. I asked him how he could possibly not remember all the discussions we had had about the navy contract, and he kind of wandered back and forth saying he just couldn't remember. From his phone demeanor, I suspected he thought I might be recording the conversation, which I wasn't, against the advice of our attorney. When I asked just what the hell I would be doing in the Boise Solicitor's Office, he said I'd probably be counting tombstones in the Boise cemeteries. I asked what happened to the conflict-of-interest statements I had submitted, and he denied ever receiving any. This confirmed for me that the Department of the Interior's chief ethics official was lying to cover his ass with Hodel, and the box I was put in just got welded shut. I told him I could do productive work at AMS and asked him to put me on leave-without-pay until further notice to avoid any question of conflict of interest, which he did.

| 268 |

The charge of misuse of aircraft was particularly galling. When I became OAS director in 1973, I told my wife that I was entering another arena, and although it was not purely political, it really was. There would be enemies. There were going to be unfounded criticisms. People would make up stories to get at me. They would fabricate lies. They will think there is no way an aircraft chief over such a large operation wouldn't abuse his opportunities for free rides. I told her this was to be our world, and I was not paranoid. Therefore, whenever possible I would ride commercial airlines in coach. I would only ride in government-owned or contracted aircraft if absolutely no other means was available, and this would be documented. I told her she and our kids would not step foot on any aircraft under my jurisdiction.

I had lived by this creed for eight years, and predictably there came an allegation that I had been riding around the country on Flight International's Learjets like the high and the mighty. (Flight International had the Navy contract.) The subpoena demanded copies of all the Flight International aircraft flight reports over the years to see whether or not I had been a passenger. There were thousands of them, and of course, I was never on them. Information got back to me that the owner of Flight International was upset with OAS because we had been holding his feet to the fire to meet his contract requirements. Word was that he'd complained to Don Hodel, and that was what blew the lid off, triggering an investigation by the Office of Inspector General.

The Federal Grand Jury

The grand jury marched on under the direction of Assistant U.S. Attorney Jeff Ring in Boise. I learned that Ring had been one of our customers at my wife's Scandinavian furniture store in downtown Boise, but due to his involvement with me, he no longer did business with her. While probably appropriate, this was nevertheless another discouraging aspect of our spiraling, downhill situation, which was complimented by rumors from other sources that Jan had received her

SBA store loan as the result of some sort of high-powered influence from me on the SBA.

Initially, the attorney for both Larry and me was Dick Greener, who later, sensing the political ramifications of the investigation, suggested we split up and I retain Jim Risch (now U.S. Senator James Risch from Idaho) as my attorney. At that time, Risch was the Idaho state senate majority leader, and Greener felt his influence could be beneficial. It apparently was. Armed with a copy of the letter I had received from the department's own attorneys in Sacramento stating there would be no conflict, Risch told Ring that the department's own attorneys said there was no conflict, so how are you going to prosecute this guy? They relinquished, and the inditement effort was terminated. I was now out from under the black cloud, or so I thought. I called Hite and asked him to speak with Hodel about reinstatement, which he did. The answer came back that Hodel, having lost his effort to make me a felon, was going to initiate administrative actions against me, so no reinstatement would occur.

AMS Activities

I moved over to the AMS Office and joined Larry Stevens. We also had an office in Atlanta, Georgia, staffed by Dean Shealy and Len Small, who had quit OAS to join us. They were riding herd on the Flight International navy program and searching for more business prospects. Larry Stevens actually ran AMS, and due to my reputation, I was the figurehead president. Restrained by introversion, I had no salesman ability, but that was what the corporation really needed. Thus, I played a minor support roll. Eventually we became involved with U.S. Navy combat-readiness training operations supporting the 6th Fleet the Mediterranean, which triggered Len Small occasionally traveling to Naples, Italy. Also, under the foreign military sales program, we put a contract together for a Learjet target-towing program on the East Coast for training Saudi Arabian gunboat crews on boats manufactured in Bremerton, Washington.

This may sound like a lot of business, but income-wise we were actually stretched thin, even though I had no salary. One day the General Services Administration (GSA) approached us about developing an aircraft management information system nationwide for the government, and this prospect generated much excitement for us. Preliminary discussions took place for a while and then mysteriously stopped. When we inquired why, GSA said that OAS had contacted them and proposed that they could do it, and GSA liked the idea better than having to contract it out to the private sector.

We had to turn this around, so I met for lunch with two OAS employees to challenge them on why they were doing this. I asked about their rationale and they replied they could do the job better, which flabbergasted me because Larry Stevens and I had developed the programs they were using before either of them was ever employed by OAS. I then implored them to at least give us a chance to compete for the work under the OMB circular A-76 requirements, which favored the private sector doing commercial-industrial work unless the government could demonstrate it could do it cheaper. They responded that circular A-76 didn't apply but couldn't tell me why.

Finally, I told them were it not for my decision to try to save OAS, they would have been out on the street, but I had done it in spite of my reservations that OAS might become a competitor to AMS. I said my concern for their well-being had been the only reason I did it, and it was becoming obvious they had no concern for me. I told them I had saved their jobs, that I was in my early fifties with no income or retirement, and now they were screwing me, just like Larry Stevens had warned they would do a year ago. They were unable to look me in my eyes. The whole tirade had no effect, and I departed, drove to a city park, parked the car, and broke down with frustration and anger. I felt the business could no longer afford me and that I had reached a dead end, so I would need to exit Aviation Management Services as well.

My Last Gasp

Early retirement was an avenue still open to me, so I asked about getting it approved with my 28 years of service. Reported by Hite, Hodel said no because he didn't want me to receive *any* retirement. With that, my financial well was dry, so I threw in the towel and resigned from the Department of the Interior. A short time later I also resigned from AMS.

I believed that against great odds, I had created a highly-efficient OAS aviation organization, recognized as such by both the private sector and in many government agencies. The thanks I received from the Interior Department was their effort to make me a felon for creating an agency within its department that "had received the only favorable GAO report in its 101-year history." OAS still exists as of this writing under the name, "Office of Aviation Services".

My destiny now was to team up with my wife's furniture store, where I would remain for the next seven years in our family business.

38

1982 - 1988

After OAS—The Furniture Store

At this stage of our life, a furniture store, which Jan had created several years earlier with the assistance of an SBA loan, was our sole means of income. It was a franchise of the Scandinavian Designs firm in Chicago. We were the only Scandinavian furniture store in Idaho, and I had been amazed she had been able to establish this business with no help (and very little encouragement) from me. The store was located in The Alaska Center that sat on Main Street in the core of downtown Boise directly across from The Owyhee hotel. It was generally viewed as a unique furniture store for Boise and attracted many clients who were educated, well-traveled, and hungry for sophisticated furniture. During these years, it had been quite successful and a noted addition to downtown Boise.

In what can only be described as a breathtaking change of pace from my aviation career, I primarily worked out of sight in the back room repairing furniture damaged by the trucking companies. Moving furniture around was a constant activity, orchestrated by my wife to keep us in shape. The store had a mezzanine, and on occasion the drill seemed to require taking everything downstairs and moving it upstairs and vice versa. I also did deliveries, as did our son J.T. and a muscular lad named Tom. J.T. did deliveries on and off after school during periods he had not been fired by Jan. One time Jan called him at home and asked why the hell he was not at the store since there was a delivery that had to be made. When J.T. responded that he was home because she had fired him, Jan told him he was now unfired and to get his ass back to the store.

Rural Delivery

I was trundling west along the I-84 throughway in our little furniture van headed for a remote home in the Idaho backcountry, about a three-hour drive from Boise. The home was occupied by two old ladies who had visited our store and had purchased two Norwegian Stressless Royal recliners, which we were obligated to deliver under the purchase contract. They sold for about $1,000 each.

Shortly after turning off I-84, I encountered a dirt road threading itself through rolling sagebrush hills for almost thirty miles in lonely cattle country. At the end of the road, the only house I'd seen for the last 20 miles came into view, and I pulled up, got out, and knocked on the door. One of the old ladies greeted me with, "Oh it's so nice of you to come all the way out here, but I have to tell you we've changed our mind."

Stifling the urge to say, "No, you goddamned haven't!", I talked my way inside and had tea with the old biddies while extolling the virtues of the recliners. They were still reluctant, so I dragged the recliners inside and had them try them once again. About an hour later, full of tea, I drove off in the empty van, happy that I had saved the sale but harboring an intense dislike for old people.

Later

The years passed by, and eventually, during the waning months of 1987, our second three-year store lease would have to be renewed. Jan and I were becoming tired of furniture store operations, so we decided to liquidate. In Idaho, there was a state law that prevented furniture stores from staging "going-out-of-business sales" without actually going out of business. Since we really intended to close our business, we felt it known by the public to be for real would give us a substantial sales boost.

To prepare for the event we imported more container loads of furniture from Scandinavia and virtually stocked the store to the rafters. The entire plan was kept secret until the sale was advertised in the papers and on TV a week earlier. Just prior to the publicity release, we closed the store, papered over all the street-side display windows, and posted the going-out-of-business sale date. Early in the morning of the sale, customers were lined up around the block, and by evening we had cleaned out virtually all the store inventory. Shortly thereafter we sold our house, put most of our belongings in storage, and rented an apartment. All ties to our most recent former life had been cut, except we did decide to at least leave our kids our forwarding address.

Now ensconced in our comfortable apartment in its park-like setting, it was time to contemplate what we might do next. Both kids had left the nest. Joy, our daughter, was in Dayton, Ohio, living with her husband's parents and pregnant with our forthcoming grandchild. J.T. was in Lincoln, Nebraska. He had been taught to fly by Harry Barr and was now selling accident insurance to farmers. Jan and I were as free as birds. Jan was thinking about either spending some time at the Mercy Center in Burlingame, California, or returning to Anchorage to be with Chet, her aging father. I was contemplating returning to Alaska and building something on our Hewitt Lake property. Everything was up in the air.

The Proposition

Lee Svoboda, the OAS Alaska flight operations chief, came to Boise on business and called to suggest we hoist a beer or two together for old times' sake. He had taught Harry Barr and me how to fly Argosy's years earlier, and I had worked closely with him on the development of that program. Two and a half beers into the reunion, Lee asked if I would be willing to come up and fly 30Z, the paracargo Argosy, as a seasonal pilot in Fairbanks. He was short an Argosy captain for the season and available pilots rated in that aircraft were next to impossible to find.

I was interested, but there were two problems: first, after flying very little for the last 14 years, I was rustier than a discarded boiler off an 1874 railroad locomotive, and second, Don Hodel was now the secretary of the interior and was unlikely to have forgotten losing his battle to abolish OAS. Lee realized this but believed it likely I would be the only qualified applicant for the job, and therefore, Hodel would have no grounds for disallowing my application, even if he did still feel I was an unreliable traitor. I agreed to give it a shot and said I would apply for the position. If it failed, I could always go hammer nails at Hewitt Lake.

A Reincarnation

I had to somehow get current for piloting in general. Harry Barr invited me to come out to Omaha where he would wire me up with Con Agra's Lear fleet for some exposure, but first, I attended a Flight Safety Lear Model 35 seminar in Wichita, Kansas. Then for several weeks I flew right seat for Con Agra and lived in Lincoln at J.T.'s apartment with his friends who were insurance salesmen. The partying was intense, but I managed in a back room with lots of pillows on my head. They had a cat named Carl whose head was screwed on 90 degrees as the result of some sort of accident. When Carl was walking, his face always looked to the left, which simplified his task of looking around corners if he planned to go left. I think if he wanted to go right, he probably had to turn around and walk backward. Carl was weird.

Since J.T. and his salesmen friends drove the back country roads selling insurance to farmers, they usually got speeding tickets, which they ignored. The fellow that delivered the summons time after time was a cop who stopped by so often, he'd come in, sit down, watch TV with them for a while, hand them the summons, and depart. His name was Carl, so they named the cat after him.

39

1988

Reentry

By late April, we had completed all the preparations to cut our strings with Boise and return to Alaska. At this point we undertook the long drive coupled with rides on various marine ferries in our two vehicles through the Inside Passage to Haines, Alaska, and then on to Anchorage via the Yukon Territory. In Anchorage, we found an apartment for Jan, and she settled in. I drove our van to Fairbanks where I was to be based for the summer to hunt for a place for myself. Our plan was to reunite when I returned from Fairbanks at the end of the fire season, about three months hence.

In Fairbanks, I settled into an apartment at Sophie Station, literally a stone's throw away from the ranger station I had lived in 32 years prior in 1956. Urban sprawl had obliterated my few memorable landmarks, such as the Igloo Motel, Dan and Alice's Watering Hole, and the black spruce forest along Airport Road. Instead, there was a hodgepodge of the usual small businesses with hub attractions like Fred Meyer, leaving me thinking, *Zoning—who needs it?* However, the driveway into the ranger station, which had since been transferred to the state of Alaska, remained a somewhat scenic path through a stand of now more mature birch trees, but the 1959 (then new) dispatch office, smokejumper building, and log cabin home were gone, with nothing in their place.

I wondered why buildings only 29 years old or younger had been re-moved or destroyed. There was no sign of fire.

At some point in the intervening years, the BLM had pulled the fire control responsibilities out of their Fairbanks and Anchorage districts and consolidated them under the newly- formed Alaska Fire Service, which is essentially what Roger R. Robinson had created decades earlier, only with hardly any people. So now I call it the Alaska Fire Service 2.0. This is what Joe Kastelic, George Kitson, John McCormick, and I had lobbied for years ago but had failed to convince the unimaginative, incompetent souls in Washington to consider. Apparently, someone had finally gotten through to them. The fire and aviation programs had moved to the U.S. Army airfield at Fort Wainwright, which used to be Ladd Air Force Base.

At the appointed hour, I drove through the Military Police gate on Fort Wainwright and pulled up at the Alaska Fire Service mess hall. The weather was cool and overcast with gusty winds. Inside, Svoboda had convened an informal "get acquainted" Argosy training session. The Argosy has a crew of three: pilot (captain), copilot, and flight engineer. Bill Babcock was the captain, and I was to be the copilot until (if ever) I was requalified to be a captain. Mark Goertzen was the flight engineer. I had not been inside an Argosy for over 15 years, and the aircraft I would be flying was a military variant of the civilian models I flew in the past.

Captain Babcock sat across the table from me and didn't say much. His eyes were expressionless. He appeared to be the stereotype pilot: leather jacket, aviator's sunglasses, khaki pants, mid-forties, clean cut, and *quiet*. Svoboda had told me he had been a Cobra attack helicopter pilot in Vietnam. He was casually puffing a cigarette and contemplating something in the far corner of the mess hall. Svoboda, on my left, was talking primarily to me about systems, speeds, and procedures. Such things as, "Jim, you remember the engine-out procedure, don't you? After you identify which engine has failed, it's HP cock to feather, feather switch to feather, LP cock closed, and checklist." Thinking back 14 years, I nodded knowingly.

He continued, "Also remember that when that when you call for landing flaps, push forward on the control column and grab a handful of aft trim to help you on the flare-out." He continued: when to split or not split the main bus bars of the electrical system—if done wrong you lose all your electricity and that means you're in deep shit; No. 4 engine is usually started first, but since the hydraulic pumps are on nos. 1, 2, & 3 engines, there's only accumulator pressure available until the pumps come on line; don't use nosewheel steering and brakes at the same time because the two systems fight and cancel each other out, etc. (My mind was groping to recall what I had known so many years ago.)

After the meeting, we went out on the flight line and boarded the Argosy. I noticed the wind was almost directly across the runway and gusting to about twenty-five knots. Someone outside started up an auxiliary power unit and the instrument panels in the airplane lighted up like a Christmas tree. Svoboda seated himself in the captain's seat, motioning me to climb into the copilot's position. Babcock was on the back bench somewhere, and Mark Goertzen, the flight engineer, was flipping switches on his engineer's panel behind me, on the over-head panel, and on the pedestal between me and Svoboda. This Argosy was the RAF military version, configured for paracargo dropping, and its flight deck configuration was unlike the Argosy's I had flown in yesteryear.

Eventually, with all engines turning, I was told to take over the controls, and we began the ride to reacquaint me with an Argosy by shooting several touch-and-go landings. Thanks to the wind, I was super uptight. I think Svoboda perhaps wanted to demonstrate to Babcock what a great pilot I was (but I knew I was a rusty has-been). I was concerned that I would commit some unforgivable screwup that would ruin my reputation and disgrace me forever (such as crashing the Argosy into the Fire Control Headquarters building). That didn't happen, and while my performance didn't confirm my worst fears, it was, in my view, anything but stellar. Finally, Svoboda must have decided that I could still get an Argosy off the ground and back again without breaking it and moved on to have Babcock take his turn. Sitting in what was now a pool of tepid sweat water, I experienced a feeling that my toenails were gradually uncurling.

The Nostalgia Flight

The next day I stood on the tarmac watching the loadmasters stuff the Argosy with 25,000 pounds of freight that we were going to haul to the Galena Air Force Station, about 270 miles west on the Yukon River. Svoboda had flown back to Anchorage content that things were hunky-dory up here. The weather was overcast and cool, but not so windy. It matched my mood: depressing. Our takeoff was scheduled for 11:30 a.m. and had been carefully planned so we would arrive at Galena when their mess hall opened for lunch at 1:00 p.m. (The work schedule was 9:00 a.m. to 6:00 p.m.)

This was a change from the way it used to be 16 years ago. These days I found that *all* scheduling of the Argosy revolved around eating. There was absolutely nothing of higher priority. In yesteryear (a term I was beginning to use more and more), scheduled eating for Argosy crews had yet to be invented, and in its place, we practiced the fine art of defensive eating I've described to you and we ate at every opportunity, never sure when our next one would be. When defensive eating clashed with our need for sleep, eating usually won. The bureau's safety aviation policies in those days did not exist.

I had recovered a little from yesterday's ride in the Argosy, but not much. I was emotionally disheveled and thinking that my idea of getting back into aviation may have been a mistake. I had been away from it too long, and now I was perhaps getting a little too long in the tooth. Even when running OAS, I rarely flew in order to avoid the inevitable accusations of misuse of aircraft. The thought of building myself a hermitage at Hewitt Lake and escaping from humanity was appealing. I was totally devoid of any enthusiasm for today's milk-run mission, the first of the season for the Argosy. Instead of being an asset, I regarded myself as a liability. The dream of taking up where I had left off years ago was beginning to seem unrealistic. During my drive back to Sophie's Station the previous night, I had debated over whether to study the airplane manuals or just get drunk. I decided to study the manuals but couldn't concentrate. Then I tried the booze, and it didn't taste good, so I just went to bed early.

Now in the right seat of the Argosy, I copied the air traffic control clearance coming over the radio: "Argosy 1430 Zulu is cleared to the Galena Airport via direct Nenana, Victor 452 Galena. Maintain 12,000 feet. Squawk 1513. Departure 118.1." I read back the clearance and requested taxi instructions, and we started moving like Queen Mary coming out of her berth. In the far distance people were holding their ears and scurrying behind doors. With four screaming Rolls-Royce Dart turboprops, popularity was not our forte.

Our departure was wonderfully uneventful, and we turned westward, climbing slowly under broken clouds. Eventually the Fairbanks departure controller said, "Argosy 1430 Zulu, Anchorage Center on 133.1, Good day."

I switched to center frequency and said, "Good morning, Anchorage, Argosy 1430Z is out of 2.7 for 12,000."

The center replied, "Argosy 1430 Zulu, radar contact 12 miles west of Fairbanks." It struck me that the controller's voice was very familiar. Sitting hundreds of miles away in Anchorage, in the dark confines of the Air Traffic Control Center with his face lit by the glow of the computerized radar screen, was a controller with whom I had spoken hundreds of times in years past! Yet we had never met, and I didn't even know his name. But nostalgia closed around me. I idly wondered why he was still there. Certainly, by now he must be past retirement age. He hadn't sounded like a kid 20 years ago. Maybe he retired once, became bored, and decided to return. If so, I hoped his reentry was going smoother than mine.

Harry Barr nursing Argosy 30Z with oil.

After a while, below me, the Minto Flats were passing under the right wing. It is a large, poorly drained land mass with lots of winding sloughs, lakes, waterfowl, scrub spruce, muskeg, and mosquitoes. Nearby was the native village of Minto; the villagers at times hunted muskrats. In the spring, when the previous season's grass was dry and just before the new grass sprouted, they would set fire to it along the riverbanks to chase out the little critters. The BLM used to call them "ratter fires" and wound up hiring the Minto fire crew to put them out.

Every spring there had been a tug of war between the BLM and the ratters of Minto. One year, the BLM went so far as to not hire the people from Minto to put out their own fires. It had been a drastic step. One spring the retardant bombers were on their way to a fire near Manley Hot Springs when the fire control officer, in a Cessna, spotted a ratter in a canoe floating down a slough setting the dry grass on fire. He directed an 800-gallon F7F Tigercat air tanker to salvo his load on him, which he did. The retardant was white borate, which simultaneously put out the fire and swamped the canoe in shallow water. It was an abhorrent act and not one of BLM's best PR moves. Today it would have made national news headlines.

Eventually, we came up on the village of Tanana near the junction of the Yukon and Tanana Rivers. Thirty-two years ago, in 1956 when Alaska was still a territory, BLM had sent me there for four days to research the Territorial Records for several mining claims because Tanana was the seat of the Fourth Judicial District of Alaska. That day it had been almost 40 below zero and kind of dark with patchy ice fog. Since I was new to Alaska and the BLM, this was my first flight of any consequence into the bush, and it would serve as my introduction to "the way we do things up here." I wound up being the only passenger in a Twin Beech, which was the same kind of airplane I had been jumping out of several weeks previously, only somewhat rattier looking. The pilot had also unnerved me. He communicated by grunting; had a dark, heavy beard, and glaring eyes; and was about 6'3" tall. He wore a huge parka with a wolf-fur-rimmed hood; pictures of our Neanderthal ancestors flashed into my mind.

The airplane had no seats in the passenger cabin. It was full of cargo, piled within two feet of the ceiling. My seat was next to the pilot in the cockpit, and I was directed (via grunting sounds) to crawl over the cargo and sit down in it. Someone shut the door from the outside, the engines started, and without ceremony we took off for Tanana. The airplane's cabin heater appeared to work only marginally, and when we plunked down at Tanana, my toes were getting numb. I squirmed my way aft over the cargo to the top of the door because I was claustrophobic and couldn't wait to get out. Outside, someone suddenly yanked it open, catching me by surprise, and I departed the airplane headfirst onto the frozen snow. After retrieving my bag, he slammed the door shut; the pilot, who had never shut down an engine, spun the Beech around, sandblasting me with snow, and pulled out onto the runway. A moment later he was gone—a grunting aberration disappearing into the gloom. There was dead silence. I turned to my "baggage handler," and he grinned (no teeth), pointed to a small building, which I assumed was some sort of roadhouse (only with no road), and shuffled off.

The repository for the Official Territorial Records of the Fourth Judicial District of Alaska was an abandoned two-hole outhouse in a snowbank behind the roadhouse. To reach the records, it had taken me an hour of shoveling to clear away the snow piled against the door. After three days combing through pages of land deeds, etc. while sitting at the roadhouse dining table, I returned to Fairbanks.

Fire 119

During my 14-year absence, Alaska had cycled through a prolonged period of low-intensity wildfire seasons. Over the barbecue, from people who had not been here in "yesteryear," I encountered opinions that Alaska really didn't have fire seasons of any real consequence. I told them in jest that that was about to change due to my arrival, and it did. Lightning ignited

A 500-gallon rollagon full of helicopter fuel is ready to be pushed out the back with two 64-ft diameter cargo chutes.

Fire No. 119 near Selawik and about 350 miles west-northwest of Fairbanks fairly early in June. Eventually it started spreading into areas requiring action with the result that a substantial fire control effort materialized requiring supply via paracargo. This fire burned for much of the summer, eventually consuming more than two hundred thousand acres, and provided constant work for our paracargo Argosy. We were in constant demand from many other fires too.

By this time, I had moved to the left seat, and there were two Argosy crews, alternating shifts, each making two paracargo runs to Fire 119 daily. I had settled into a groove and was no longer paranoid about my age. Babcock ran the other crew, and something of a contest developed to see which of us could drop the cargo closest to the center of a target on the ground. It was almost like a game of mammoth lawn darts with 500-gallon Rollagons of jet fuel instead of darts. I started comparing this relatively stress-free work environment to my crisis-loaded years running OAS and concluded that, except for some low odds of unanticipated cataclysmic death, there was no comparison. The cargo-dropping activities on Fire 119 went on for weeks and became one of the prominent missions for us throughout the summer.

A Dynamite Drop

One morning, after the loadmasters had stuffed the Argosy with five Rollagons of jet fuel to drop for helicopters, we were directed to taxi over to a deserted area of the Fort Wainwright Airport, shut down, and take on 4,000 pounds of explosives for fire line construction. The Military Police had the area cordoned off and traffic on the nearby road shut down. A pickup truck full of boxes backed up to the Argosy's rear ramp, which had been lowered to pickup-bed height, and loadmasters in the truck were tossing the boxes of explosive to others standing on the ramp. While watching this, a BLM employee who I didn't know sidled up to me and started talking about how happy he was to be getting rid of the explosives. When I asked why, he stated that they had been storing the stuff for eleven years in an ammunition bunker and it tended to become unstable with age. About that time one of the load-masters missed a catch, and a box tumbled down onto the tarmac with a resounding thwack. I heard someone comment how fortunate we were it hadn't exploded, and I figured the word *fortunate* was somewhat of an understatement.

We were dispatched to a fire about 30 miles northwest of Fort Yukon, which was currently under instrument flight conditions in heavy smoke. Babcock was flying this leg, and I was the copilot. At the completion of the instrument approach, we could barely see the terrain beneath us and cancelled the instrument clearance, continuing on to the fire. The terrain around the Yukon Valley is quite flat so we could live with the marginal forward visibility and eventually located the fire. In the cargo hold, the smoke-jumper loadmasters slid the first fuel Rolligon on roller tracks to the aft lip of the open cargo ramp and attached static lines to the two 64-foot cargo chutes. (Static lines pull the parachutes open after the cargo slides out the back. One end of the line is attached to the cargo chute being dropped, and the other to the aircraft.)

Upstairs on the flight deck, we were maneuvering the Argosy in a slow-flight condition, not much above stall speed, and barely 500 feet above the ground, approaching the drop target in heavy smoke. We were two seconds from communicating the "kick it" order on the intercom when the loadmaster shouted, "Stand by!" upon which we overflew the drop zone, wondering what was happening downstairs.

After a moment of silence from below, Babcock asked what was going on down there, and the loadmaster again shouted, "Stand by!" with no further information. At this point Babcock told the flight engineer to get the hell downstairs and find out what was happening, which he did. A moment later a white-faced flight engineer emerged onto the flight deck and announced that one of the 64-foot cargo chutes had slipped off the cargo and they were trying to keep it from falling out the back and deploying. The accidental deployment of a 64-foot chute attached to the Argosy only 500 feet above ground while just above a stall would result in an unforgettable spectacle, especially when augmented with 4,000 pounds of explosives mixed with 2,500 gallons of jet fuel in addition to the aircraft's regular fuel capacity.

This was a moment for fondling the rosary beads.

A moment later, the loadmaster announced the problem was under control, and we continued with the paracargo operation uneventfully. Some serious alcohol consumption was undertaken in Fairbanks that evening.

Struck by Lightning

I've been struck by lightning several times over the years, but this instance was different. One afternoon we departed Fairbanks headed west for Galena with a cargo of sixty 55-gallon drums of jet fuel. It was a hot day with thunderstorms, and we were climbing out IFR (on instruments) with the Anchorage Center giving us radar traffic vectors.

We could see a cell dead ahead on the weather radar. Although we could see nothing but grey beyond the windscreen, the color started to progressively darken ominously as the medium through which we were passing became denser.

I commented to the copilot that the Center appeared to be guiding us into a storm and asked them to route us around it, but they said they couldn't, due to other air traffic. Moments later a bolt of lightning hit our nose, the impact of which caused a powerful jolt to my rudder pedals. Simultaneously, a chorus of alarms sounded with flashing lights, and we dealt with each, eventually silencing the chaos. At this point, the head loadmaster appeared on the flight deck. He was a big fellow with a heavy Oklahoman accent and intoned, "Jim Thurston, I've seen the light! I've seen the light, and I ain't gonna ride with you *no more!*"

He relayed to me that the loadmasters down in the cargo hold had had quite an experience of their own. The lightning had been a ball-lighting strike which traveled from the front to the rear of the cargo hold, bouncing off both walls of the fuselage and passing only two to three inches above the 60 fuel drums. After landing at Galena, we found no visible aircraft damage, and all systems had returned to normal. While some might say we had been lucky, I realized I had missed a golden opportunity to have some fun. I had good rapport with the head loadmaster, and we joked around a lot. Had I collected myself soon enough after the lightning strike, I could have told the copilot and flight engineer to slump over and play dead while I did the same (with the airplane on autopilot) because I knew the head man would come thundering up to the flight deck to see what had happened. Truly a missed opportunity.

40 |

1989 - 1992

Return to Anchorage

At the close of the 1988 fire season in early September, I relocated to Anchorage, moved into Jan's apartment, and we eventually purchased a home on the Anchorage hillside. Similar to the Boise home, it was a fixer-upper on Prospect Drive, only about a quarter mile removed from our old Kasilof Hills lot, which had been incinerated in the 1971 hillside fire earlier described. (I figured the odds were with me that the hillside certainly wouldn't dare to burn over as frequently every 20 years or so.) I now was basically unemployed during the off-season with free time available to start remodeling, however, from time-to-time OAS would call me out to fly miscellaneous missions.

When the 1989 fire season commenced, I was again flying the Argosy and other aircraft under an arrangement that continued until I retired in May 1992. Also, in the summer of 1989, J.T., having been bit by the Alaska bug, quit his job selling farmers accident insurance in Illinois and moved to Anchorage, where he took up the art of selling title insurance to mortgage brokers. He has a natural sales ability and over the years has convinced me to purchase or do many things I would not have normally considered.

In 1989, before starting our cabin, I rode out to Whiskey Lake with Merle Akers in his airplane. It was late February, but the days were sunny and cold. That winter, there had been an unusual amount of snow, and accessing his cabin was, in itself, a struggle. We socialized with Carl Lind and others at

Hewitt Lake and two days later planned to return to Anchorage. Merle fired up his airplane and planned to create a packed takeoff trail for our departure. Unfortunately, in the deep powder snow, during a taxi turn, his left landing gear failed, and there was other damage to the left-wing tip and propeller tips. It was almost -30°F, and field repairs needed to be initiated. Carl made a quick round trip to Anchorage in his airplane for equipment, and work started to stabilize the airplane. Once stabilized, Carl, Merle, Merle's dog, and myself returned to Anchorage in Carl's airplane. I then departed on a cruise to Mexico while those guys successfully salvaged Merle's airplane.

Having purchased a 40-acre lot on Hewitt Lake 26 years earlier, I figured it was about time to build a small cabin on it, and to enable this, I purchased a Cessna 185 on floats. Hewitt Lake is 75 miles northwest of Anchorage and 45 miles from the nearest road, so flying materials in was the only realistic option. Several years earlier, J.T. had been taught how to fly by Harry Barr in Lincoln, Nebraska, and would be useful for our cabin-building project if he knew how to fly floatplanes, which he didn't, so I taught him.

Moving building materials involved flying with both internal and external loads. External loads were lumber, plywood, etc., which had to be lashed onto the crossbars of the floats. Large 4'x10' plywood sheets with their 40 square-foot surfaces tend to lend a degree of instability to flight and create a minor uncomfortable feeling to the pilot at first exposure, but it goes away after a dozen flights or so. Sixteen-foot-long dimension lumber, even when strapped down with the forward ends only a couple of inches aft of the propeller arc, extend so far aft that during rotation at takeoff the ends drag in the water making it difficult to become airborne. J.T. mastered all these techniques and finally the cabin was enclosed, but not finished, before the snows arrived.

Mount Redoubt Volcano

The 10,200-foot Redoubt Volcano, located on the west side of Cook Inlet in Southcentral Alaska, 108 miles southwest of Anchorage, erupted explosively on over 20 separate occasions between December 14, 1989, and April 21, 1990. Fourteen lava domes were emplaced in the summit area, thirteen of which were subsequently destroyed. In one eruption, the ash plume reached Texas. In another, the Drift River Oil Terminal, located at the foot of Mount Redoubt, was said to have reported on its hourly FAA aviation weather sequence as, "Visibility one-eighth mile in falling rocks." The eruption in 1989 spewed volcanic ash to a height of 45,000 feet and caught KLM Flight 867, a Boeing 747, in its plume, at which time all four engines failed. After the aircraft descended 13,000 feet, the pilots were able to restart them and land safely at Anchorage with their flock of frazzled passengers. The damage to the aircraft was approximately $80 million, and ash blanketed an area of about 7,700

Courtesy of USGS Wikipedia Commons.

sq. miles. This eruption caused other economic losses estimated at over $160 million, making it the second most costly eruption in the U.S.

Alternating snow and ash layers on Merle Aker's storage shed at Whiskey Lake.

One day Mount Redoubt blew its top and I was unavailable because I was flying my Cessna 185 on skis with Jan to our Hewitt Lake cabin. We did not see the eruption because we had been flying under a layer of broken clouds at about 3,000 feet. After landing and while settling in at the cabin, I routinely turned on the CB radio to monitor for local calls, and a friend in a cabin nearby immediately called and asked if I had encountered any fallout during my flight. My first thought was that a hydrogen bomb had been dropped somewhere and World War III was probably underway until she clarified that Mount Redoubt had just had a major eruption, and a huge ash cloud was said to be heading for Anchorage.

Apparently, I had unknowingly narrowly escaped an encounter with it since there was no fallout at Hewitt Lake, but the CB radio network nevertheless came alive with fallout chatter. As time passed, the ash cloud reached Anchorage and gummed up everything, compromising car and other engines of all sorts if they were operated and creating a general mess. It also grounded many of the air force cargo and fighter-interceptor flight operations at Elmendorf Air Force Base next door, along with army flight operations at Fort Richardson.

The situation would not change until it rained and settled the dust, so I figured we would stay at Hewitt Lake until that happened. Four days later it rained, and we flew back to Anchorage. A week or two later it blew up again, and the ash covered the Hewitt-Whiskey Lake area but not Anchorage (where I was at the time), so I had lucked out both times. The volcanic activity, however, turned out to be a godsend for me during the winter since it provided some extra part-time income.

Augustine Island Volcano
(one of my sniffing targets).
*Courtesy of Cyrus Read, Alaska Volcano
Observatory, USGS.*

Shortly after the initial 1989 eruption, The U.S. Geological Survey's Alaska Volcano Observatory wanted to monitor Mount Redoubt and other Cook Inlet volcanos up close with special equipment mounted on an aircraft. Since these volcanos are of the type that can erupt suddenly and catastrophically without warning, they needed to find both an appropriate aircraft and a suitably dumb pilot willing to go sniffing around up close to these active volcanos.

They immediately found me, and I was engaged for about two years sniffing around all the Cook Inlet volcanos (Mount Spur, Mount Redoubt, Mount Iliamna, Mount Saint Augustine, and Mount Douglas). OAS pro-

vided a twin-engine Cessna 402 jerry-rigged to accommodate the sniffing equipment. The Volcano Observatory had set up a special radio frequency over which they could warn me of any eruptions, hopefully in time for me to escape the blast area. One day I tested it and received no answer. I found out later they were on lunch hour and that maybe I shouldn't have called and bothered them.

Due to my extraordinary vibrant personality, I think I became the scientists' favorite pilot (willing to fly next to their explosive volcanos) and was assigned the job of keeping them happy. I cultivated this work —not due to my joy of sniffing, but due to my home being only 100 miles from the job. I could easily see Mount Redoubt out the window of my home office on the Anchorage hillside. When it erupted, I figured I would be called to fly. (My use of the word *sniffing* is misleading.

The mission actually involved flying circles around the volcano in close proximity to it and under the plume. This allowed the spectrograph equipment onboard to peer upward and acquire data far too complicated for me to describe concerning the nature and amount of materials being disgorged.)

Exxon Valdez Oil Spill

On the evening of March 23, 1989, the oil tanker Exxon Valdez departed the port of Valdez, Alaska, bound for Long Beach, California, with 53 million gallons of Prudhoe Bay crude oil onboard. At four minutes after midnight on March 24, the ship struck Bligh Reef, a well-known navigation hazard in Alaska's pristine Prince William Sound. The impact of the collision tore open the ship's hull, causing some 11 million gallons of crude oil to spill into the water. It was the worst oil spill in U.S. history until the Deepwater Horizon spill in 2010. The spill in Alaska covered 1,300 miles of shoreline and killed hundreds of thousands of seabirds, otters, seals, and whales. The catastrophe spawned a major industry for oil spill cleanup personnel, scientists, and of course the inevitable hordes of attorneys. It also provided some work for me.

Prior to my involvement, the U.S. Fish and Wildlife Service (FWS) was in charge of the effort to quantify the spill's impact on waterfowl and the other species in Prince William Sound, such as the mortality count for ducks, eagles, etc. I was told they presented a plan to accomplish this that the U.S. Department of Justice deemed wholly insufficient as a basis for prosecuting Exxon. The FWS plan called for shooting hundreds of ducks with shotguns, tagging their little necks with numbered radio tracking devices, dumping them into the water around Bligh Reef, and monitoring where they floated before either sinking or beaching onshore. Somehow this, along with ducks actually located, would supposedly provide a float/sink ratio basis for the extrapolation of mortality estimates firm enough to hold up in an Exxon lawsuit. The Justice Department, dissatisfied with this plan, took over the project, believing that shotgun pellets in the ducks would make them sink prematurely and compromise the evidence.

Thus, it was deemed that the ducks would be captured and killed by batting them over the head, and to further the reality, they would be dumped into a barrel of North Slope crude oil. After throwing them into Prince William Sound, an aircraft with electronic monitoring equipment would patrol the spill area, detect and locate the bludgeoned, oil-soaked ducks, and gather data on the scene of the disaster. This is where I came in, but when I was told this story, I found it so hard to believe I discounted it.

Because the Interior Department's U.S. Fish and Wildlife Service was involved, OAS provided the aircraft and crew. The aircraft utilized was N780, the infamous Aleutian Goose, a one-of-a-kind heavily modified Grumman Goose with turboprop engines, extended fuselage, and increased fuel capacity configured for offshore wildlife surveys. Dave Henley, who was a Kodiak-born OAS pilot, and I were the crew. A couple of FWS technicians rode in the cabin that was set up with their electronic tracking gear.

The operation involved flying about 500 feet above the water, mainly tracking the shorelines of the mainland and the sound's numerous islands. This went on for several weeks, usually flying 8-hour missions out of Anchorage. Every so often, the technicians would call out, "I've located number 78. He's about 100 feet offshore under our right wing," or "Number 131 is in a tree abeam us near the center of Green Island." I found it interesting that the guys in back could distinguish that some ducks were on a beach, while others still floating, and others up in spruce trees where presumably eagles had deposited them.

Since we had to rerun these surveys over the same areas each day, by the time we finished I was intimately familiar with the intricacies of Prince William Sound. Had I been able to look into the future, I probably would have been able to spot the *MV Wanderlust*—a 42-foot trawler serving on the spill cleanup effort as a medical boat. Before long, it was to be the first boat Jan and I ever purchased—a direct result of an unrelenting sales effort by our son, J.T.

Arctic Search

A survey of bowhead whales in the Arctic Ocean north of the Alaskan coast was scheduled for October of 1991 with Dave Henley and me crewing the Aleutian Goose. Unfortunately, the survey was cancelled, and we joined with other aircraft to search the Arctic Ocean for several people missing on a polar bear survey. To do this, we operated out of the Naval Arctic Research Laboratory (NARL) hangar at Point Barrow. At this latitude and time of year, the days shorten to no sun at all, with only dusk-like visibility, and rapidly keep getting shorter. Each day, we departed Point Barrow northbound into our assigned search area up to 400 miles away. In the search zone, we flew a grid pattern at low altitudes, usually 200 to 500 feet, looking for survivors between the fog banks. The ice below us was not without fissures and stretches of open water.

The usual scenes were of the most desolate, unforgiving environments I had ever encountered, and I was contemplating our being out there with a twin-engine aircraft while wishing we had four engines. To me, it appeared obvious that if we ever went down this far from civilization, it was over. Even though we were an amphibian, if we had to land in the water, the short daylight hours would have prohibited any search effort to reach us before the next day, weather permitting, which was questionable with all the low fog. (The people we were searching for were in a twin-engine aircraft, just like us.) Our sighting of polar bears was numerous. In some areas, their tracks meandered endlessly on the snow-covered ice. Because they are carnivores, we paid particular attention to any converging track patterns that might lead to a source of protein.

In Barrow, the relatives of some of the missing people were hard to encounter after returning from the search with no results each day. We were met with hopes we had to dash. One of them tended to blame us for operating in an environment so hostile it promoted others (like their loved ones) to do the same, inferring we were somehow irresponsible. She was borderline hostile.

One evening, in our Barrow hotel, Dave and I were clutching our beers while we relaxed watching the TV news. The news commentator came on with an article about the government's oiled-duck survey in Prince William Sound and how the irate public was demanding an investigation. We looked at each other, and Dave said, "Shit! I think we may be un-indicted conspirators!" Fortunately, we never heard anything more about it. After two weeks the unsuccessful search effort was terminated. Dave and I returned to Anchorage, glad to be home. The subjects of our search were probably lost forever.

41

1992

My Last Official OAS Act

At 5:30 p.m. on May 24, 1992, I had just returned to OAS-Anchorage from Dillingham, Alaska, in the "volcano sniffer" after ferrying two VIPs back from a meeting. It was after hours, and OAS was locked up with no other souls around. For this I was grateful since the moment was poignant —it was the last moment of my

My sayonara flight log.

30-year run as a federal employee with service dating back to 1953, 39 years prior. Happy that I now qualified for retirement in spite of Don Hodel's desires, I stood on the uninhabited aircraft ramp wrapped in nostalgia for a few moments before going into the office. Soft, late-afternoon sunlight and a calm wind added to the mood. After unlocking the door, I deposited the aircraft and office keys on their hooks, placed my final OAS flight log on the dispatcher's desk, and departed the premises. This was my last act as a federal employee. Being one who favors clean breaks in life's chapters, I have not stepped foot on those grounds since.

My plan was to celebrate by going home, getting cleaned up, and stepping out for a quiet, two-martini dinner with Jan. I don't remember where, but Harry Barr, whom I assumed was back home in Nebraska, materialized out of nowhere and ushered me into a surprise retirement party at a hotel filled with acquaintances. This was a major contrast to the feelings I had just experienced on the OAS ramp and was greatly appreciated. I enjoyed reliving some of my past experiences with friends, many of whom I had not seen for years. It was a perfect ending.

Hewitt Lake

Courtesy of Google Earth.

Our Hewitt Lake cabin became my favorite location for after-retirement relaxation and general, all-around puttering. It is remote— 75 miles west of Anchorage next to the foothills of the Alaska Range with the highest mountains in North America in view from our cabin's outhouse. Summer access is via floatplane and boat while winter access is via ski-plane and snow machine. The lake is three miles long and about 115 feet deep in front of our lot. Abundant rainbow and lake trout were wiped out in the early 1960s by the human introduction of northern pike into the nearby tributary river system. The forest is mixed-wood mature birch and white spruce and is inhabited by black bears, brown bears, and moose. In the fall, red salmon come to spawn, and the dead fish litter the shoreline, which in turn attracts numerous bears. At the time of our cabin construction, there were a total of only about 16 cabins on the lake, and solitude reigned.

Hewitt and Whiskey Lakes are next to each other and connect with a snow machine/ATV trail. On the overview photo, our property includes the 5-acre pond on the left side of Hewitt Lake while Carl Lind's place is on the opposite side where he constructed a runway connecting the lake with an adjacent muskeg bog. Merle Aker's lot is in the secluded cove on the east side of Whiskey Lake. Both Carl and Merle had constructed cabins during my 14-year tenure in Idaho, so I was a latecomer to the party.

First Winter Visit to Our Cabin

After purchasing a Cessna 185, J.T. and I had constructed our cabin during late fall of 1991. By the first heavy snow in mid-October, it was enclosed but lacked some insulation when we had to quit and switch from airplane floats to skis. Being deep, Hewitt Lake takes a while to freeze up in the fall, and so I didn't try to access it until late December, alone in an airplane packed full of essentials to survive the cold weather in a shell of a cabin not yet totally insulated.

Arriving over the lake, I checked for signs of overflow and could see none, which really meant nothing. There was an unknown depth of snow on the lake. Overflow is common because lake water seeps up through cracks and accumulates on the ice surface under the snow, generally invisible from above until you step or land a ski-plane on it. Leaving an airplane sitting with its skis underwater could result in it being frozen in, especially when it is seriously cold. Thus, for the winter's first arrival, I landed by touching down and fast-taxiing for half a mile or so in front of our lot, never stopping, and then I took off again to circle and view the ski tracks from the air. They were full of water except for one 30-foot-long dry spot, so I landed a second time immediately next to the water-filled tracks, fast-taxied, and stopped a few feet abeam the dry spot with my skis not in the overflow water. At this time of year, the days are only about six and a half hours long, and I had already used up four of them getting ready to go and flying here, so I had a lot of work to do before dark. The temperature was -12°F.

At this point, the drill involved strapping on snowshoes, trudging to the cabin, lighting a fire, digging out the snow machine, creating a snow machine trail, and returning to the airplane to start hauling freight. Creating the snow machine trail was very difficult because on the land the powder snow was at least five feet deep, and I kept getting stuck, whereas on the lake it was only about two feet deep. Once, while trying to wrestle the snow machine out of a hole it made for itself, I managed to sink up to my chest next to it, and I still remember the frustrating feeling of having sunk so deep I could not even see over its seat. It took over an hour of physical labor to break in a trail for this relatively short distance, and it now was almost dark.

After unloading and securing the freight, I secured the airplane by removing the battery and placing covers over the wings, windscreen, horizontal stabilizers, and engine compartment. These covers prevent frost and snow from adhering to the wings and tail surfaces and were necessary because airplanes don't fly well (or at all) with frosted wings. The engine cover was heavily insulated to hold heat for later when a Thermax heater would be actuated to warm the engine prior to departure. (The battery would reside in the warm cabin until departure time to prevent losing its charge during below-zero weather. In several instances over the years, I fired up the airplane in near 40-below temperatures, took off, and returned to Anchorage.)

That evening the temperature dropped to -28°F, and staying warm in my semi-insulated cabin was a challenge since the paltry amount of firewood I had stored had not been thoroughly dried and burned only reluctantly. The next morning over coffee, I contemplated my to-do list, the first of which was to cut some burnable firewood. Due to the difficulty of snowshoeing through the deep powder snow, I harvested a small spruce tree near the cabin, split the logs into thinner pieces and stored them in the cabin near the fire place to at least get a start drying out.

Then I undertook to construct a snow runway, which is a means to avoid overflow problems during the winter's season. This involved running the snow machine back and forth over an area on the lake about 50 feet wide and 1,200 feet long to pack down the snow, following which it set up into a firmer mass. Next, I attached a WWII army metal cot frame and bed springs behind the snow machine with ropes and dragged it back and forth over the compacted runway, neatly soothing it out. (Carl Lind had taught me this, and it worked magically.) The snow, compacted by the snow machine and smoothed over by the army cot, would set up suitably and eliminate the overflow problems. Afterward, I cut and placed spruce bows along both runway edges every 200 feet to provide definition under flat-light and whiteout conditions during landing approaches. Since, during my absences in Anchorage, snow would cover this work of art, it might have to be re-done, but at least the original base would be there.

The Great Snapback

One winter there was a very high snow accumulation, and several cabins in the general area collapsed (although I believe not at Hewitt Lake). I contemplated the five feet of snow on the roof of my little cabin and started imagining what it would be like if it collapsed while I was in it—perhaps asleep in the loft. It could be deadly, so I contrived a plan to deal with it. In Anchorage I purchased 300 feet of 3/8" nylon line, and on my next trip back I undertook to implement my scheme. This involved using my extension ladder and the Danforth anchor borrowed from my skiff.

Climbing up to the end of the cabin roof ridge, I tossed the anchor onto the uppermost section of the snow mass and tossed the remaining 200 feet of rope down to the lakeshore 30 feet below. (The cabin sits on a ridge immediately overlooking the lake.) The plan was to pull the snow mass on that half of the roof loose by yanking the line hard with the snow machine racing across the lake. Theoretically, pulled by the anchor, the whole snow mass would slide off the roof in a spectacular avalanche, and then I could do the same to the other half. (This is what wilderness puttering is all about.)

Impressed with the ingenious nature of my plan and brimming with great expectations, I tied the other end of the 200-foot nylon pull line to the snow machine and took off across the lake at full throttle. Shortly after, the machine slowed down, and seconds later it stopped altogether with the throttle still wide open. When I released the throttle, I suddenly started going backward at an accelerating speed and then abruptly stopped. The ability of nylon line to stretch was amazing. Looking back at the cabin, I could see the line had not come off the roof, although it had slid about two-thirds of the way down. The snow mass remained unmoved, and I was powerless to find out what happened until it slid off next spring.

In June, I discovered the anchor had pierced through one of the metal roof panels and had ripped it open (much like gutting a fish) down to where it encountered a major crossbeam, which is what had stopped me. Fortunately, the upper point of the metal gash was just over the outside deck and did not compromise the interior. I recovered my anchor and replaced the roof panel while mentally cataloging yet another of my life's many debacles.

Feeding the Beaver

The five-acre pond on our lot included a family of beavers. We quietly coexisted for a number of years until papa beaver started a logging operation on the smaller birch trees near the cabin. He seemed attracted to the area because my snow machine trails were easier to traverse than the deep, unbroken snow. Often, I saw him waddling along one of my trails dragging a part of one of my beloved young birch trees, and while this pissed me off, I had no desire to harm him.

Following him one day, I found the beaver hole in my pond near the shore to which he was transporting his food, and this prompted an idea. There were several large birch trees in close proximity to this hole, each containing weeks' worth of succulent, delicious branches, not to mention a vast inventory of beaver-building materials. Cutting one of them down, I carefully aimed the tree to land on top of his hole, thereby holding down to a minimum his calorie requirement to find new food. Weeks later, after he had removed the branches (and was considerably fatter), I returned and sawed up the main stem for firewood. It was a classic win-win situation (except possibly for the beaver's unhealthy weight gain.)

Local Trivia

I had chosen the name, "Bear Wallow" for my CB radio handle in the local area. This was the name of the Forest Service lookout in Idaho I had worked out of in 1953, and it held kind of a wilderness nostalgia. The topography of the 40-acre lot beyond the pond was a hillside of successively higher hollows, thus making me contemplate changing the name to "Bear Wallow Hollow." To fight the mosquitoes, I built half a dozen swallow houses and installed them around the cabin. So, what would you think of, "Swallow Hollow at Bea Wallow"? I don't think so, and the name remains "Bear Wallow."

Anyhow, while not one damn swallow ever showed up, four "camp robber" birds did. They became very friendly companions, always looking for a handout, of course, and I made them happy. One morning they tried joining me at the table to watch me eat, but one pooped on my pancakes, and the others kept flying into my windows, so I had to keep them out. When riding the snow machine or ATV, one occasionally rode along on my shoulder. I named them after Donald Duck's nephews: Huey, Dewey, Louie, and Smirnoff—the last because I was one duck short and loved vodka. One day visitors stopped by, and while on the deck pointing to a landmark across the lake, Dewey landed on my pointed index finger looking for a handout. The visitors loved it. Later I checked the literature and found these camp robbers were actually Canada Jays.

The CB radio provided interesting company. I could listen in on the conversations amongst other remote cabins around our part of the country. Some had unique names like "Chicken Coop" or "Little House on the Prairie." One winter morning I nearly broke up hearing the following dialogue:

"Gertrude, you got your ears on?"

"Yeah, Agnus. Good morning. What's up?"

"Do you got a chainsaw available? Ours broke, and Virgil needs one out on the lake. He's ice fishing."

"Sure. How soon does he need it?"

"Well, you see, he's hooked onto one that's too big to fit through the hole, and he needs to cut it out bigger. So I think he needs it pretty soon!"

Renegade Moose

One sunny winter day I landed and taxied toward the two ice tie-down lines I had installed for the airplane but had to stop because an enormous bull moose was standing directly between them staring at me. We were nose-to-nose about 50 feet apart. Several times I tried to get him to move off by revving the engine, but this had no effect, so I gave up and left the airplane in place until later.

The next day, Jan decided to take a walk on the lake while I split firewood at the cabin. The snow on the lake was firm enough not to require snowshoes. The day was marvelously sunny, and she had progressed far out on the lake when she looked back and saw a monster bull moose was a couple of hundred yards behind and apparently following her. She increased her pace, but the moose was closing the distance, and now she became very concerned. After splitting wood for a while, I happened to look up and saw my wife way out on the lake plodding along, but a hundred yards behind her was that huge bull moose, apparently stalking her! I jumped onto the snow machine and raced down to the lake to pick her up, passing the moose that essentially ignored me with its eyes focused on Jan. Scooping her up, we returned to the cabin, and the second part of our moose episode was over.

Earlier, J.T. had informed us he planned to come out to the lake from Anchorage later that day in his airplane to join us for a day or two. "Later that day" finally came and went, and night arrived with no sign of J.T., so we assumed he had changed his mind and wasn't coming, which was not an unusual phenomenon. Later, Jan and I were heavy into a game of gin rummy when we heard the sound of an airplane circling overhead in the darkness. Forgetting I had the airplane battery staying warm with us in the cabin, I jumped on the snow machine and raced down to the airplane so I could call him on the airplane radio (if it was him) and find out what the hell he was doing.

Realizing my mistake upon reaching the airplane, I returned to the cabin, grabbed the battery, and raced back to the airplane. By the time I got the battery hooked up so I could call him, the sound of the airplane overhead had quit. There was just silence. I called anyway, but there was no reply. Frustrated, and with frozen fingers, I returned again to the cabin where we settled in, wondering what was going on. Before long, J.T.'s voice came over the cabin CB radio—he was calling from Carl Lind's cabin across the lake!

Night Ski Landing

So, it turned out J.T. had a story of his own. His planned arrival was to be when the full moon, scheduled for this clear night, would be out and thoroughly illuminating the lake for landing. (I have been out on the lake under these conditions, and you can literally read a newspaper under that light.) His one minor problem—he had read the schedule wrong, and the moon had not yet risen. Meanwhile, while he circled above and while I was running back and forth like a chicken with its head cut off, Carl was at his airplane installing a Thermax heater for his planned departure in the morning. Hearing the overhead airplane, he turned on his radio, called, and J.T. answered. They discussed the situation, and Carl volunteered to place his snow machine at one end of his snow runway with its light shining down the landing path, and J.T. undertook the landing.

The airplane swooped in above Carl's head, and at the same instant, a monster bull moose materialized out of the darkness and crossed the runway inches below J.T.'s skis. It was a very near miss, and I'll bet money it was the same moose we'd already been encountering. Eventually the full moon did materialize—it was gorgeous—and the moose went away somewhere; we all settled down for a relaxing evening while I tried to nurse my blood pressure back down to normal.

Bear Tales

I was told the nearby Yenlo Hills were a prime breeding area for grizzly bears. I was also told that years ago someone in our area with an axe to grind went around and smeared bacon grease on the cabin doors of folks who displeased him. The bears wreaked havoc on those cabins. I don't know how accurate these stories are, but for years I encountered no real bear problems at Hewitt Lake, although I was aware they were thick during the fall red salmon spawning period. During the summer and fall when traveling through the brush on our lot, I carried a Mossberg 12-gauge pump shotgun loaded with slugs on my shoulder and never had an occasion to use it. Other than that, I was unarmed.

One year I decided to enlarge my land holdings and purchased half of an adjacent 40-acre lot. Part of the deal was that I had to pay for and provide the required subdivision survey. I hired surveyors in Talkeetna, a community 70 miles north of Anchorage, and flew two of them to the lake where they worked for three days. I was doing the cooking, and one morning I served pancakes and bacon. After eating the meal, I found to my horror that instead of using PAM cooking spray on the frying pan, I had sprayed it with Johnson's wax. The two yellow spray cans are quite similar. None of us had noticed the difference, so if you ever run out of PAM cooking spray, you know what to do.

At the end of the first day, the surveyors left their transit and equip-ment set up on the partially surveyed subdivision line, figuring no rain was forecast. The next morning, they found that while it hadn't rained, a bear had attacked their equipment and damaged the transit, requiring me to fly it into Anchorage for repairs. Eventually, we received title to the land and now have a total of 60 acres with about 1,400 feet of lake frontage.

On one of my last visits, I discovered our cabin had been ransacked by a bear. It appeared that he first tried entering through the Texture 1-11 plywood wall next to the metal door since a large area of the exte-rior plywood had been stripped off, revealing the interior framing and insulation. At this point, instead of attacking the inner wall, he turned his attention to the metal door, which was locked and hinged outward. Instead, he pushed it inward through the door jam, bent it double, and stomped on it for good measure. Inside the cabin he tore the kitchen cabinets off the walls, overturned the propane stove, overturned the sofa, created a general mess, and shit on everything for special effect.

I was unable to figure out what attracted him in the first place since aside from things like salt and pepper, there was nothing else I would think attracted bears. Also, the cabin had supposedly been bear-proofed because we had nail mats in front of both doors. (A nail mat is a partial sheet of plywood through which numerous nails have been pounded in such a manner that a bear would have to stand on the nails to position himself in front of a door. They don't always work.)

I flew home devastated that my little refuge had been so violated, and I did not want to ever return. J.T., Jan, and a friend flew out and cleaned up the cabin while I remained home sulking. After replacing the door, J.T. coated a pressurized bottle of bear spray with peanut butter and hung it by a string in front of the door. The next trip out, he found the bottle had tooth punctures, and apparently the bear had received a healthy jolt of bear spray in his mouth. We did not have problems after that, however, there were lots of other bear problems at our lake. Most of the cabins had been broken into, and at one, I could see several large craters 4 to 6 feet in diameter dug in their front yard. In the background the cabin front door was hanging by its hinges. Another neighbor told me there had been a dead salmon on his dock, and instead of snatching it off the dock surface, the bear came up underneath and tore a hole through the dock to get to it.

Carl Lind told me what happened at his place. Having gone on a family trip, he allowed some friends to use his cabin to go bear hunting. They arrived in a charter plane, settled into the cabin, and decided there was enough time to go on a hunt. Having seen no bears, they returned to find the cabin door had been broken and the cabin interior trashed. They repaired and reset the door, cleaned up the cabin, and settled in for the evening. Suddenly, the bear appeared outside and was trying to get in, so they shot it through the door.

My trip frequency to Hewitt Lake began to dwindle. The bear problems, along with our discovery of Halibut Cove, 100 air miles south of Anchorage, had altered the direction of my life's energy.

42

1993 - 1995

Our Discovery of Halibut Cove

One day Jan told me she wanted me to fly her and drop her off at a five-day watercolor painting class in Halibut Cove. I told her I'd heard of it but didn't know where it was and looked it up on a chart. I was surprised to see it was tucked in off Kachemak Bay across from Homer. In the mid-1960s, Carl Lind and I had flown our Taylor-

Halibut Cove

craft on floats over much of the bay, but somehow Halibut Cove had never come to our attention. Arriving over the Cove in our Cessna 185, we were both taken by the beauty of the setting, and I was amazed I had never stumbled upon it in the past. I think I must have always been too busy going somewhere else. I dropped Jan off at the Quiet Place Lodge and returned to Anchorage, planning to pick her up in five days. Three days later she called and said this place was really interesting and suggested I plan to stay a couple of days when I came down, which I did. For two days we toured the Cove, met a few folks, and started discussing how nice it might be to have a small weekend cabin here, unaware that land was virtually unavailable at the time. Halibut Cove is hemmed in by native-owned land, the Kachemak Bay State Park, and hardly any private holdings were for sale.

The MV Wanderlust

J.T. used to play poker, and one day a player mentioned he had a boat for sale in the Anchorage boat yard. When J.T. checked it out, he decided we absolutely had to buy it. During that quiet afternoon in March 1993, I was home dutifully paying bills when he called, all excited because he had found a 42-foot boat for sale. It was a reasonable price, and he said I needed to come down to the Anchorage boat yard and check it out immediately. I told him no—everybody knows a boat that size would be just a big hole to pour dollars into, and I wanted nothing to do with it. Satisfied I had successfully cut that potential financial hemorrhage off at the pass, I went back to my bills.

Before long, Jan called. She had been downtown; after talking to me, J.T. had called her and talked her into looking at the boat, which she had. She said she liked the boat, and I really should come down and check it out. She also liked the boat's name: *Wanderlust*. It was now apparent that forces were amassing to overthrow my resistance, and I should get the hell down there to protect my interests, so I capitulated and hurried down to the boat yard.

The boat was out of the water on blocks. It was late March, and there were still about two feet of snow on it with alternating layers of Mount Redoubt's volcanic ash. My first impression was that it was huge compared to what I had been expecting. J.T. told me it was 42 feet long with a 13-foot beam (width), and it appeared to my uninformed mind like a lot of boat for the $65,000 asking price, considering I knew people were paying $20,000 to $30,000 for small boats in the 20-foot range. He said the owner had leased it out as a medical boat for the oil cleanup on Prince William Sound.

Using the built-in pulldown ladder at the stern, we boarded the vessel and took a tour inside. The stern stateroom contained two queen beds, a closet, and a full bath with bathtub. The cabin contained the steering station and controls as well as a kitchen with a refrigerator, sink, and dining table for six. The forward stateroom had a double-decker bunk bed and bathroom with shower. Up top, the bridge contained a second steering/control station. The engine room, accessed via a hatch in the main cabin floor, contained two diesel engines, a 5KW generator, and lots of other machinery beyond my comprehension. The boat was loaded with teak, inside and out. I was impressed but made no commitment.

As time went by, I couldn't get my mind off the boat, plus J.T. kept the pressure on, using his best salesman techniques. In the same sense that two plus two equals four, my mind started to rationalize that the *Wanderlust* plus Halibut Cove equaled "Buy it!" and began to fantasize about Jan and me taking carefree trips around the pristine waters of Kachemak Bay and Prince William Sound from our comfy little cabin in Halibut Cove. It would be a new world for both of us, notwithstanding the reality that we could barely spell *boat*, much less operate and maintain a vessel that size. My only boat experience had been operating our 16-foot skiff at Hewitt Lake. Prior to that, in the few instances I had happened to be on a small boat, there had always been an alpha-fish personality on board who automatically assumed command with the unspoken understanding that myself and others should sit back and keep our hands off the controls.

A month went by, and I finally relented and told Jan I couldn't stand it anymore and wanted to buy the *Wanderlust*. I was flabbergasted when she blandly informed me that she was no longer interested, which I couldn't understand since she had been so gung-ho over the idea in the first place. Following this setback, it was a most natural phenomenon that a realignment occurred featuring J.T. and me vs. Jan on the *Wanderlust* issue. More time passed, Jan caved, and we finally bought the boat. After shoveling the snow off the boat and inspecting things in more detail, it became obvious that considerable woodwork on the teak was in order due to its general disrepair, so I hired a cabinetmaker of excellent reputation named Charlie Horsman. To cope with the problem that aside from the engines, I didn't know what I was looking at when gazing upon most of the engine-room machinery, I hired an ex-navy guy named Chris Christensen, who appeared to have great mechanical knowledge coupled with the disposition of MacGyver. (He told me his navy experience had largely been working closely with Admiral Rickover, so I hoped he knew his way around a non-nuclear boat.)

The proud, naive new owners.

Meanwhile, Jan and I hired a Coast Guard Auxiliary fellow to homeschool us on the ABCs of marine boating so we wouldn't look like complete idiots when time came to actually go somewhere in the boat. On June 27, the boat was ready to launch on a midday high tide, and we planned to sail to Halibut Cove with a stopover in Homer. I had hired a very large truck/crane to pick up the *Wanderlust* and lower it into the water. After lifting it and while transporting the dangling boat toward the water's edge, Chris almost had apoplexy when the right-front wheel of the truck came off the ground and the crane threatened to roll over and fall 20 feet into Cook Inlet. I pictured the *Wanderlust* sinking with the truck/crane on top of it in front of the crowd of onlookers, with follow-up on the Channel 2 TV evening news. But fortunately, it turned out OK, and the boat was gently lowered into the water. It had been close, though.

At this point, Chris climbed down onto the boat to check for leaks and started screaming that water was gushing into the lazarette (the aft-most boat compartment). The hull drain plug had either popped out or had not been installed. I fretted that now we may have to lift a boat out that was already heavier than when we put it in and again risk a rollover, but the drain plug was located, and the problem solved. After disconnecting the crane, I paid the operator, and we all boarded the boat for our initial cruise. Aside from Jan and me, others included J.T., Chris (as temporary marine mechanic), and the Coast Guard fellow as captain. Just as we were about to depart, a beluga whale materialized a foot or two behind the boat and seemed to be sniffing us. To Jan, it appeared to be an omen for smooth sailing. After all the unanticipated crane drama and flooding, I didn't know what the hell it meant but was glad to finally get underway.

Our planned departure time was selected to take advantage of the swift Cook Inlet current that was outgoing and would add numerous knots to our boat's slow cruising speed of eight knots. The current neatly swept us south past the mouth of the turbulent Turnagain Arm and abeam the northern Kenai Peninsula shore where conditions were calmer. Later, when the tide reversed, we were, for a while, making virtually no headway in the incoming current. After a couple of hours, Chris put his arm around my shoulders in a fatherly manner and said, "Jim, it's always a good idea to periodically check the engine room and make sure everything is in order, so I'm gonna lift the hatch, climb down, and make sure all's OK." Seconds after he descended below, he was screaming, *"We've got a f**king leak! Shut the port engine down!!!"* This was followed by, *"Get me a goddamned pencil. Now! Now! Hurry! Hurry! Sonofabitch!!*

From the intensity of the screaming, I thought we were on the verge of sinking and was picturing a wall of water surging into the engine room! With shaky hands I located a pencil and passed it down to him, thinking that instead of finding a pencil, maybe we should be finding our life vests? What was he possibly going to do with a pencil? Document details for possible later litigation? Take notes for a fascinating chapter in the *How Not to Run a Boat* book he was going to write? Actually, he stopped the leak by sticking the pencil into a hole on the corroded manifold for the port engine's seawater cooling system. Moments later he emerged out of the engine room, no longer screaming but muttering profanities, with water droplets dangling from his nose, chin, and eyeglass rims. He then announced, "I got the f**ker stopped —for now! Fire up the port engine, and let's see if it holds." It held, and we celebrated our "non-sinking" with a round of Budweiser's for all.

That evening as we cruised down the Cook Inlet, the sky was clear, the water calm, and it was a long, sunny June 27 day. Jan, J.T., and I spent time on the flying bridge taking in the beauty of the setting and wondering if another mechanical surprise would materialize. Several hours later, it did. Jan and I had retired to the master stateroom and snuggled into our luxurious queen beds, hardly believing we were actually underway in such splendid comfort in our own boat! About 4:00 a.m., I awoke and lay there, peacefully contemplating the reassuring throb of the twin diesel engines.

After a while I began to sense a very minor hint of diesel fumes and wondered if it was just my imagination. Eventually I couldn't sense any fumes at all and discounted it. Since the sun had already gained considerable altitude, I got up and decided to check the main cabin. The Coast Guard guy was at the helm alone while J.T. and Chris were probably asleep in the forward stateroom. We were coming up abeam Homer on our port side and about 20 minutes from making port when suddenly there was a loud *thunk*, and we lost propulsion on our starboard side. Chris immediately exploded out of the forward stateroom in a manner that reminded me of Captain Hazelwood's sudden rush from his stateroom to the Exxon Valdez's bridge after it collided with Bligh Reef.

While our starboard engine was still running, apparently the starboard propeller was not turning, and we made our grand entry into Homer Harbor limping on the port engine. Chris descended into the engine room and could smell an exhaust leak, plus he observed the 18-foot-long starboard propeller shaft had separated from the engine coupling. It was now apparent that the planned stopover in Homer would be a couple of days at least to deal with our rapidly increasing inventory of colorful malfunctions. (I had an urge to say something to Jan about her beluga-whale-smooth-sailing omen but didn't have the heart to pop her bubble.) Fortunately, we had prepositioned an airplane at Homer to return Jan, J.T., and the Coast Guard gentlemen to Anchorage, which I did, making a brief Homer-Anchorage-Homer round trip while Chris worked to address our assortment of maintenance problems.

During my absence, Chris found Cecil Cheatwood, a local diver who frequented Homer Harbor performing underwater boat maintenance and repair. Cecil found that the propeller shaft needed work and removed it. Chris also removed parts of the leaking exhaust manifold and seawater fittings, both of which would have to be repaired in Anchorage. We hauled the propeller shaft to Otto's Machine Works in Homer, left it, then flew to Anchorage with the other parts. Since Chris had good connections in Anchorage, we were able to fly back to Homer that evening with both parts repaired. After working on the boat for two days in Homer, I came to know Cecil, and before long it was apparent I'd get to know him even better because the boat required many dives. Weeks later I realized that I had used Cecil so much he had memorized my phone number. (When a marine salvage and maintenance diver knows your phone number by heart, that's got to be a bad omen.) By this time, I was contemplating changing the name of the boat from *Wanderlust* to *My Lemon*.

With repairs completed, Chris and I sailed to the public dock at Halibut Cove. This small dock was built by the state of Alaska, was unattended, and had no water or electricity. Chris was also an experienced boat captain, and I had been unaware of this at the time I hired the Coast Guard gentleman, but by now it was a moot point. Thus, it was Chris who taught me how to handle the *Wanderlust*, and he began by having me practice docking the boat repeatedly. On the third try, I lost control of the boat because the starboard throttle control suddenly became unresponsive. Chris lunged to the controls and prevented impact with the dock, after which we found that, once again, the starboard propeller shaft had disconnected from the engine coupling. This time, Chris donned a marine survival suit and did some underwater propeller fixing that allowed us to operate on both engines. Eventually he had to return to Anchorage, so we took the boat back to Homer, and I flew both of us home.

The Community of Halibut Cove

Halibut Cove (often referred to as "the Cove") is on the southern Kenai Peninsula 115 air miles due south of Anchorage and about 10 miles east of Homer across Kachemak Bay. It is a tiny village situated around the sheltered waters between Ishmailoff Island and the mainland. Although I had flown around Kachemak Bay frequently in the early 1960s, I had never entered Halibut Cove nor was I really aware of it because I was always going to a different destination. Actually, my only awareness of the Cove was associated with the name Senator Clem Tillion, which I had heard frequently on Anchorage news broadcasts in regard to state legislative activities.

When Jan and I first arrived in our floatplane, we were struck by the unique flavor of the Cove's scenery, waterfront boardwalks, cabins, and clear, jade-green waters. It was like an idyllic scene out of Disneyland, and an unattended state dock presented us a great place to base the *Wanderlust*. The Cove residents were primarily artists, commercial fishermen, a restaurant operator, retirees, and builders of docks, cabins, houses, and boardwalks. There were no roads, and skiffs were the primary transportation within the Cove. There were only about a dozen winter residents, but the population grew to perhaps 80 during the summer. We immediately began contemplating acquiring a small lot with the hope of someday building a weekend cabin on it since the floatplane we owned took only about an hour to travel to the Cove from Anchorage.

MV Wanderlust

A few weeks later, the *Wanderlust* was moored at the public dock, and I was getting more acquainted with Halibut Cove and its residents. One day, a stranger came down the dock, walked up to me, introduced himself as Grant Fritz, and inquired if I was Jim Thurston. When I said yes, Grant told me he lived in Kasilof (on the Kenai Peninsula) but also had a place here in the Cove. He said a Kasilof neighbor named Pat McElroy had heard that I had shown up in Halibut Cove; Pat had told him, if he ever ran across me, be sure to have me tell him my fire story. I responded, "Fire story? What fire story?"

Grant said, "The story about how you managed to burn down your own U.S. Army tent while on fire guard duty during a winter bivouac at Fort Richardson in 1957 when you guys were going through basic training!" I only vaguely remembered McElroy's name and was amazed that almost 40 years later, I might have generated a reputation across the outer reaches of Alaska for this colorful incident. Because my civilian occupation at the time had been a fire control forester with the Bureau of Land Management, the escapade had been somewhat awkward and not something I wanted to broadcast. When I told Grant the tale, he laughed so hard I was concerned he might wet himself, but he didn't. My introduction to the Cove was off to a rocky start, and I wondered how McElroy came to discover I was here. Later, I learned that Halibut Cove had a highly efficient "tom-tom" system, which was, in effect, their precursor to our modern-day Facebook.

Clem Tillion

During her watercolor class visit previous to my introduction to the Cove, Jan had become friends with Diana Tillion, the renowned Halibut Cove artist who taught the class that Jan had attended and specialized in painting with octopus' ink. One evening, Jan was at a social gathering at Diana's home and met her husband, Clem, who impressed her as a memorable character.

Courtesy of Roy Corral.

My first encounter with Clem was when I caught a ride on the *Stormbird*, the mail boat he operated twice a week to Homer. I was a passenger sitting on the bench seat behind him in the wheelhouse, taking in the unique characteristics of this individual: red hair, probably of Scottish descent, very loud voice, about 10 years older than me, saltier than Morton's salt, a walking encyclopedia of the local area's history as well as history in general, and apparently one of Alaska's premiere pioneers. At one point he turned and inquired who I was, and when I told him my name, he lit up, talked about meeting Jan, and invited us to visit his home.

The next few weeks, as I came to know Clem and his wife better, I concluded they were the most unusual and colorful Alaskans I had ever met, or perhaps would ever meet (except possibly for Bill Adams). Over time I spent many hours in his living room, sitting in a chair across from him, transfixed with tales of his WWII South Pacific Seabee experiences, his days as a pharaoh card dealer in Fairbanks, his arduous overland hike across and down the Kenai Peninsula from Anchorage to Seldovia in 1947 before any roads existed, his discovery of and settling in Halibut

Cove, his commercial fishing exploits, and his eventual assumption of political power as president of the Alaska State Senate, followed by his appointment to head up the North Pacific Fisheries Commission. Clem was a self-educated, well-read rough-cut diamond who possessed profound political insight, integrity, and depth. He wanted people to settle in the Cove and graciously encouraged us to do so, which we eventually did.

43

1995 - 2004

Our Next Chapter in Life

Our quest for a Halibut Cove cabin site was achieved in the summer of 1995 with the purchase of a waterfront lot. At this time, my efforts shifted to the Cove at the expense of our Hewitt Lake cabin. We had acquired a gem of land with spectacular views, good shore frontage, electric service, tideland and drinking water rights, and excellent exposure. After several years of building, we erected a 3,500-square-foot Lindal Cedar home on the site and settled in. Eventually we decided to leave our former life in Anchorage behind and live in Halibut Cove permanently. Since then, we have built many structures, including a lodge, and as of this writing in 2022, we are still here, where access is only via boat, helicopter, or floatplane.

After arriving in Halibut Cove, my piloting activities continued with shuttling between Anchorage and the Cove in our Cessna 185. In 2004 the insurance company jacked up my premium because I had turned 70, even though I had never had an accident or incident. One day that fall, I handed my son the airplane keys and instructed him to fly it to Anchorage and sell it. The sun was beginning to set, and I was nearly overcome with nostalgia as I stood alone on the dock and watched the Cessna gradually fade in the distant northern horizon along with my career as a pilot. It was the bookend to 47 years of aviation that had started when I first soloed at Patrick Henry Airport in Tidewater, Virginia.

I thought back to 1956 and how things have changed from when I first came to Alaska. That was before the jet age, and many folks in the Lower 48 envisioned Alaska as cold, remote, and inhospitable. Indeed, when actually selected by the Federal Bureau of Land Management for the position of Fire Control Forester in Fairbanks, my expectations of perpetual snow and igloos abruptly evaporated.

At that time, Alaska was still a territory, and no state or borough governments existed. Washington, D.C., practically ran everything (except the Territorial Governor and Legislature liked to think they might have a little influence). Washington was often derided for not caring about Alaska beyond its strategic position in the Cold War with Russia. The federal Bureau of Public Roads, for example, was referred to by Clem Tillion as the "Bureau of Parallel Ruts," but in some respects life was simpler without so many regulations and increasing levels of government.

Back then, winters were considerably colder, and color TV did not exist, although black and white national TV news was flown up from Seattle to Anchorage a week later and then forwarded another week later to Fairbanks. It was the same for NFL football coverage. I often contemplated how cheap they were not to have made two copies and sent one each to Anchorage and Fairbanks respectively, but I was probably only concerned because at the time I was actually living in Fairbanks.

During my early Alaska years, I became aware of how much Alaska was dependent upon aircraft for virtually everything (and still is). Today, Anchorage is just over three hours from Seattle, whereas it took over seven hours to fly to Fairbanks in 1956. The late 1950s saw a major transition from dog sleds to snowmobiles throughout the native villages. I remember flying on skis into remote villages to be met on airstrips with numerous snow machines, freshly purchased as the result of a bountiful firefighting season the previous summer. Village dog sleds were becoming a memory. In many villages many of the natives did not speak English.

Aircraft instrument approach aids were almost exclusively the ancient low-frequency, four-course, non-directional radio ranges (now long defunct). More modern VHF navigational systems only existed at Anchorage and Fairbanks. GPS navigation was far off in the future. Domestic trash-burning in 55-gallon barrels outside houses and apartments was often the norm. Today, burn barrels hardly exist. Forest fires were occasionally still reported by telegram or mail, if reported at all. Vacant public land was still open to 160-acre homesteading on the hillside immediately overlooking Anchorage and in Fairbanks, homesteading was still active inside the city limits. Pristine lakes in close proximity to Anchorage and Fairbanks had few or no cabins on their shorelines. Today there are hundreds. In 1956 Alaska's entire population was around 200,000, while Anchorage's population approximated 47,000 and the road sign on Airport Road in Fairbanks proclaimed Alaska's second-largest city had a population of only 5,002 souls.

In retrospect, time since then has passed at warp speed, and its velocity keeps increasing. Early on, I was 22 years old when timidly tending the rumbling heating plant at the Fairbanks ranger station in the dark of the -50°F winter. With no radio or TV, no human companionship during off-hours, and not enough money to even buy a book, it felt like the passage of time had frozen, and months were dragging on like years.

By midlife, though, it was the opposite. Time had speeded up, and it seemed I never had enough time to plan things as carefully and methodically as I wished. It felt like somebody or some situation was always pressing to demand my attention. Months were passing like weeks. My procrastination on little things was rampant.

I no longer have such pressing responsibilities, but in spite of this, weeks zip by like days, and at some unknown point, this increasing velocity of time as I perceive it will terminate, and so will I. Looking back, it's been quite a ride and one hell of a good life!

I contemplated all this while standing on the dock, my airplane with my son at the controls almost fading from view in the northern sky. Upon writing these nostalgic reflections today, it occurred to me that I had arrived at an appropriate place to finish this journal.

Thanks for taking the time to read it.